The Execution of Willie Francis

THE EXECUTION OF
Willie Francis

*Race, Murder, and the Search
for Justice in the American South*

GILBERT KING

BASIC
CIVITAS
BOOKS

A Member of the Perseus Books Group
New York, NY

Copyright © 2008 by Gilbert King
Published by Basic Civitas,
A Member of the Perseus Books Group

Books published by Basic Civitas are available at special discounts for bulk purchases in the United States by corporations, institutions, and other organizations. For more information, please contact the Special Markets Department at the Perseus Books Group, 2300 Chestnut Street, Suite 200, Philadelphia, PA 19103, (800) 255–1514, or e-mail special.markets@perseusbooks.com.

Designed by Timm Bryson
Set in 11 point Janson

Library of Congress Cataloging-in-Publication Data
King, Gilbert.
  The execution of Willie Francis : race, murder, and the search for justice in the American South / by Gilbert King.
    p. cm.
  Includes bibliographical references and index.
  ISBN 978-0-465-00265-8 (alk. paper)
  1. Francis, Willie. 2. Capital punishment--United States. I. Title.

HV8699.U5K55 2008
364.66092--dc22
[B]
                                                2007042051
10 9 8 7 6 5 4 3 2 1

In Memory of
Susan Marie King

and for
Emily Rose King

After the first death, there is no other.

—DYLAN THOMAS

Contents

the curse of st. martinville

*So I had it after all the months. For nothing is lost, nothing
is ever lost. There is always the clue, the canceled check, the
smear of lipstick, the footprint in the canna bed, the condom
on the park path, the twitch in the old wound, the baby
shoes dipped in bronze, the taint in the blood stream. And
all times are one time, and all those dead in the past never
lived before our definition gives them life, and out of the
shadow their eyes implore us.*

— ROBERT PENN WARREN,
All the King's Men

Before I left on my first research trip to St. Martinville, a sleepy Acadian (Cajun) town in southwestern Louisiana with a population of
just a few thousand, people familiar with the community told me to
expect "a whole different world." I'd been poring over countless
books on the region, including Sister Helen Prejean's *Dead Man
Walking*, and had noted the author's surprise on the second page
when she was told that Elmo Patrick Sonnier, the condemned man in
her story, was a "Cajun from St. Martinville." As Sister Helen herself

had found the town to be, in her words, one of the "friendliest, most hospitable places on earth," she observed that if murders were prone to happen anywhere, "this is the place one would least expect."

Once I arrived, it didn't take very long for me to discover that St. Martinville, the oldest settlement in an area known as Acadiana, had not changed much over the years. The pictures I'd seen of Main Street in the 1940s looked very much like the Main Street of St. Martinville today. In the center of town the Italianate and Greek Revival architectural treasures that surround St.-Martin-de-Tours Catholic Church are pleasing reminders that St. Martinville was once known as "le petit Paris." Not far from the church, along the Bayou Teche, stands the Evangeline Oak, immortalized by Henry Wadsworth Longfellow in his epic poem *Evangeline: A Tale of Acadie*. The tree has long been recognized as the symbol at the heart of Cajun culture.

The people of St. Martinville love to talk, even to strangers, and I found myself spending entire afternoons in the company of some of the friendliest, most hospitable people I've ever met. Yet something struck me as odd about many of my encounters. I would tell people I was working on a book about an old murder case in St. Martinville, and invariably they would ask if it was about Patrick Sonnier.

"No," I'd say, "Willie Francis."

The name was met with blank stares, which were usually followed by "never heard of him." On a visit to the former New Iberia Parish jail, which is now used to store files above the New Iberia courthouse, the maintenance man giving me the tour inquired if I was ready to see Sonnier's cell. (Sonnier was later executed in the same electric chair that Willie had walked away from nearly forty years earlier.)

"Sure," I told him, then asked if I could also see the cell that had held Willie Francis.

"Who?"

It was as if the idea of another infamous murder in these parts was incomprehensible. It wasn't until I began talking to some of the older folks in St. Martinville, people who had been around during the 1940s, when the State of Louisiana sent the Negro teenager to the electric chair, that I began to get nods of recognition. With these folks, the name Willie Francis resonated. And time and again the responses I received were the same: "Willie Francis didn't kill anyone," or "There are people in St. Martinville today who know what really happened," or "That boy was innocent."

The people in St. Martinville who shared these responses with me were priests, morticians, farmers, teachers. Some were black; others were white.

Willie's own version of the story was elusive, as he did not take the stand at his trial. A pamphlet—*My Trip to the Chair*—that he had written in 1947 to raise money for his U.S. Supreme Court appeals was proving impossible to find. In it, Willie was purported to have described, in his own words, the events leading up to, during, and just after he survived his own execution. I had spoken to people who had seen the document, and I'd contacted countless universities, research centers, and private collectors—all to no avail. The only known copy had been catalogued in a file of rare African American pamphlets at the Library of Congress in Washington, but it had been missing for almost two decades. Nearly every month for three years during the writing of this book I called the Library of Congress, hoping that somehow, against all odds, the file would turn up. One afternoon, with my deadline fast approaching, the telephone rang. It was Patrick Kirwin from the Library of Congress.

"Are you still looking for that Willie Francis pamphlet?"

Within hours, I had a copy in my hands—the holy grail of Willie Francis research that I had all but given up on—and the document would now allow me to present not only eyewitness accounts of Willie's botched execution but Willie's own account of that fateful day in St. Martinville—in Willie's own unmistakable voice. "I wonder if I will ever get to read the thing," Willie wrote. The document would also provide and confirm a telling detail in the murder that would send Willie Francis to the electric chair.

I thought back to a story told to me by James Akers, St. Martinville's unofficial town historian, caretaker of the Acadian Memorial, and, he claims, the only white person at the funeral of Willie Francis. It was my first day in town, and we were standing in Akers's office on South New Market Street overlooking the Teche, with the Evangeline Oak overhead. The sun was just beginning to set, and Akers didn't appear to be in a rush to go anywhere. A tall, gangly man with gray hair, a beard, and a Cajun accent that belied his Norwegian descent, Akers attempted to recall memories of the name that had been all but forgotten in this town where almost everyone, black and white, spoke French.

"Willie Francis," he said, sighing. "Willie Francis. That was a shame. Of course, that wasn't the first time. Something like that's happened here before."

The Cajuns have a word for it. *Corrompre*. Corrupt. "It was a dirty town," I'd been told.

"If you go into that courthouse there, look up the name Isabelle Robertson," Akers said. "Happened in August of 1891, in that pretty white house on the corner. That's where Mrs. Robertson lived with her daughter. One morning they found both bodies. They'd been stabbed and choked to death."

Akers's eyes widened. "Many months later the sheriff arrests a black man by the name Louis Michel. They took Mr. Michel behind the courthouse under a big oak tree, just like the Evangeline. Thirteen steps up the scaffold, there's rope waiting for him. The sheriff reads the death warrant and asks Mr. Michel if he has any last words. Michel says he does. He says, 'You remember that night you came to hang me? I was hiding under the house with my Winchester rifle and I could have killed three or four of you but didn't because, being innocent, I fear no man.' Then he looks into the crowd and says, 'There are people looking at me now who know I am innocent. I did not kill anyone.' But no one in the crowd said a word. Because of their silence, Mr. Louis Michel had one more thing to say. He put a curse on St. Martinville. Cursed the town so that it would not prosper, and grass would grow in the streets."

Akers paused and held up a finger. His story was not finished. "The sheriff slips the noose around his neck. Louis Michel was Catholic, and a priest was there to give him his last rites. When that was done, the sheriff gave the signal and Michel dropped down from the scaffold. But you see, they had too much rope. And Mr. Louis Michel was a tall man, six foot four or more. When he dropped, his toes could still, just barely, touch the ground. So do you know what the sheriff did? He got himself a shovel and he starts digging a hole right under Louis Michel's feet. Dug until the man's toes no longer touched the ground, and he was properly strangled. And the people of St. Martinville watched him twitch and draw his last breath, all the time wondering about that curse."

Akers looked out over the Teche, the last of the day's light glowing on the Evangeline Oak. The story of Louis Michel continued, even after his death. Just weeks later, Akers told me, there was a man on a train who caught the attention of a newsboy. The man's name was Paul Cormier, and the newsboy remembered him from town as a man who disappeared from St. Martinville just after the Robertson murders. The sheriff took him into custody, and Cormier was eventually tried and convicted for the murders of Mrs. Robertson and her daughter.

"Louis Michel was innocent," Akers said. "Just like he says before they hanged him."

I took careful notes. Akers is a colorful character and tells intriguing stories of St. Martinville and its rich history. But I was skeptical. I doubted that this tale rose to much beyond town lore, a story passed down for so many generations that its origin is no longer important. The abandoned storefronts and cafes on Main Street speak the only truth that matters.

Akers had more advice for me and gave me names of people he thought I should talk to. "When you look at what happened to poor Willie Francis, maybe you think St. Martinville is cursed," he said. "It's like Mr. Louis Michel said, there are folks in this town who know the truth. Same goes for Willie Francis. But you won't find the truth in the courthouse records."

Corrompre.

Months passed, and I'd made several trips back to St. Martinville. I would ask people from time to time about the hanging of Louis Michel and his curse on St. Martinville. There were only vague recollections of the crime but adamant confirmations of the curse. On my last visit, I went to the courthouse with names and dates, but with low expectations. Just as Akers had said, I found a newspaper story from 1891 documenting the mysterious killings in St. Martinville. I also found court records detailing the trial, conviction, and hanging of Louis Michel, who went to his death proclaiming his innocence, as well as confirmation on the arrest of Paul Cormier for the murder of the Robertson woman and her daughter on Main Street.

I looked out the window of the courthouse, across the lot where the redbrick jail once stood in this cursed town—the very spot beneath a giant oak where two young black men, generations apart, were denied not only justice but a proper execution. I wondered if Willie Francis had known about the curse, and if the strange fate of Louis Michel had ever crossed his mind as he waited in a dirty cell for the sheriff to lead him up those thirteen steps to the electric chair known as Gruesome Gertie.

As history has shown us, if you peel back the layers of the pastoral and the genteel in the American South, you sometimes find shameful, haunting reminders of the past. Murder, secrets, lies. All buried in a world gone by.

As I would learn, St. Martinville is a whole different world.

face of a killer

Side by side they sat, Captain Ephie Foster and Vincent Venezia, not saying much, as the old truck rattled along, deep into the heart of Louisiana's Evangeline country. With squinted eyes, they barreled across the prairies and Atchafalaya swamplands, then cut through endless cane fields that stretched west into the big, low sun. Live oak trees lined the gravel road before them, the mossy branches catching and trapping the last of the day's light in gauzy, backlit canopies. Behind them, the tires kicked up columns of dust that hung in the windless air like smoke from the captain's cigar.

If the truck had been equipped with a radio, they might have heard the news from the West Coast earlier that day of May 2, 1946, when six inmates overpowered prison guards in a deadly but unsuccessful escape attempt from a federal penitentiary on an island in San Francisco Bay. By the time the "Battle of Alcatraz" ended, two guards were dead and seventeen more were injured. The riot made front-page headlines across the country, and it might have given the two men from the Louisiana State Penitentiary something weighty to talk about on their ride south from Angola, where they passed their days in the company of some of Louisiana's most hardened criminals—men who wouldn't think twice about slitting their throats if the opportunity arose. But there was no radio, and by all reports, Foster and Venezia were not talkative men, so the only sound from the truck was the steady rumble of the engine. With Venezia at the wheel, the captain could gaze absently into the setting sun, pinching a cigar between fingers that he dangled out the passenger side window. Ephie Foster liked his cigars and always kept one in his mouth, even when it wasn't lit.

The truck was a 1941 International Harvester K–3 two-ton cornbinder, from the manufacturer known at the time for its production of heavy-duty farm equipment. Painted red, it was mounted with a large, gray sheet-metal trailer, unmarked and nondescript. In fact, the only thing odd about this cornbinder was the additional muffler and exhaust pipe that extended from the roof of the van. The truck would not have turned heads, at least not until it pulled up to park behind a Louisiana parish jail. Then, as photographs show, people would stop dead in their tracks and stare, as if some ancient beast of classical mythology was lurking behind the thick, metal doors. And when Captain Foster emerged from the truck, they'd stare at him, too—their somber eyes carefully registering the face of a killer.

Earlier that Thursday afternoon, Foster and Venezia had climbed into the truck that Warden Dennis J. Bazer kept in a garage on a hill at Angola, and they'd assured the warden they'd get the job done proper and be back in two days. On most of these parish trips, Bazer would follow behind the truck in a state car; but there was trouble back at Angola, and the warden was forced to stay behind for an emergency meeting with Louisiana Governor Jimmie Davis. On May 2, 1946, Foster and Venezia were on their own.

Ephie Foster, forty-three years old, had been a farmer from Avoyelles Parish, Louisiana, just west of the Mississippi border, before he took a job as a captain at the Louisiana State Penitentiary in nearby Angola. Camp captains like Foster were recruited from the "lower class of Louisiana's rural dwellers" and were mostly "redneck farmers and French speaking 'cajuns.'" One captain was put in charge of each camp, and these "semi-literate" officials were permitted to dish out punishment as they saw fit "with little or no interference from wardens or general managers." Discipline, one report noted, usually came in the form of floggings on a scale just "short of rank torture," and a newspaper columnist would later observe that "most of the white trash who infest the [Louisiana] penal service are no better than their victims."

Poor white captains like Foster lived an "idyllic life" on Angola's fertile grounds. The prison provided them and their families with housing and supplies and Negro inmates to cook and clean for them. Foster would have enjoyed an existence that "mimicked that of the passing plantation aristocracy."

Vincent Venezia, thirty-eight, was the son of Italian immigrants—one of ten children born to his mother, Josephine, and his father, Anthony Venezia, who worked as a dryer in the sugar industry. With "sallow complexion, green grey eyes, red hair, fair teeth" and "large out standing ears," Venezia sported scars on his upper left arm, his right ear, and his right knee. By the time he was twenty-two, Vincent wasn't living at home in New Orleans with the rest of his family. He was instead an inmate at the Jefferson Parish jail, where he listed his former occupation as "proprietor" of a "Pressing Establishment." In and out of the state penitentiary three times during the twenties and thirties for convictions on charges ranging from burglary to fraud, Venezia was serving hard time at Angola in the spring of 1946 and, as a prison trusty, had become an assistant to the chief electrician, U. J. Esnault. Foster and Venezia were no doubt pleased to be away from the prison as they drove past the sugarcane wagons and pecan trees into New Iberia, where they would stay for the night.

On Thursday nights, the bars on Main Street were packed with what the locals called "oilfield trash," recent transplants from dust bowl states who had come to New Iberia during the oil boom of the 1930s. In one case, the Texas Company (Texaco) moved the entire population of the town of Smackover, Arkansas, to New Iberia. These new arrivals, most of them Baptist, were not particularly welcomed by the French Catholic "sugar elites" who had prospered for generations in southwestern Louisiana and did not appreciate the encroachment of the oil industry into their cane fields.

The mixing of oil and sugar laborers in the bars of New Iberia made for rowdy, hard-drinking crowds, so Foster and Venezia would have had no trouble finding a place to imbibe on their night away from Angola and the warden. Past the antebellum homes and burial crypts along the Bayou Teche thrived several saloons—places like the Teche Club and the Jungle Club—where French-speaking men with fiddles and squeeze boxes crammed into corners and belted out the Cajun music popular with both the oil and sugar men. One song sure to be heard that night was the Cajun favorite "Jolie Blonde." A ballad written by a prisoner in nearby Port Arthur, Texas, in the 1920s about a pretty blonde woman who left her Cajun lover for another man, it had become a kind of Cajun national anthem.

Even bearing in mind the purpose for their journey, it was still a good time to be away from Angola. The U.S. Department of Justice Bureau of Prisons had recently released a damning report that deemed the conditions at Angola's state penitentiary, which had been built on a slave plantation, to be "deplorable" and falling "far short of desirable standards . . . in practically all respects." Sanitary conditions were "decidedly inadequate," and gambling was the prison's only "organized" form of recreation. Mary M. Daugherty,

Angola's registered nurse at the time, described the penal farm as a "sewer of degradation," where "sex offenders, stool pigeons, homosexuals and degenerates of every type were huddled in bedside companionship with the new arrivals."

Angola "gun bulls," who guarded inmates in the prison's notorious Red Hat cell block, were known to have arbitrarily shot and buried troublesome convicts in the farmland along the Mississippi River. And trouble at Angola came aplenty. Housed in sweatboxes in Camp A, the hardest prisoners worked from sunup to sundown along the levee in their black and white "wide stripes" and straw hats that had been dipped in red paint to identify their menacing status. The Red Hats saw escape from the farm as the only way to free themselves from a life of hard labor, and because they had nothing to lose, repeated attempts were the norm. Prison understaffing led to the development of the "trusty system," whereby select inmates like Venezia (who had demonstrated good conduct during "the greatest cane harvest in penitentiary history" and "exceptional service and merit of unusual value during the West India Hurricane") were assigned duties in the penitentiary ranging from errand boy to armed guard. Trusties were granted more privileges than other inmates, but the system bred rampant abuse and corruption. Lore had it that the trusty guards at Angola, who were mounted on horseback and armed with sawed-off shotguns, had to serve the time of any convict that escaped under their watch.

Expecting a storm of controversy following the release of the Bureau of Prisons report in May of 1946, Governor Davis traveled to Angola to meet with Warden Bazer. Together they would propose a "modernization program" to ameliorate the prison's inhumane conditions. Their efforts failed as conditions only worsened. Whippings and beatings "increased disgracefully." Not long after promised reform, thirty-seven convicts slashed their heel tendons with razor blades in protest against the overwork and brutality by camp captains in "America's Worst Prison." It was Davis's emergency visit to Angola that kept Bazer behind on May 2, thus affording Foster and Venezia the opportunity for their night on the town.

Venezia's ears must have pricked up when he learned he'd be going on an overnight trip to New Iberia without the warden, or anyone else except for Foster. There was a bar called Bruce's Place on West Pershing Street, between St. Peter's Cemetery and the railroad tracks, run by a man named "Back of Town" Bruce Broussard. Local prostitutes, who gathered on the porches of shotgun shacks flanking the bar, had gained this redlight district of New Iberia a certain renown that had surely reached Angola. For the penned-up Venezia, a visit to Bruce's Place would have been the highlight of the trip, and his fellow inmates back at the state penitentiary would be clamoring for all the lurid details when he returned.

Before midnight, Foster and Venezia showed up at a different bar called the Green Lantern, an old brick and wood saloon set off by itself on West Main and North streets, where the jukebox played Cajun music and patrons waltzed on a cement slab dance floor in a dimly lit room. Locals knew the place to be rife with shadowy "sinister characters," whose flying bottles of Regal beer and fistfights were nightly occurrences. Foster and Venezia sat up front by the paneled bar, where the owner, George "Squirrel" Etie—a tall, former bootlegger who had lost an arm in an automobile accident in the late 1920s—observed them laughing, drinking, and talking loud about the job in the morning.

It was getting late, and the two men down from the prison in Angola were having one last drink on the other side of the tracks. At five foot nine or so and with a heavy build, Foster was an imposing presence in the saloon. His demeanor was serious, and he seemed capable of trouble. But the whiskey appeared to have softened him a bit. Tomorrow. In St. Martinville, Foster told them. They drank some more. Then Foster invited them all to come watch. Dared them to show up at noon behind the courthouse in St. Martinville.

Foster and Venezia left the bar and stood in the dirt lot as light from the moon illuminated the marble crypts in the nearby cemetery. Maybe the oil and sugar men didn't believe what Foster had told them. He could have convinced them, though. He could have swung open the back doors of the truck and shown them. The large oaken chair facing outward, awaiting its next guest—the death mask draped over the seat back, leather belts and straps dangling from its legs, its arms, and its headrest—in the Louisiana moonlight.

Say hello to Ole Gertie, he could have told them.

Gruesome Gertie was the nickname the prisoners at Angola had given the portable electric chair. What Ephie Foster delivered with his truck was death. Or justice—it depended on whom you were asking. Either way, he took it from parish to parish to carry out grim business for the State of Louisiana. After each trip, the chair would return to the hill—its victim another notch on the leather straps. Behind it, mounted on the floor of the truck, was a bulky, oversized gasoline engine—the dynamo that gave Gertie her juice.

Gertie's next guest was just across the cemetery, in the pure white and stately New Iberia Parish Courthouse that loomed to the east. Foster knew he was in there. He knew that the boy—the one he called "the nigger"—was up there in a cell above the courthouse, waiting for dawn and probably not sleeping too well. Tomorrow, Foster told them, we're going to fry a nigger. Show starts at noon.

Standing there in the dirt lot outside Bruce's Place, with Gertie in the truck and the five-dollar whores of New Iberia on the porches, he might have wondered if any of these oil or sugar men would have the guts to come to St. Martinville in the morning to see Gertie do what she was built to do.

like shines in a rooster's tail

But, as he lay in the morning light, his face for a moment
Seemed to assume once more the forms of its earlier manhood;
So are wont to be changed the faces of those who are dying

— HENRY WADSWORTH LONGFELLOW,
Evangeline: A Tale of Acadie

Willie Francis opened his eyes as the first rays of Louisiana sunlight spilled through the window bars and onto the eighteen-inch-thick concrete walls of his narrow, solitary cell. This was to be the last sunrise he'd ever see. He rose from his cot and peered out over the small, clapboard houses that surrounded the New Iberia Parish jail. Tin roofs gleaming in the sun. The spire of St. Peter's Church jutting into the clear Acadiana sky. Dogs barking. A rooster crowing. His heart was already beating fast, and the sound of jingling keys and footsteps coming down the corridor brought a lump to his throat.

In contrast to the natural beauty just yards away, the jail had a putrid smell—numerous alcoholics and drug addicts were incarcerated there at the time—and the pipe extending to the seatless toilet leaked so that a slow, steady stream of water flowed across the cell floor, under the bars of the gate. Willie's cell was on the fourth floor; it had pink walls and gray bars.

Willie recognized the footsteps of Gilbert Ozenne, the Iberia Parish sheriff, whom he'd gotten to know well over the last eight months. But there was a second set of footsteps, which, Willie would discover, belonged to a fellow prisoner from the west wing. When they reached the cell, Ozenne and the inmate found Willie clutching the Bible his father had pressed into his hands at the end of a visit months earlier. Willie's mother had wanted him to read from it while he waited in his cell for this day to come, only she'd been too overcome with emotion to present it to her youngest son herself.

"Mornin', Willie," the inmate said, standing sheepishly before him. In his hands he held a bowl with soap, a razor blade, shaving brush, and a pair of scissors. He mumbled a brief apology for what he had come to do, and Willie gave him a nod as Sheriff Ozenne opened the cell.

The inmate stepped inside. Willie looked over at the pink walls, specifically at the words "Of Course I Am Not a Killer," which he had scrawled himself in big, dark letters one night a month earlier, when he'd been unable to sleep. But his day in court had come and gone, and Willie was done with words. His new barber tried making small talk as he began to clip Willie's hair, but Willie "didn't feel much like answering back."

Willie had often walked by the City Barbershop on Main Street back home in St. Martinville, where white men would pass part of a lazy afternoon in the chair with the barber, Sidney Dupois. That was a chair you could relax in. Like you had all the time in the world. Willie would walk by and see those white men in Mr. Dupois's chair, and sometimes he'd stand outside and talk to Little Sid, Dupois's young son.

The razor scraped roughly over Willie's scalp. He had to be bald, the inmate said, so that the electricity could pass cleanly into his body through the crown of his head. What he didn't tell Willie was that, if any hair was left on top, it would smolder beneath the leather hood he'd be wearing, and it might possibly catch fire—and create a sickly odor the witnesses would have to endure while they watched 2,500 volts of electricity course through the body strapped to the oaken chair just a few feet in front of them.

Willie closed his eyes while his fellow prisoner wiped the razor on a towel and continued to shave Willie's head. He was thinking about going home to St. Martinville to die. The town where Willie was born and had lived his whole life was just nine miles away from the jail in New Iberia. "It's just a little town where everybody knows everybody else," Willie said. "We have two sections, one for the white people and the other for the colored, and everybody gets along fine. The white tend to their own business and the colored tend to theirs." Willie had been brought to New Iberia because the small jail in St. Martinville wasn't set up to hold or guard prisoners for any length of time.

"They said I would like it much better here because the death cell is bigger and more comfortable than in St. Martinville," Willie said. "It didn't make much difference. They hadn't said when they were going to kill me, so I didn't care where they put me." There was also some fear that Willie might be lynched if he was held in town.

The day before, he had confided to his priest that he was scared of spending his last night on earth in a small cell by himself. And scared of going home in handcuffs to sit in a chair that was going to electrocute him to death. He worried about going to heaven. Not far from the only house he'd ever lived in was a small cemetery where blacks in town were buried. It's where his body would likely end up after the funeral. Willie was the youngest of his mother's thirteen children, and he'd be the first to die. His fears in the face of his scheduled death were real, and the boy had spent the last eight months trying hard to be a man.

Just a month earlier, the State of Louisiana had set the date. Willie had seen the death warrant: a big, official-looking document with the dreaded day—May 3, 1946—typed in. The document sentenced him to "a current of electricity of sufficient intensity to cause death, and the application and continuance of such current through the body of the said Willie Francis until said Willie Francis is dead."

District Attorney L. O. Pecot, in a letter to St. Martinville Sheriff Leonard (E. L.) Resweber on April 5, 1946, informed the sheriff to advise Willie of the date and time of his execution well in advance, "in case he desires to prepare himself to enter into the unknown veil of eternity." Pecot concluded his letter to Resweber with more preparatory instructions for Willie's execution: "If you follow these instructions, you will be in the clear all the way through and as this is your first experience, I am sure that you will use every possible precaution to follow the law as I have given it to you."

The language in his death warrant made Willie smile. So specific was it in its instructions as to who was allowed to watch him die that it struck Willie that the State of Louisiana had every angle covered in dense legalese in case he might kick up a fuss and say, "You can't kill me because you have a word wrong on that paper!"

In fact, the State of Louisiana had got a few words wrong—specifically the sentence stating, "no person under twenty-one years of age to be allowed in said execution room."

Willie Francis had just turned seventeen in January.

•   •   •

Willie hadn't been in New Iberia long when he was looking out his cell door window and saw a man walking down the corridor—a man "who was dressed just like a priest." Willie began to yell and wave his arms, and when he caught the man's attention, he asked him to come over to his cell. "I guess he thought I was crazy because of the way I acted," Willie said, "but he came in anyway." The man was Father Charles Hannigan, who belonged to a religious order called

The Holy Ghost Fathers, and he was immediately drawn to the excited boy who had called out to him from his cell.

On May 2, the day before Willie would be taken from New Iberia to St. Martinville for execution, Father Hannigan visited Willie one last time. A frequent visitor during the months of Willie's incarceration, Father Hannigan was a fifty-nine-year-old Irish Catholic from Philadelphia who had studied at Duquesne University of the Holy Ghost in Pittsburgh and was serving at St. Edward's, the local black church not far from the jail. Father Hannigan had become the person Willie relied on to prepare him for his impending death, yet despite all the preparations, the priest could not help but note that Willie was in a state of terror. Willie had always stuttered, but now his stammer virtually paralyzed his ability to speak. So Father Hannigan took it upon himself to do most of the talking. Slowly, his words began to calm the boy.

You're a lucky fella, Willie, he told the boy, without conviction. Lucky in that you know when you're going to die, unlike those who get "squashed by trucks" or "die between clean sheets by surprise."

Father Hannigan let that thought settle for a moment, then went on to explain that on leaving the jailhouse he himself might tumble down the staircase and break his neck. Unlike most people, Willie had the chance to "prepare himself for that moment," he pointed out.

Hannigan told Willie that he must face his death bravely and start a new life when he "got up from the chair the next day." He shouldn't "start it like a little crybaby." But Willie was worried how painful his death would be. This is your chance to die like a man, Willie, Father Hannigan told him. One of the hardest things in life is to make "yourself learn how to die right."

The priest's words began to resonate with Willie. Dying like a man was important to him.

Besides, Father Hannigan said, you have nothing to fear, Willie. The electric chair will not hurt you. It will only tickle "for a little while," and then it will be all over. You're not being hanged, Willie. "That would be a terrible way to die."

By the end of their talk, Willie felt calmer. Nobody wants to die, Willie thought. But since he couldn't do anything to stop it, there was no point in crying or worrying anymore. Father Hannigan had done what he could to help Willie meet his destiny.

Just as the sun was beginning to set that last evening, Sheriff Ozenne had visited the cell to discuss Willie's last supper. He could have whatever he wanted, Ozenne told him. But the youth was only interested in ice cream, and Ozenne prompted Willie into adding a steak to his order. An hour later, Ozenne returned with what he considered the best steak in town. And, Willie thought, "more ice cream than I could eat."

Now that the end was near, Willie was getting along well with Ozenne and his deputies. They never spoke harshly to him, and since Willie didn't get "sassy" much, they'd give him the little things he asked for, even if it meant bending a rule or two.

After his dinner, Willie had laid down on his cot in the dark cell. But he couldn't take his mind off the electric chair. Why was it called the "hot seat," he wondered? Father Hannigan had told him it only tickled, but if the seat was also hot, it must also burn. And burning did not tickle. Finally, Willie tried to put the chair out of his mind. He had promised Father Hannigan that he was going to be a man and not a child. He would not cry. "Boy, you sure feel funny when you know you're going to die," Willie thought. "Almost like you know something only God should know."

Dogs barked at all hours in the yards across Iberia Street, and the sounding of the bells from St. Peter's Church across the railroad tracks marked the time. For Willie, the evening dragged on.

At one point he took hold of his Bible and flipped through its now worn pages. Born into a Roman Catholic family, Willie went to church on Sundays at Notre Dame de Perpetual Secours Church in St. Martinville, just a block from the jail where he was to die tomorrow. In truth, he wasn't very religious. As he'd confessed to Father Hannigan, he spent a lot of time at church thinking not of the Lord but of what he was going to do once he got home and changed out of his Sunday best. Once his days had become numbered, however, Willie had finally been able to concentrate on the words in the Good Book. Over the past eight months, he'd labored his way through his Bible in his attempt to get ready for his new life—as Father Hannigan had recommended.

Willie knew that tomorrow he would be dead and that "they will bury me in a cold cold grave." He pictured himself looking at his own "grave-marker." For the last time, he got down on his knees and prayed. "God, tonight is the last time I will sleep in a bed because tomorrow I will have to sit down on that chair and die. Please help me to die." That night, Willie dreamed of "a bunch of us boys sitting on the bayou banks but I was the only one who wasn't having a good time." In his dream, everyone was laughing, but Willie just stood on the bank. "I was looking to the other side of the Bayou but I couldn't see anything. It was all fuzzy and blurred about in the middle of the Bayou."

•   ♠   •

Willie reached up and ran his hand across his freshly shaved scalp. The inmate wiped the razor clean against a towel, then stepped back and paused to admire his work. "Well, Willie," he said. "I guess that's one haircut you won't have to pay for."

Willie smiled, then broke out laughing. He knew the inmate was only trying to take Willie's mind off the electric chair. Soon Sheriff Ozenne and his deputy were laughing, too. After that the four of them began trading jokes. "For a little while," Willie reflected, "dying didn't seem such a bad thing."

About an hour before noon, Sheriff Ozenne returned to Willie's cell and asked him if he was ready to go home. Willie nodded, and the deputies prepared him for the ride to St. Martinville—his legs were shackled, his hands cuffed in front of him.

His cell door was unlocked, and Willie began to lead the sheriff and one deputy down the seven-cell corridor of the east wing, where a hand-cranked row of bars was opened. At the end of the corridor, he paused to take one last look at his pink cell. His stomach was beginning to turn—a "funny crawling feeling" he got upon leaving the "death cell." He took a deep breath while the other prisoners stared on in respect. And fear. Willie walked through the area known as "the bullpen," where the deputies and guards gathered to listen to the radio or play bourré, the Cajun card game. Sheriff Ozenne looked more serious and somber now; a heavier mood had set upon him as he pointed Willie toward the elevator. The inmate who had shaved Willie's head gave him a small farewell wave of the finger.

The New Iberia jail was located on the fourth floor of the courthouse, and after the elevator doors closed, Willie was sure the sheriff and his deputy could hear his heart pounding, hear how loudly the fearful thoughts were screaming through his mind. As the elevator descended, Willie felt a wave of nausea consume him. He closed his eyes for a moment and hoped he wouldn't get sick. The elevator stopped and the door opened. Willie began walking through the courthouse lobby toward the large aluminum doors. Outside the courthouse, he squinted his eyes and blocked the sun with his cuffed hands. In front of him stood the large bronze statue of Lady Justice at the top of the stairs to the courthouse. A robe draped over her, she had one hand extended for justice; the other, for equality.

At the front of the stairs, a black Ford sedan was waiting with its back door open. Willie carefully maneuvered his shackled legs down the courthouse stairs. When he got to the sedan, he took one final look at the small rectangular window of his jail cell on top of the courthouse.

A deputy got in the sedan first and slid all the way across the backseat. Transfer protocol required prisoners to be seated between two police officers, so Willie got in next, and Sheriff Ozenne followed. Ozenne liked Willie, and he would have liked to have given him a clear window view on his last ride, but he didn't want to put any ideas of escape into Willie's head.

The sedan pulled away from the New Iberia courthouse. Willie tried to concentrate on all Father Hannigan had told him about being brave. His tongue felt stuck to the roof of his mouth, and his ears were ringing. He couldn't have spoken if he had wanted to. Ozenne, Willie, and the deputy sat in stony silence as the sedan turned down Main Street, away from New Iberia and toward St. Martinville. A large sign, suspended by wire between two telephone poles, hung over Main Street at its end and offered a friendly farewell: "Come Again."

Willie looked down at his feet, noticing his shoes were "nice and shiny." He figured he'd only get to make about "fifty more steps in my nice clean shoes and then I would be dead."

"Don't worry, Willie," a deputy said, "it won't hurt you very much. You won't even feel it."

But Willie wasn't worried about the pain. He was "more worried about the fact that it was going to kill me."

The car glided down the flat, two-lane gravel road that cut through the endless sugarcane fields Willie knew so well. The fields terrified black children, because they'd heard the stories of whites who forced blacks to strip before "running" them naked through the razor-sharp stalks. They would emerge with hundreds of bloody, searing cuts on their bodies. After the sedan crossed the Bayou Teche, Willie's knees began shaking uncontrollably. Outside the car window lay the banks of the bayou where Willie once swam with his friends, fished, and climbed trees. "More than anything else we liked to eat figs," Willie remembered. "We would snitch them and go sit on the bank and see who could throw them the farthest out into the water." Willie noticed, too, the baseball field he and his friends would claim whenever they could find a ball and a broomstick.

For the drive, Sheriff Ozenne had arranged one final favor for the boy he had come to like so well. He had the driver make a left turn down Randolph Street instead of going straight to the St. Martinville jail. Willie had lived at 800 Washington Street his whole life, and as the sedan slowly drove its length, Willie craned his neck in the hope of catching one final glance of his mother inside the small, wooden, one-story, dull gray house in the black section of town. She was there, but Willie did not know that she was sick in her bed, and he could not see her. He kept his eyes on the house until it faded from view, while pebbles from the road kept popping up against the fenders like hard rain on a tin roof.

The sedan turned left on Main Street, where the large, white-pillared courthouse commanded the view. It was there, eight months earlier, that Willie had been tried and convicted of the murder of Andrew Thomas, the popular Cajun owner of the town pharmacy. On that last visit to the courthouse, the judge had sentenced him to death. This morning, Willie's name had made the front page of the St. Martinville *Weekly Messenger* under the headline:

NEGRO MURDERER TO DIE HERE TODAY

● ● ●

When the sedan pulled up to the curb, dozens of townfolks ran up to the car for a "last look" at the boy. Sheriff Ozenne and his deputy moved Willie through the crowd, much of it sad, more of it angry. Many blacks had shown up in support of Willie, men and women who were convinced that Willie was the victim of a frame-up and disgusted by the sham of a trial that had condemned him. Whites had come out in larger numbers, mostly to see Willie Francis pay the price for the murder of a beloved town figure.

Willie searched the crowd, hoping for a final look at his father, but he did not see him before he was taken behind the courthouse, to the squat, redbrick, two-story building that was the St. Martin Parish jail. An eight-foot wooden fence surrounded it, and the mossy branches of a live oak loomed over the tiny jail. Over the years this oak had claimed its share of Negroes, whose bodies were hanged by rope under its branches, until the State of Louisiana, in 1940, decided upon the more humane method of death by electrocution.

A truck was parked on the street behind the jail; the chair had reached its destination. Captain Foster and Vincent Venezia had arrived at the St. Martinville courthouse around 8:30 in the morning. They'd driven the truck around back and parked it on Saint Martin Street, behind the jail. The execution room was on the second floor, so they were going to have to haul the bulky oaken chair up a staircase—not a pleasant prospect in light of the already sweltering heat and the fact that they had barely slept after their late night in the saloons of New Iberia.

Residents of St. Martinville, once they caught sight of the odd vehicle, had begun to gather behind the jail. Children had also gathered around Louisiana's unmarked truck, and some had climbed trees. They gawked at the two gruff men from Angola who together swung open the back doors of the truck and began to unload the chair. An unlit cigar hung from Foster's lips. Formidable-looking and loud, he hadn't shaved, and onlookers kept their distance as he barked instructions at Venezia. When they'd gotten the chair out of the truck, deputies from the St. Martin Parish sheriff's office came out to discuss the logistics of the operation with the executioners from Angola. Indeed, the chair would have to be carried up a narrow staircase to the second floor. Foster decided they would run the wires out the second-story window and back to the truck, where they could be connected to the large generator that powered the chair.

After hauling the chair to the second floor, the two executioners returned to the truck. The chair was so heavy that there was no need to secure it to the floor. An onlooker that day would later testify that he saw Venezia hand Foster a flask and both men drink from it. Foster then went back into the jail with an eight-foot high, green steel electrical switchboard, "polka-dotted with needled dials," which he proceeded to connect to the wires running through the window. Venezia stayed inside the van of the truck and hooked the wires on his end to the generator made by International Harvester. Once the chair was in position and the switchboard fully connected, Venezia fired up the powerful engine. The sound was deafening. Because the truck was parked so close to the jail, the deputies had to shout to be heard, even inside the small execution room.

Foster told Venezia that the chair was ready to be tested, but the first run indicated a problem with the electrical connection. Foster wet his thumb with his tongue, then wiped some dust and grime off a glass dial. He didn't like what the needles were doing, so he went back down the stairs to the truck, where he and Venezia reworked the wiring from scratch. Certain that the chair was now in working order, they slipped behind the truck for another pull from the flask. Then, at ten minutes before twelve, they fired up the generator and let it run to build up the necessary voltage for a fatal blast.

Meanwhile, Sheriff Ozenne and his deputy led Willie up the stairs inside the jail. The three of them entered the L-shaped room, which was not much larger than a tennis table. Willie finally got a glimpse of the chair that was to take his life, and it scared him to look at it. It was propped against the northern wall of the jail; its leather buckles and straps dangled ominously to the side. "I wished I had seen my father instead," Willie thought. Thick black cables entered from the window, ran, like snakes, across the wooden planked floor, and were attached to the chair's tall back. At its top was a crown of metal and gauze bolted to a leather strap—a crown that would be dipped in salt water and fastened to Willie's freshly shaved head, then secured to the back of the chair. Already this chair had snuffed out the lives of twenty-two men in Louisiana. And one woman: the comely and slender Toni Jo Henry, who, just two and a half years earlier, had cried when she was told her head had to be shaved. "Look," she said, "I've been condemned to execution, not mutilation."

The half-dozen witnesses crowded the room. Their white faces were familiar to just about everyone in town and to each other, but they engaged in no conversation. Willie could feel their silence beyond the deafening, ghastly roar of the dynamo just outside the jail. He met the gaze of one of them, just a step away from him. It was Sidney Dupois, the barber.

"What are you doing here?" Willie asked.

"I came to be with you, Willie," Dupois answered.

Willie wanted to ask how Little Sid was doing, but his mouth was dry and he was scared. Cuffed and shackled, Willie shuffled toward the chair that would take him from this world. When he turned and tried to sit, Sheriff Leonard Resweber grabbed him by the arm and walked him out to a cell across the hall.

There, sitting on a cot, was Father Maurice Rousseve, the bespectacled priest from Notre Dame, the black church just outside the jail. Father Rousseve, a tall, scholarly man who was ordained in the country's first class of black Catholic priests, had known Willie for years. He had instructed the nuns at Notre Dame to bring the schoolchildren into the church, where they would pray for Willie's soul at the time of his execution. Willie had attended public school in St. Martinville, but education for blacks in town ended in the sixth grade. Willie only got as far as third.

Sitting beside him on the cot, Rousseve told Willie that he had nothing to be frightened of because he was just minutes from heaven. In "rich, round tones," the Creole priest assured Willie, too, that he personally would take good care of his family and counsel them through the sad days to come. When Willie rose from the cot, he'd been comforted by Father Rousseve's words. He appeared to be ready to accept his fate. At that point, Sheriff Resweber walked over to Willie's side and read the State of Louisiana's death decree:

> Now, Therefore, I, James Davis, Governor of the State of Louisiana, do hereby direct and require you, the Sheriff of the Parish of St. Martin, to cause the execution to be done on the body of said Willie Francis so convicted and condemned, in all things according to the judgment and sentence of said Court and the law in all such cases made and provided, by electrocution, that is, causing to pass through the body of the said Willie Francis a current of electricity of sufficient intensity to cause death, and the application and continuance of such current through the body of the said Willie Francis, until said Willie Francis is dead.

Outside the jail, Willie's father, Frederick Francis, was pacing helplessly, first back and forth, then in circles. Busy arranging for a hearse, he had just missed Willie's arrival from New Iberia. Relegated to the noisy area outside the jail, he was trying frantically to catch one last glimpse of Willie alive. But as the hour drew closer to noon, he grew more forlorn as he minded the hearse and coffin that would carry his son's body from the jail. Already exhausted, he was becoming increasingly delirious from the long wait under the hot sun. Francis had spent the previous night getting a small tombstone in place over a bumpy patch of land beneath a pecan tree in the back of the cemetery for St. Martinville's blacks. For this proud, grief-stricken father of thirteen children, who had sent one son, Adam Francis, off to fight for his nation in World War II, the state-planned execution of his youngest child was more than he could bear. Staring at the second-floor window of the room where Willie was awaiting a life-ending jolt of electricity, Frederick Francis continued to pace.

The bells at Notre Dame de Perpetual Secours Church sounded at noon, their peal barely audible above the din of the generator. Willie's time had come. Leaving the cell, Sheriff Resweber gave Willie a nod, and the boy followed him across the hall to the execution room and shuffled over to the chair. This time Resweber let him sit. Deputies approached. They removed the handcuffs and leg shackles. Willie's dangling feet barely touched the floor.

The deputies began strapping Willie down, starting with his slender arms. Leather straps drew his biceps to his sides and secured them to the back of the chair. Straps fastened his wrists to the armrests. One thick strap seat-belted him tightly at the waist. One deputy ripped his left pant leg; another placed an electrode on his calf to improve conductivity once the current surged to Willie's body.

Willie looked into the eyes of his red-faced executioner, Captain Ephie Foster, who stared back at him. Foster instructed the deputies to buckle the strap onto Willie's left thigh. Everyone seemed to be buzzing around him. The deputies continued fastening, clipping, and buckling things. Willie broke into a sweat. The coldness he felt seemed to increase with the roar of the generator.

Willie was breathing hard. For several minutes in the small, cramped death room, the witnesses were still, as if they were waiting in silent, keen anticipation for that precise second on the clock to arrive when they could get to the part they had all come for. They stood about uncomfortably, saying nothing. Carrying a view camera mounted on a tripod, Father Rousseve stepped to the front of the room. Sheriff Resweber had consented to the portrait, so Rousseve adjusted the tripod, slipped his head under a dark cloth, and snapped a picture. Rousseve had photographed many of the couples who appeared before him on their wedding days, and he'd done portraits of countless children on the day of their First Holy Communion at the church across the street from the jail. Now he had just photographed one of his young parishioners strapped into Louisiana's electric chair, his head slumped forward. "A beaten animal," ready to accept his fate.

Captain Foster allowed Rousseve to finish. Behind him, George Etie, the one-armed owner of the Green Lantern and one of the New Iberians who had taken up Foster's offer to see the nigger fry, stood against the rear wall of the room. Finally, Foster broke the silence. "OK," he said, and with that, Sheriff Resweber stepped forward.

"Is there anything you'd like to say?" the sheriff asked.

Willie shook his head no. Resweber paused for a moment, in the event Willie might be gathering himself for a final statement. Father Rousseve again came forward, this time with a steel crucifix, which he pressed to Willie's lips for him to "kiss the cross." Then, along with the sheriff, Rousseve stepped to the back of the room. Another moment passed. A sudden movement behind him made Willie flinch. Someone pulled something, a hood, maybe, over Willie's face; the leather mask caught him by surprise. Black and thick, it clung tightly to his face, although a small slit near his mouth made it possible for him to breathe. The man then tightened the gauze crown—soaked in water so that the electricity could travel unimpeded to Willie's head—and secured it to the chair. Roughly, he attempted to gag Willie's mouth with a leather band that he strapped to the back of the chair. Willie's head banged back against the hard wood.

"It hurts me the way you're doing it," Willie mumbled.

"It'll hurt more after a while, Willie," Captain Foster replied.

Gagged with the leather band, Willie sat in darkness now, the deafening noise of the engine amplifying his terror. Father Hannigan had told him the chair wouldn't hurt.

Captain Foster crouched over the electrical switchboard resting on the floor, another half-smoked, unlit cigar clamped between his lips. He was waiting for the generator to build to 2,500 volts, the level he wanted for delivering a powerful, fatal surge of electricity. When the needle on the switchboard finally indicated the machine was fully charged, Foster took one final glance at the black boy sitting in his chair.

Outside the jail, Frederick Francis was too agitated to take comfort from those who had gathered around him in support. Down the street at Notre Dame, black schoolchildren continued to pray alongside the nuns, the dull drone of the dynamo within their earshot. Perched on the branches of the giant oak, whites vied for a better view.

"Good-bye, Willie!" Captain Foster's cruel voice boomed above the rattle of the chair's noisy engine.

Willie, surprised by the captain's farewell, tried to say good-bye. But his stutter and the leather band in his mouth prevented it.

In a grandiose manner fit for the stage, Foster reached down and slowly pulled the switch. Willie's hands immediately clenched into fists. His body tensed, then stretched, as the first currents of electricity began to surge into him. He groaned audibly. He strained against the leather straps. He writhed in his agony. It felt like "a hundred and a thousand needles and pins" were pricking him, and his left leg felt like "somebody was cutting it with a razor blade." His lips swelled gruesomely, their flesh puffing out from the slit in the leather mask. His nose got flattened. Just thirty seconds into the electrocution, Willie's body, involuntarily jumping and seizing, convulsed under the current. The heavy, oaken death chair began to rock and slide across the floor before angling away from the witnesses, aghast at what they were seeing.

Then, just as suddenly, the current stopped. Aside from the generator, the room was quiet. Dr. Sidney Yongue, the parish coroner, stepped forward to pronounce Willie Francis dead. "Well, let's examine him now," he said.

His assistant, Dr. Bernard DeMahy, took one look at Willie. "It's no use to examine him," DeMahy said. "He's breathing."

Yongue looked up. Willie, slumped forward in the chair, was gasping for breath. Before Yongue could make a move, Foster, who had overheard the two doctors, spluttered, "Well, we'll give him another one," and threw the switch again.

The electricity tore through Willie's body and again sent him into convulsions. Captain Foster was closely watching the boy in his chair and, sensing trouble, yelled out the window: "Give me some more juice down there!"

Venezia yelled back from the truck: "I'm giving you all I got now!"

Foster let the current flow, but clearly, something was wrong. Willie's body continued to convulse, tense, and stretch under the voltage, each muscle fiber straining against the leather straps, until finally he screamed.

"Take it off! Take it off!" Willie shouted. "Let me breathe!"

Foster stared, incredulously. "You're not supposed to breathe!" he shot back, and let the electricity continue to surge at full strength.

Willie gasped, and summoned one final cry:

"I AM N-N-NOT DYING!"

The clarity of Willie's pained, stuttered voice stunned Foster, who was beginning to realize that the State of Louisiana might not be getting its pound of flesh on this strange afternoon. Resweber turned to Foster and motioned for him to end it. Foster turned off the switch, stopping the current. Willie's body sunk in the chair. The noisy generator shut down a moment later, and the room fell into a pristine silence.

Willie believed that he was dead. Without a word, the deputies began unstrapping him from the chair, and Willie was struck by the fact that, even in death, he could still "feel hands all over" his body—the same way it feels when you're alive, he thought. It was strange to him that Sheriff Resweber and his deputies moved so fast.

"It seemed like they were in an awful hurry to get me out of that chair so they could bury me," Willie thought.

Quickly, they pulled the mask from his head, and Willie blinked at the sudden light. His eyes slowly adjusted and met the faces of the "spellbound" witnesses to his execution. All of them, including the barber, Mr. Dupois, were stunned at the sight of Willie staring back at them, his eyes squinting and blinking, his chest heaving and gasping for breath. One by one, they began speaking to each other, their voices rising in a cacophony of excited chatter. Only moments before, he had screamed that he wasn't dying. Then, everything went quiet, and he thought he must be dead. His head was ringing, and his body ached, and he could not understand what the voices around him were saying. But none of that mattered to Willie.

I'm not dead, he thought. The chair didn't kill me.

The deputies loosened the straps, then peeled away the electrodes from his skin. Sheriff Ozenne grabbed Willie by the arm and helped him out of the chair. His body and head were still buzzing, but aside from a few unsteady steps at the beginning, Willie walked away from the electric chair. "Quivering with fright," he did not look back. Still holding him by the arm, Ozenne led Willie past the stunned witnesses and an irate Captain Foster into the holding cell across the hall, where Willie lay down on a cot. A few minutes later, Dr. Yongue arrived with his doctor's bag, and he and Dr. DeMahy examined Willie. They later noted in testimony that he was "stunned" and continued to have breathing difficulties, but that he would recover. Sheriff Ozenne offered to take Willie outside for some fresh air or bring him something to eat, but Willie shook his head.

"I just want to rest," he said.

•　　♦　　•

Word traveled down the block to Notre Dame Church, where someone rushed down the aisle to inform the still praying nuns that

Willie Francis had survived the electric chair. There was a great deal of excitement in the pews, with the nuns proclaiming a miracle of divine intervention in the small Louisiana town.

Frederick Francis did not wait around to see his son. Instead, he climbed into the Model A hearse and rushed home to bring his family the news that Willie wasn't killed.

Back in Sheriff Resweber's office, the mood was more somber. Foster had just finished delivering the news to Warden Bazer, and now Resweber was on the phone with Jimmie Davis at Angola, charged with the unusual task of explaining to the governor what had gone wrong with the chair at the execution of Willie Francis in St. Martinville. Davis was incredulous. When Resweber asked if they should fix the chair and return Francis to it later in the day, Davis said he wanted to confer with his attorney general, Fred LeBlanc.

Would it be possible, Davis wondered, for the State of Louisiana to send Francis back to the chair after failing in the first attempt? LeBlanc considered Davis's proposition and determined that there were "too many complications." "On one side," LeBlanc stated, "Francis was sentenced to die on a specific date. However, on the other hand, he was sentenced to be subjected to electric shock until dead. We'll have to decide whether he can be put in the chair again under the original sentence."

The decision was made, unanimously among the state officials, in less than an hour, and despite LeBlanc's initial concerns. The State of Louisiana would send Willie Francis back to the chair where he would absorb electrical current until dead. And they would make sure to do it right this time. The officials conceded, however, that a second attempt that afternoon would be in poor taste, so they granted Francis a brief reprieve. Davis suggested a second attempt be made in one week, but Warden Bazer noted that the chair would be in Leesville, Louisiana, for another execution on that day. It was impossible, Bazer said, for the State of Louisiana to perform two executions in one day. They decided, therefore, to schedule Willie's second execution for May 9, 1946—just six days after the first attempt.

Governor Davis phoned Sheriff Resweber with the decision. After receiving Davis's order, Resweber returned to the jail and gave his now twice-condemned prisoner the news. Willie Francis had six days. On May 9, he would once again make that long, quiet drive from New Iberia back to the same, two-story redbrick jail and sit in the same chair while the State of Louisiana would again send "a current of electricity of sufficient intensity to cause death, and the application and continuance of such current through the body of the said Willie Francis, until said Willie Francis is dead."

The whole ordeal confounded Willie. One minute he was happy to be alive; the next he found himself again condemned. "It's sort of like being glad you can sit on a gravestone without having the gravestone sit on top of you," he'd later say.

How can they make me sit in that chair again? Willie wanted to know.

Resweber had no response. Instead, he focused on getting Willie back to New Iberia. On unsteady legs, Willie followed Sheriff Ozenne and his deputy out of the holding cell. He caught a glimpse of Captain Foster, who was now taking apart the electrical equipment; he was not in the best of moods. He shook his fist at Willie and cursed him: "I missed you this time, but I'll kill you next week if I have to do it with a rock!" Foster shouted.

Willie smiled. And he kept his eyes and smile on Foster as he walked past, as if, though for only a moment, he would enjoy a small victory over his executioner. "I didn't like the idea of going through that all over again," Willie explained, "but I was so glad to be alive I didn't say anything."

Willie said good-bye to Father Rousseve. He was following Sheriff Ozenne out of the jail when he turned back again to the priest and said, "The Lord was with me that time." Father Rousseve nodded.

Outside the jail, Willie surveyed the disbelieving crowd. They had expected him to be carried out in a box. They had seen his father with a coffin and hearse. They had heard the roar of the generator. But now the condemned boy was leaving the jail on his own two feet, just paces from the spot where the feet of another condemned man, Louis Michel, mistakenly reached the ground in a botched hanging half a century ago. Fear, joy, and superstition confounded the onlookers in this cursed town until someone broke the surly silence:

"They couldn't kill the black bastard!"

Once in the sedan, Willie continued to glare at the white onlookers. As the car drove away from the St. Martinville courthouse square, Willie spotted a friendly face in the crowd and managed a wave with his manacled hands.

The drive back to New Iberia was just as quiet as the ride in to St. Martinville two hours earlier. They crossed the Bayou Teche, passed by the same banks, the same cane fields, and the same mossy oaks that hung over the two-lane gravel road. During the earlier ride, fear, dread, and sadness had rendered Willie incapable of speech. But now he was changed. Not only had he faced his own death, he had walked away from it—and from the chair that had haunted his sleep for nearly a year. As the sedan pulled up in front of the stark white courthouse in New Iberia, Willie glanced up at the top-floor window of the cell he'd been living in those long eight months. He was coming home. Because today the Lord was with him.

Sheriff Ozenne led Willie back up the stairs, across the verandah, through the large aluminum doors of the courthouse, and back into the elevator where he had nearly been sick earlier. He wasn't in the cell long before Father Hannigan arrived to pay him a visit. The priest had already received word that Willie had cheated death, but he still couldn't hide his surprise at seeing the lanky teenager alive. Equally excited to see Father Hannigan, Willie began telling him the whole story of the day's strange events. Still slightly dazed from the ordeal, he wanted Father Hannigan to know that he had gone to that chair like a man, that he had been ready to die with dignity.

"Yes," Father Hannigan assured him, "you were brave, Willie. God has been good to you, son."

Willie surprised Father Hannigan with his response. "Why, Father—God is always good!"

Quiet for a moment, the teenager had one more thing to tell Hannigan, who later recalled that it was "the closest thing to a reproach" he ever heard from the boy. "Father," Willie stuttered, looking very seriously at the priest, "you were right. It did tickle me. But it sure hurt me, too!"

•   ♠   •

As far as anyone knew, no one had ever before walked away from the electric chair. Willie Francis was the first, and news of this extraordinary occurrence was beginning to spread throughout Louisiana. Earlier, an irate Ephie Foster grumbled, "the chair didn't work." A wire, he said, must have been loose. Asked his name by reporters, Foster answered "Harry Dwyer," who was a plumber back at Angola. By late afternoon more newsmen were arriving in St. Martinville with hopes of interviewing Willie. Sheriff Resweber, when asked what happened to the kid in the electric chair, told reporters, "He wasn't even scorched." But they wanted to hear from Willie himself, so they drove to the New Iberia jail. Seeing that Willie had no objection, a worn-down Sheriff Ozenne relented and led several reporters and a photographer down the narrow corridor to Willie's cell.

Willie was lying on his cot when the throng of scribes in their customary brown hats and Pall Mall cigarettes in hand descended upon him with notebooks drawn. Still dizzy, Willie tried to concentrate on the barrage of questions directed at him.

"Willie! What was it like being in the electric chair?" one shouted.

Willie took a deep breath. "They walked me into the room and I saw the chair," he began in his slow, Louisiana drawl. "I knowed it was a bad chair. I didn't think about my whole life like at the picture show. Just 'Willie, you goin' outa this world in this bad chair.' They began to strap me in the chair, and everything begun to look dazey. It was like the white folks watching was in a big swing, and they'd swing away and back and then right up close to me where I could hear them breathing. Sometimes I thought so loud it hurt my head. When they put the black bag over my head, I was all locked up inside the bag with loud thinkin'."

The reporters scribbled furiously.

"The electric man could of been puttin' me on a bus for New Orleans the way he said good-bye," Willie said. "And I tried to say good-bye, but my tongue got stuck and I felt a burnin' in my head and my left leg and I jumped against the straps. When the straps kept cuttin' me I hoped I was alive, and I asked the electric man to let me breathe. That's when they took the bag off my head."

"How'd it feel, Willie?"

"Plumb mizzuble," Willie stuttered. Earlier, he had told a reporter that the chair "tickled" him. "But I'm telling you that chair sure isn't full of feathers."

"What went wrong?" another reporter asked.

"God fool'd with the electric chair," Willie answered.

"How's that? What do you mean?"

Willie drew another deep breath, as if to cement the idea of divine intervention in his mind. "The Lord was with me," he said.

The questions persisted, and Willie gave answers that filled up their pads.

"What was it like to taste death?" one reporter wanted to know.

Willie responded literally. "Like you got a mouth full of cold peanut butter," he said, and added that it looked like "little blue and pink and green speckles, like shines in a rooster's tail."

"I reckon," he added, "dying is black. Some folks say it's gold. Some say it's white as hominy grits. I reckon it's black. I ought to know. I been mighty close."

The *New York Daily News* would publish the interview with Willie, which caught the attention of Walter White, executive secretary of the National Association for the Advancement of Colored People (NAACP). In a column of his own, White wrote, "What a miracle that a virtually illiterate (but far from ignorant or untalented) boy should think in imagery as deeply moving and beautiful as any contemporary poet."

What would he like to do if the State of Louisiana decided to keep him in jail and didn't send him back to the chair? "I'd be happy to be a cook in the pen," Willie answered. "I use to cook for my daddy pretty good and he says I got a knack with mustard greens and sidemeat."

When the questions finally abated, a photographer asked for a picture. Willie obliged. The flash fired. The photograph pictures Willie calmly seated on the cot, alone in his cell, his bald head shining in the light from the naked bulb. Willie had given them a local story for the ages, a real bell-ringer, and they rushed off to meet deadlines for the next day's headlines. Willie's picture would, over the next few days, show up on the front page of newspapers around the country, with headlines declaring him "Indestructible" and "Lucky Willie Francis" above captions that read: "The Lad Who Cheated Chair" and "Negro Slayer Cheats Death." One reporter dispatched to the small Cajun town noted, "Speaking of rumors, this place is chocked full of them. Like bees from a beehive, rumors fly fast here surrounding the Willie Francis case, giving it a background of treachery, danger and wanton murder." The reporter added that there were people in St. Martinville who were "disappointed in Francis' survival of the chair. . . . Alive he may yet reveal something that has not been uncovered in the case."

As newspapermen converged on this sleepy sugar town, Ephie Foster and Vincent Venezia were heading in the opposite direction. They loaded the chair back onto the truck and drove slowly up Claiborne Street before turning left on Main. They had a long drive back to Angola, and they stopped for gas in the black part of town, near Willie's house. Velma Johnson and some of her schoolmates from Father Rousseve's elementary school at Notre Dame were watching from nearby as the two Angola men got out of the truck and swung open the rear doors, giving the children a clear view of the chair inside. While Venezia put gas in the truck, the big one, Foster, stared menacingly at the young black children before slamming the doors shut. "He made sure we all got a good look at that chair," Johnson recounts. Then Foster and Venezia got back in the truck and put the cursed town of St. Martinville in their rearview mirror.

With his would-be executioners retreating across the horizon, Willie closed his eyes and drifted. His insides still tingled and buzzed. A train always blew for the crossing at Iberia Street, the whistle followed by the rumble of the long, heavy freight on the nearby tracks. Free, he could hop this slow train and take it nine miles to St. Martinville, then hop off, and in just a short walk be at the house on Washington Street. They'd all be there, his brothers and sisters, his parents, and they'd wrap their arms around him. On the wall of his cell, the words Willie wrote one month earlier were still visible—words anyone could see.

Of Course I Am Not a Killer

to dry the tears of those
who still weep here

I like that guy.

— Bertrand DeBlanc

Hours had passed since Frederick Francis had driven home with news of his youngest son's miraculous encounter with Louisiana's deadly chair. Inside the Francises' small clapboard house, shock quickly turned to celebration as Willie's brothers and sisters screamed, laughed, and cried with joy at their baby brother's fortune. They had gathered to mourn—had readied themselves for a painful day of grief and funeral preparations—yet here they were, shaking the floorboards of their house with excitement. They didn't kill Willie!

"Merci Dieu!" Willie's mother, Louise, wailed in Cajun French, then collapsed to the floor. She had not been able to bear the prospect of accompanying her husband to the place where her son was going to die, so she had stayed at the "weather-beaten" house on Washington Street just blocks from the St. Martinville jail.

"Le bon Dieu," she cried repeatedly, her "wrinkled hands" clasped and raised to the heavens.

As the celebration on Washington Street began to die down, Frederick Francis became agitated again. A mixture of fury and

34

helplessness came over him once the euphoria of his son's miraculous escape from the chair finally subsided. The sheriff, the deputies, and the law had left him standing outside the jail with a coffin and hearse, waiting and pacing, without a final good-bye to Willie. Without money, he was helpless to defend his son and was forced to rely on the state for that, too. By law, by the formality of the death warrant, Louisiana would kill his youngest son. Again. And like his son, he, too, believed that the Lord had spared Willie's life. That it was God's will.

So Frederick Francis, Roman Catholic father of thirteen children, slung a sledgehammer over his shoulder and walked into the darkness, toward the tracks where the rumble of the Northern Pacific Railroad trains wobbled by. He walked until he came to the patchy, uneven lot that was the Union Baptist Cemetery. When he reached the very back of the lot, he stood beneath a pecan tree to collect his thoughts. He looked down at the tombstone that was to mark his youngest child's grave—the stone he had borrowed money to purchase the day before. Then, with all the strength he had in him, Frederick Francis raised the sledgehammer over his head and brought it crashing down onto the tombstone. It smashed into pieces.

●　●　●

On Saturday morning, May 4, Bertrand DeBlanc was sitting in his small wooden house on Claiborne Street, just paces from the St. Martinville courthouse, drinking his usual Cajun-style coffee—strong and slowly dripped into an enamel pot—when an old Negro man appeared on his steps. The man looked tired and drawn; he had tears in his eyes as he stood at the doorway. DeBlanc met the man's eyes. It was a look he would never forget.

The man at DeBlanc's door was Frederick Francis, born in 1879, just sixteen years after Abraham Lincoln signed the Emancipation Proclamation. Francis was a subsistence farmer who grew onions and bell peppers and took odd jobs around St. Martinville when he wasn't working in a local sugar factory. DeBlanc had seen him around town before, just as he'd seen Willie—doing odd jobs here and there. Both of them seemed friendly enough to DeBlanc.

Frederick Francis's father, Joseph Francois, had also been a farmer and had spent his whole life in St. Martinville. Early U.S. census reports for St. Martin Parish in the 1800s list the name Francis as "Francois," and by 1830 there were twenty-six slave inhabitants at the R. Francois Plantation. It is likely that Joseph Francois and his family were slaves—the property of this wealthy St. Martinville family whose surname they bore into the twentieth century.

In 1900, a fourteen-year-old "boarder" named Louisiana Taylor was living in the Francois household along with twenty-one-year-old Frederick Francois. When Frederick Francois registered for the draft in 1917, he could not read or write and placed an X on his draft card where his signature was required. As Frederick's wife, Louise Taylor would give birth to thirteen children—the last born in 1929 and baptized "Willie Francis."

The St. Martinville where the Francois family had lived and worked as slaves in the nineteenth century was not much different from the St. Martinville of the 1940s. Though slavery was by then part of the past, in 1947, 81 percent of black families in the United States had incomes below $3,000 per annum (double the percentage of whites), and segregation of schools and public facilities was the norm in the South. Louisiana's poverty level was among the worst in the nation. Francis at the time was making $9 a week in the fields. But Frederick Francis didn't need facts or statistics to tell him what he had certainly known long before he found himself waiting beside a coffin for his son's body outside the St. Martinville jail. Most whites, he knew, had difficulty accepting the notion that blacks were even members of the same biological species. (In the 1940s, the U.S. Army and many hospitals still separated blood supplies by race.) So, while not all of them felt hatred toward Willie Francis—some genuinely felt pity and even sadness for the boy and his family—without equivocation, most whites in Louisiana in 1946 did not deem blacks their equals.

DeBlanc looked in Francis's eyes and saw the tears of a desperate, aching man. He knew why Francis had come.

Like Frederick Francis, DeBlanc was born and raised in St. Martinville, and like Francis's ancestors, DeBlanc's had lived in town for generations. The son of a railroad lawyer, Bertrand was the only child of his father's second marriage. Daniel's first wife had died young, and with five children, he needed a woman to care for them. At age fifty-two, Daniel DeBlanc and his new bride, thirty-six-year-old Marie Louise Bertrand, became proud parents of Bertrand DeBlanc, born on January 20, 1911. Bertrand grew up on Bridge Street near St. Martinville's Church Square, but he enjoyed the privilege of attending better schools in New Iberia, as well as St. Paul's, the prestigious catholic school for boys in Covington.

In 1935, while home in St. Martinville on a break from his law studies at Louisiana State University in Baton Rouge, DeBlanc attended a "Home Sweet Home" Cajun country dance. These communal dances were known in southwestern Louisiana as *fais do-dos* ("go to sleep" in Cajun French) because they'd last all night, and Cajuns would bring along their children who would eventually go to sleep there. Young Cajun men would be restricted to holding pens known as *une cage aux chiens* (dogs' cage), unless they were busy fighting outside or dancing. Young ladies arrived with their mothers as chaperons. At that *fais do-do* in 1935, law student Bertrand DeBlanc met a local girl, sixteen-year-old Lillian Vincent. Lillian was one of ten children fathered by Edmond Vincent, who owned a farm on the outskirts of town. (The Vincents on Edmond's side were descendants of Jean Lafitte, the nineteenth-century French smuggler and privateer, who settled in southwest Louisiana toward the end of his life.)

DeBlanc, who loved to do the two-step, found the nerve to approach the Vincent girl and ask her to dance with him. Quickly taken by her beauty and grace, he was determined to stay out of the *cage aux chien*. "He was there with some friends and he picked me," Lillian would later say. The two of them spent most of that night on the dance floor.

Three years later, they married, and DeBlanc, on receiving his law degree from Louisiana State University and a master's degree in French, returned to St. Martinville to practice law. "His hero was Huey Long," Lillian says. "He dared to be like Huey Long." A charismatic small-town lawyer from north-central Louisiana, Long was a forceful radical populist who rose to power by taking on the state's political hierarchy, as well as the Standard Oil Company, which he accused of exploiting the state's natural resources. DeBlanc had attended law school with future Louisiana Senator Russell Long, Huey's son, and he had seen "the Kingfish" deliver the "Evangeline speech," one of the most famous pieces of oratory in American politics, in June of 1927 under the giant live oak tree in St. Martinville. DeBlanc was as inspired by Long's vision for Louisiana's future, which he attached to the growth of the celebrated tree, as he was by Long's passionate rhetorical style. In 1927 the French Cajuns were still a despised white minority in Louisiana, viewed by many upper-class whites as being "lower than niggers." But Long took a different view, and after the band had whipped up the Cajun crowd's enthusiasm, the undeniable Huey Long launched his campaign ("Every man a king, but no one wears a crown") with a message that in 1928 would win him the governorship of Louisiana in a landslide:

> And it is here, under this oak where Evangeline waited for her lover, Gabriel, who never came. This oak is an immortal spot, made so by Longfellow's poem, but Evangeline is not the only one who has waited here in disappointment.

Where are the schools that you have waited for your children to have, that have never come? Where are the roads and highways that you spent your money to build, that are no nearer now than ever before? Where are the institutions to care for the sick and disabled? Evangeline wept bitter tears in her disappointment. But they lasted through only one lifetime. Your tears in this country, around this oak, have lasted for generations. Give me the chance to dry the tears of those who still weep here!

An impressionable Cajun with an interest in law and politics, the young Bertrand DeBlanc would have found it difficult to forget the occasion of Huey Long coming to the little town of St. Martinville with so much drama and spirit.

At the beginning of America's involvement in World War II, the DeBlancs were living in a big house on Bridge Street in St. Martinville, where Lillian had given birth to the couple's first three children: Daniel, Dolly, and Veronica. Bertrand DeBlanc hadn't yet established much of a law practice, and money was tight for the family in St. Martinville. The young lawyer came home from work one day with an announcement: Bertrand had decided to follow in the footsteps of his father and grandfather by enlisting in the military; he was going to fight in the war raging overseas. Like DeBlanc, Cajuns enthusiastically enlisted in the military following the Japanese attack on Pearl Harbor. Nearly 25,000 Cajuns joined the armed services during World War II, the majority from Acadiana. Captain Robert L. Mouton of the U.S. Marines traveled the swamps and bayous of Acadiana in a pirogue (a shallow-draft boat) to recruit Cajuns for the war effort. "They can shoot straight," Mouton said, "they can handle a knife, they're good physical specimens and they love a scrape. . . . If that doesn't make good Marine material then *moi, je suis fou* [I'm crazy]." Lillian DeBlanc had learned, as would many of Bertrand's colleagues and adversaries later on, that once Bertrand made up his mind to do something, there was no stopping him.

"I have to go, too!" Lillian remembers him saying, and by September of 1942, DeBlanc was serving overseas. As a member of the 3118th Signal Services Battalion, DeBlanc's unit participated in the D-Day invasion by creating deceptive radio signals to convince the Germans that invading Allied forces were forming elsewhere. Like most Cajun servicemen, DeBlanc was fluent in French. The U.S. Army found his translating skills useful, and among other duties, he operated a teletype machine. General Dwight Eisenhower awarded his outfit for its outstanding work in communications, and in addition to the unit citation, by the time he had completed his service, Pfc DeBlanc was decorated with a European Theater Ribbon bearing one battle star and a Good Conduct Medal. In October of 1945, the *Weekly Messenger* ran the headline "Pfc B. DeBlanc Gets Army Discharge" above a story announcing DeBlanc's return to St. Martinville, to "his home on Bridge St. with his wife and children." Still, money remained a concern, and soon after his return from Germany, DeBlanc sold the house on Bridge Street and moved his family to a tiny wooden shack on Claiborne Street, across from the courthouse. The tiny house would also serve as his office until he could get his law practice off the ground. So Bertrand DeBlanc hung out a shingle and, eager for business, tried to reestablish his presence around the St. Martinville courthouse. His close proximity to Court Square kept him in the know, but although he was kept busy enough with notary work, cases were tough to come by in the small town. Nor was everyone who showed up at his door looking for representation.

On the morning of what was supposed to be Willie Francis's last day on earth, DeBlanc had been sitting in his house when Sheriff Resweber stopped by to ask if he would be willing to serve as a witness to Willie's execution. "No," DeBlanc had replied, "I like that guy." He'd seen Willie around town, and DeBlanc had found him to be a gentle, affable young man. Many whites around St. Martinville shared these sentiments. Maybe it was the softness in his eyes that distinguished Willie from so many of the other boys in town, white or black. So Bertrand declined to be a witness—because he liked Willie.

With Frederick Francis, the sixty-two-year-old father of a convicted murderer, now standing in his house, DeBlanc was acutely aware of his family's own past in the Acadian town—particularly the reputation of his grandfather, Alcibiades DeBlanc, the most powerful man in St. Martinville in his day and a celebrated hero to Cajuns. Bertrand was also aware that the family of Frederick Francis and the other blacks in St. Martinville had surely lived in terror of Alcibiades DeBlanc and the marauding band of loyal white supremacists he'd assembled to spread fear and death throughout southern Louisiana.

Jean Alcibiades Maximillian DeBlanc, born in St. Martinville in 1821, went on to become a lawyer, a lieutenant colonel, and the commander of Louisiana's 8th Volunteer Infantry Regiment during the Civil War. He was a practicing attorney in St. Martinville when Confederate President Jefferson Davis appointed him to be a colonel in the Confederate army. DeBlanc fought at the Battle of Gettysburg, where he lost his right arm on July 2, 1863. He was described as "a perfect Gentleman and an excellent officer. All respected, obeyed and loved him," and at the end of the war, he was appointed by Major General Harry Hays to negotiate with federal authorities the surrender of Confederate troops in Louisiana. DeBlanc returned to St. Martinville—as would his grandson Bertrand after his stint in a later war—to reestablish his legal practice.

In May of 1867, Alcibiades DeBlanc organized a "Caucasian Club" that pledged to restore white control of the government and to support the supremacy of the white race after Republican

carpetbaggers such as Illinois native Henry Clay Warmoth, who became governor of Louisiana in 1868, sought to grant voting rights
to blacks. DeBlanc founded the Knights of the White Camellia
(KWC), a secret fraternity that would ultimately reach as far west as
central Texas and as far east as the Carolinas. It took its name from
the flowering southern shrub, which was intended to symbolize the
purity of the white race. Though the group was often confused with
the Ku Klux Klan, the Knights were more numerous, their activities
were more clandestine, and their members—physicians, newspaper
editors, lawyers, law enforcement personnel—came from a higher
social stratum than the Klan's. Their aim was to reduce the influence of blacks in politics and to prevent racial integration; their
methods were founded in terrorism and intimidation and were every
bit as oppressive as the slave patrols and vigilance committees
(which DeBlanc had also organized in St. Martin Parish) that
roamed the South during slavery. *The Republican Campaign Text Book
1882*, published by the Republican Congressional Committee, included this sensational description of the Knights of the White
Camellia:

> These, mounted, masked, and armed, dragooned the
> parishes night and day and ruled in terror and blood,
> amid assassination and outrages, and violence of every de-
> gree and kind—mutilation, maimings, and whippings. No
> age or sex was respected—none was spared. The evi-
> dence, multiplied in a hundred shapes, is overwhelming,
> and is as revolting in its terrible details as it is conclusive
> in its proofs. The historical sanguinary violence of the
> "Franco-Spanish blood"—the sources of Louisiana's
> white population—was indulged without restraint. The
> old hellish terrorism of Murat, Couthon, and St. Just,
> those cruel demons of the French revolution of 1798, was

revived in Louisiana in all its frightful horrors. Indeed, throughout the canvass, prior to election day, murder was king, intimidation rioted at absolute tyrant.

Southern Louisiana was embroiled in intense political turmoil and racial experimentation in the Reconstruction years following the Civil War. In 1872, Republican William Pitt Kellogg, an Illinois friend of Abraham Lincoln's, resigned from the U.S. Senate to run against Democrat John McEnery for governor of Louisiana—a vacancy created by the impeachment of Warmoth for political corruption. (Lieutenant Governor P. B. S. Pinchback finished the last thirty-five days of Warmoth's term—making him the first African American governor of a U.S. state.)

The election was close, with both Kellogg and McEnery claiming victory, until President U. S. Grant ultimately signed an executive order naming Kellogg the victor. McEnery responded by urging supporters to take up arms against Kellogg's "fraudulent governorship," and Alcibiades DeBlanc along with his anti-Republican Knights of the White Camellia answered the call. On March 28, 1873, DeBlanc spoke to a crowd of thousands of whites at Lafayette Square in New Orleans. "What is behind the government of W. P. Kellogg? Negro domination. Are you prepared to submit to such domination?!" he incited the crowd to cheers and a resounding, No! "A thousand times no!" he continued. "If Grant refuses to recognize McEnery and recognizes Kellogg as governor, there is but one thing left and that is to do as we did in '68—to raise the flag of the white race in Louisiana and"—more cheers—"maintain our dignity and manhood to the bitter end."

In an effort to discourage the Negro vote, the White Camellia had run hundreds of Negro families out of St. Martinville and other towns by persuading planters not to employ blacks. After the election, DeBlanc organized and commanded an army of six hundred men to resist the "usurping" government, and he successfully convinced KWC supporters to refuse to pay taxes. Kellogg was forced to send Republican police in New Orleans (Metropolitans) to St. Martinville and, later, U.S. troops to dislodge DeBlanc, but whites refused to shelter or transport the federal troops and DeBlanc's army was able to hold them off. "If white people are to be arrested for the discharge of negroes who voted the Republican ticket, make your warrant for me now," DeBlanc said.

A story in *Scribner's Monthly* in 1874 noted, "The Louisiana white people were in such terror of the negro government that they would rather accept any other despotism. A military dictator would be far preferable to them; they would go anywhere to escape the ignominy to which they were at present subjected."

Indeed, it was estimated that "half the white male population in many parishes of Louisiana" belonged to the Knights of the White Camellia. DeBlanc proclaimed that he did not wish to see bloodshed in the standoff, but some Metropolitans were killed in skirmishes around St. Martinville. DeBlanc and his group were also accused by Kellogg of terrorizing and lynching Negroes during the insurrection. In 1874 DeBlanc surrendered to U.S. marshals; he was arrested and brought to New Orleans aboard the *Lucretia*, where he was held prisoner. There a crowd seven thousand strong showed their support for the "hero of a great popular demonstration," and when DeBlanc was quickly "requited of charges with bail," there were "great cheers" for the man who had stood up to Kellogg and championed white supremacy. "Legend has it that when the horses from his carriage were spooked by the large crowd and broke away," St. Martinville local James Akers says, "the people pulled Alcibiades' carriage through the streets of New Orleans in celebration."

Just two years later, after restoration of white, Democratic rule, Alcibiades DeBlanc was appointed to the Supreme Court of Louisiana and lived the remainder of his life in St. Martinville, where he was affectionately known as the King of the Cadians until his death in 1883.

Frederick Francis likely had no knowledge of the DeBlanc's family history, and on the morning after the attempted execution of his son, Francis passed the courthouse on his way down Main Street from his small gray frame house on Washington Street. He was on his way to see a lawyer, Jerome Broussard, for whom he sometimes did odd jobs.

Willie had been sitting in jail for the last nine months without benefit of an attorney. No appeals had been filed on his behalf, no last-minute motions. The teenager had passed the time with only a Bible to aid him as he'd waited for his execution date. When that day had finally come, Willie didn't die. And now they were going to try to do it again. Frederick Francis needed help.

Broussard sympathized. He did not agree with the state's ruling that the young man should go back to the chair a second time. But Broussard handled mostly oil cases. There was also the issue of Francis's inevitable in forma pauperis (pauper's appeal) filing. The black farmer's lack of funds to pay for legal services was a factor Broussard was forced to consider, as his two-man practice was already overwhelmed with work and the Francis case had the potential to become a protracted battle. Perhaps weighing heaviest on his mind, however, was the unspoken, yet most obvious reason of all: Broussard had a well-established law practice in St. Martinville, and he could ill afford to offend his wealthy clients by taking the side of a young Negro who had been convicted of murdering a well-respected white man in town. So Broussard recommended Bertrand DeBlanc, the young lawyer in the tiny wooden building next door.

Moments after Frederick Francis left his office, Broussard called DeBlanc on the phone. "You know what happened?" Broussard asked.

"Yes, I was there," DeBlanc said. He had seen the truck arrive; it had parked right in front of his house. He'd seen Ephie Foster and

Vincent Venezia and the crowd that had gathered to watch as the chair was unloaded and carried into the jail. DeBlanc had gotten out his Brownie camera and begun to take pictures of the spectacle. The courthouse. The jail. Gruesome Gertie being carried out of the truck. He had even snapped a few shots of his children, Daniel, Dolly, and Veronica, sitting outside on the steps, watching everything.

"I know you liked him," Broussard said. "How'd you like to take the case?"

DeBlanc had already made up his mind. What he had seen the previous day behind the St. Martinville courthouse had infuriated him. From the very start, for DeBlanc, it was a matter of right or wrong, and sending Willie Francis back to the chair was clearly wrong. "The question of guilt or innocence was beside the point," DeBlanc would say. "I didn't give a damn if he got a fair trial. The question was whether the man goes to the chair twice for the same offense. . . . They's done everything they were supposed to do. The whole thing about capital punishment in my opinion is the anticipation. For the two weeks, three weeks, a month, you know you're going to die the moment they pull the switch. . . . You blow that, you blow the whole thing."

Broussard's final words to DeBlanc were meaningless: "They don't have any money."

"I don't need it," DeBlanc said, then hung up the phone and waited for Willie's father to arrive. He looked around the front room of the house that doubled as his office—a bare-bones setup if ever there was one—and into the back room where his children were usually playing on their beds, unless they were running and yelling past his desk while he was meeting with clients.

Despite the temporary calm, Bertrand DeBlanc knew as well as Broussard that the moment news got out around St. Martinville that he, a white lawyer, was representing Willie, there was going to be talk. The shock on the townspeople's faces would only be compounded by the fact that they knew DeBlanc had been good friends with the victim, Andrew Thomas. He and Andrew had co-owned the very plot of land where Thomas was killed. DeBlanc's wife, Lillian, and her sister, Stella Vincent, had even worked at Thomas's drugstore before the pharmacist was murdered. No one in town had a bad thing to say about "Drew," even though the "old bachelor" was a mystery to most. DeBlanc had heard the rumors. People wondered why Andrew Thomas lived in that house all by himself, outside of town. And they wondered why Thomas's car was sometimes seen in front of the homes of married women whose husbands were away.

Bertrand DeBlanc hadn't given much thought to any of the talk and innuendo that had consumed the small town of St. Martinville before and, more vigorously, after Andrew's murder. He liked Andrew; he'd liked visiting him at the drugstore before he'd gone off to the war. He was overseas when he'd heard the news of Andrew's death, and he'd been just as shocked, even at that distance, as anyone in St. Martinville.

DeBlanc knew that things would now be different. Possibly there would be trouble. He'd be attempting to save the life of the Negro boy who killed Andrew Thomas. While he may not have been sure what this would mean to his career as a lawyer in a small southern town, not to mention how it might affect his family, DeBlanc couldn't help but realize that these moments were of equal consequence in his life as his enlistment in the armed services.

DeBlanc had returned to St. Martinville from another part of the world where Americans, white and black, had sacrificed their lives to defend principles of freedom and justice. Nearly a million blacks had returned from that war, their eyes opened to racial inequalities in their own country. And millions of white servicemen had seen what Nazi Germany and imperialist Japan were capable of. The Jim Crow ways of the South did not sit well with many of them, either. As the young Cajun lawyer stared at a desperate Frederick Francis, father of the condemned teenager, these forces of fairness and justice were about to come bearing down on a town, a state, and a nation.

"This is the most unusual case I've ever seen," DeBlanc told Francis. "But I think it's the kind of case we can win."

so many heart-breaking scenes

Beautiful is the land,
with its prairies and forests of fruit-trees;
Under the feet a garden of flowers,
and the bluest of heavens
Bending above, and resting its dome on the walls of the forest.
They who dwell there have named it the Eden of Louisiana.

— HENRY WADSWORTH LONGFELLOW,
Evangeline: A Tale of Acadie

Catholic French colonists began settling the area that is now Nova Scotia in the early seventeenth century, despite the overwhelming harshness and desolation of the Acadian wilderness in Maritime Canada. Without much economic support from the motherland, these devoutly Catholic peasants, who had fled their country because of the religious wars in France, quickly developed into self-sufficient pioneers. (Ships carrying food and supplies to their tiny settlements were often destroyed or delayed by storms in the Atlantic, or planned voyages to Canada were simply abandoned due to French politics.) The isolation of the French Acadians encouraged the development of individual skills such as hunting, fishing, and building for the common good of the community, resulting in lifestyles that obliterated entrenched notions of class and undermined the significance of social position, which had characterized life in France.

By the start of the eighteenth century, the French Acadians had solidly established themselves throughout the coastal region of eastern Canada and were recognized by their neighbors as a unique cultural group—simple, peaceful, and prosperous. Daniel Subercase, Acadia's last French governor, was believed to have said in 1708, "The more I consider these people, the more I believe they are the happiest people in the world."

Yet all was not tranquil across the Atlantic; the French and the English had been at war since 1688. As a result, the English colonists had never been comfortable sharing the Acadia region with these "French neutrals," who refused to take a full oath of allegiance to the English king, rejected the Church of England, and clung fiercely to Roman Catholicism.

Even more menacingly, the French Acadians maintained a close relationship with the region's Indian tribes, most notably the Mi'kmaq tribe that had long been engaged in hostilities with the English. For the most part, the Acadians stayed where they had originally settled—close to the shore—and respected the Mi'kmaqs' claim to the interior. The English eventually realized that the Acadians owned the best land and had the most prosperous farms, which yielded an abundance of wheat, corn, barley, oats, and peas. Not only did they prosper, they multiplied. An English surveyor named David Dunbar wrote, "These French inhabitants increase so fast, that soon there will be no land left for other colonists."

Major Charles Lawrence, a British military officer and lieutenant governor of Nova Scotia, conspired with Governor William Shirley, commander in chief of British forces in New England, to remove all Acadians from their settlements on the Bay of Fundy's coast. The English systematically fostered rumors among the local populace of an impending French invasion to justify their confiscation of all the Acadians' weapons, while at the same time, British troops amassed in Nova Scotia. Acadian men and teenaged boys were summoned to the church of St. Charles de Grand Pre, where Lieutenant Colonel John Winslow addressed the Acadians in what became known as *le grand Derangement* (The Great Upheaval). Presenting "His Majesty's final resolution concerning the French inhabitants of this Province of Nova Scotia," Winslow informed them that the English would be appropriating all their land and cattle, although the French were free to keep their money and take whatever possessions they could carry aboard ships that would transport them and their families down the coast to a new territory. He concluded, "I hope that in whatever part of the world your lot may fall, you may be faithful subjects, and a peaceable and happy people."

While Winslow spoke to the men gathered at the church, armed British troops barred the exits. And Winslow spoke falsely. There had been no resolution issued by His Majesty; rather, the supposed royal edict was merely another part of the ruse Lawrence had concocted to rid the territory of the Acadians. Meanwhile, he had sent in British troops to occupy French Acadian villages, with orders to arrest and burn the homes of anyone who resisted. Catholic priests had been rounded up, and their churches were converted into sleeping quarters for the troops.

Winslow himself saw to it that the first group of Acadians, some 230 men and boys, were led to waiting English ships, and he noted, "I ordered the prisoners to march. They all answered they would not go without their fathers. I took hold of [a prisoner] and bid [him to] march. He obeyed and the rest followed, though slowly, and went off praying, singing and crying, being met by the women and children all the way, which is 1 $1/2$ mile, with great lamentations, upon their knees. . . . Thus ended this painful task of so many heartbreaking scenes."

The Acadian families were intentionally separated and herded aboard waiting British ships, mostly in October of 1755, with the cruel winter months lying ahead of them. None of them knew where they were going. Winslow wrote in his journal: "The inhabitants, with great sorrow, abandoned their homes. It was a scene of confusion, despair and desolation. Husbands and wives, brothers and sisters, parents and children, fiancés and friends, believing they were merely separating for a few days, were never to meet again on earth, the ships having far distant destinations."

The British ships set sail for destinations as far-flung as New York, Pennsylvania, and the Carolinas to make it difficult for the refugees to regather and attempt to return to Nova Scotia. Virginia did not welcome the thousands of these ragged exiles and encouraged them to move on as quickly as possible. A few managed to navigate their way back to Nova Scotia, while others settled in places like Maryland, where Catholic communities welcomed them. But for the most part, and with great hardship, the half who survived the journey headed south along the coast. For ten years they traveled until they reached the swamplands of southern Louisiana. Once again, they were strangers in a strange land. Once again, they would be forced to call on their resourcefulness to adapt to a different and new, but equally harsh, environment.

Over the next few years, these Acadian refugees began settling on a tract of land purchased in 1760 by Gabriel Fuselier de la Claire, born in Lyon, France. He named the area Poste des Attakapas; it totaled about 473,000 acres and was situated along the Bayou Teche across from the Attakapas chief Rinemo. This new town sprung up around St.-Martin-de-Tours Roman Catholic Church, established by Acadians in 1761, and Church Square became a bustling Victorian epicenter of commerce. By 1789, French Royalists fleeing the bloody French Revolution had begun arriving in New Orleans, but many moved west into the bayou country to live among the Acadian exiles, where the land was rich and plentiful. Incoming members of the French aristocracy traveled to Poste des Attakapas with many of the luxuries they had enjoyed in France, from silver cutlery to Louis

Seize furniture, and created in the bayou country of Louisiana a lavish imitation of the world they had known at the French court.

Lured by the rich land and the promise of profits in indigo, hemp, and cattle ranching, Creole and French families from the West Indies also found their way to the region around the same time as the Acadians. The land on both sides of the Bayou Teche, after it was drained, was easily cultivated, and the soil proved to be ideal for growing sugarcane, which soon became the region's largest crop. Acres of cane fields sprouted up around Poste des Attakapas, many of them owned by the hard-working Acadians, who also provided much of the labor. In marshes and swamps where the drainage and planting were not feasible, the industrious Acadians hunted wild game for food and fur.

At the turn of the nineteenth century, the Louisiana sugar boom was under way, and by 1817, the area once known as Poste des Attakapas had officially been incorporated as St. Martinville. Transportation by steamboat along the Bayou Teche enabled prominent Creole families to travel to St. Martinville, where they could take in the best operas and stay at fine hotels. St. Martinville was now a fashionable resort as well as a mecca of French culture, thus its nickname, le petit Paris. In spite of the harrowing exile they had endured, the Acadians—independent and self-sufficient—had adapted to their new environment and prospered. They had become "a peaceable and happy people" once again.

Much of the wealth of the aristocratic French in St. Martinville had been tied to the land they owned. They were, in general, unable to transfer their capital to the new continent when fleeing the revolutionary rabble, so without their fortunes, most of the Royalists either accustomed themselves to middle-class living or descended into poverty. The French and Creoles aligned themselves with each other, and together they attempted to cast the Acadian exiles as mere colonial peasants—a "crass and uncultured people" who lived less affluently, less ambitiously, and less genteelly. Egalitarian as always, the Acadians resented the codes of conduct that the French, with their aristocratic assumptions and pretensions, tried to impose on them. That resentment bred decades of tension between the Acadians and the Old-World French.

No matter how great the enmity between these two groups, neither was subjected to as much unearned hardship as the other group of arrivals to Louisiana in the 1700s. They were coming in large numbers, from Africa, on ships run by Yankee traders. Louisiana needed the slaves that arrived at the Acadian coast to support the booming sugar business. Unlike the English colonials who imported their slaves from the British West Indies, the slaves in Louisiana, imported under French and Spanish rule, came from Senegambia and, in time, created "an unusually cohesive and heavily Africanized slave culture." It was from French and Spanish customs and attitudes mixed with African mores that the distinctive "Creole" culture emerged. By 1820, there were more black slaves than white residents in the region.

Acadians, or Cajuns, rarely owned more than a few slaves per family, and Cajuns who worked land that they themselves did not own refused to work as serfs on sugar plantations owned by Creoles or Anglo-Americans. Yet the culture of the Cajuns and Creoles, and slave blacks, overlapped; they shared the French language, a cuisine based on seafood taken from the swamps and bayous, and eventually the Catholic religion. They overlapped, but rarely did they mix. Despite the egalitarian principles the Cajuns espoused and the Old-World French class distinctions they eschewed when they lived in Nova Scotia, Cajuns rigidly enforced group boundaries. Although these boundaries separated Cajuns from the wealthy Creoles and aristocratic French, they also automatically elevated Cajun slaveowners above black slaves and afforded them an increased social status.

Slave insurrections in Acadian territories codified the hierarchical relationship between blacks and Cajuns. Negroes were viewed not just as labor but also as a threat to "internal security." Cajuns voluntarily and exuberantly served in the local slave patrols that conducted meticulous inspections of slave quarters, often with cruel results, for slaves resisting these inspections were immediately flogged under the rule of *Le Code Noir* (The Black Code)—the French law governing local slave administration, in effect since 1724.

"Prior to the late eighteenth century," Carl A. Brasseaux notes in *The Founding of New Acadia*, "Acadians had consistently refused to recognize the innate racial, cultural, or social superiority of any group. Though initially uncomfortable with the institution, the Acadians were compelled by the threat of insurrection to protect and vigorously maintain Negro slavery. By identifying rigorous slave control with their own security, the exiles were tacitly committed to an unarticulated policy of white superiority."

With this inherently unfair way of life normalized by time, things continued on in St. Martinville much the same until an outbreak of yellow fever in 1855. That epidemic marked the beginning of the end to the most prosperous age in the town's history. Visitors from New Orleans, who had been coming to St. Martinville to escape the sweltering heat and their own city's battle with the fever, now sought out new destinations for their vacations. Then, the following year, a great fire swept through the town and destroyed many of the wooden structures surrounding St.-Martin-de-Tours Church. And on August 10, 1856, a powerful hurricane devastated the crops throughout the parish, which the ruthless storm left in ruins. Before St. Martinville could recover from these natural disasters, the Civil War brought marauding Federal troops into Teche Valley. The property destruction was enormous. St. Martinville, like the rest of the South, was changed forever.

After the Civil War and the loss of slave labor, the agricultural industry in Louisiana faced certain failure, which in turn would devas-
tate the state's economy. Just two years after President Lincoln
issued the Emancipation Proclamation, the state put severe restric-
tions on the rights of all blacks, whatever their wealth or blood lines.
Although the new Louisiana Black Code acknowledged the rights of
freed persons to marry, to acquire property, and to testify in court, it
also served to restore the plantation economy, whereby blacks became exploited laborers rather than outright slaves.

By the end of the nineteenth century, St. Martinville had evolved
from the bustling le petit Paris into a small Louisiana Cajun town.
Steamboats no longer churned their way up the bayou; the summer
no longer brought its steady flow of visitors. Railroads had become
the preferred mode of transportation. America celebrated progress,
but St. Martinville, like many small towns across the country, was
left behind. Still, the sugar mills continued to prosper, and poor
blacks continued to supply cheap labor for the Leverts, the Pette-
bones, and the Fourgeaud family businesses in town. Slavery was
gone, but sharecropping had instituted an equally effective feudal
system that kept an economic stranglehold on blacks in Louisiana,
just as it did throughout the South, well into the twentieth century.

In 1939, the writer Henry Miller began traveling around America
on an odyssey that, as he stated in the account of his journey, *The
Air Conditioned Nightmare*, he hoped would shed some light on the
American experience. Miller perceived keenly and recorded eloquently how the sugar business had been able to survive and thrive
in Cajun country:

> Supporting it all, a living foundation, like a great column
> of blood, was the labor of the slaves. The very bricks of
> which the walls of the famous houses are made were
> shaped by the hands of Negroes. Following the bayous

the landscape is dotted with the cabined shacks of those who gave their sweat and blood to help create a world of extravagant splendor. The pretensions which were born of this munificence, and which still endure amidst the soulless ruins of the great pillared houses, are rotting away, but the cabins remain. The Negro is anchored to the soil; his way of life has changed hardly at all since the great debacle. He is the real owner of the land, despite all titular changes of possession. No matter what the whites say, the South could not exist without the easy, casual servitude of the blacks. The blacks are the weak and flexible backbone of this decapitated region of America.

Miller passed through New Iberia and St. Martinville on that journey and absorbed the mystery and otherworldliness of the Bayou Teche: "Sky and water had become one; the whole world was floating in a nebular mist. It was indescribably beautiful and bewitching. I could scarcely believe that I was in America."

Along the same stretch of the Bayou Teche—which fascinated Miller so thoroughly—and in the center of St. Martinville, stands the Evangeline Oak. A grand and impressive tree, it stands at the heart of Acadian, or Cajun, culture and has represented those people's hopes and dreams for over a century. The tree attracts tourists from as far away as France, all of whom are drawn to the place where Evangeline awaits her lover Gabriel in Henry Wadsworth Longfellow's epic poem of 1847, *Evangeline: A Tale of Acadie*.

Longfellow based his poem on the tragic expulsion of the French Acadians from Nova Scotia. In the poem, the separated lovers, Evangeline and Gabriel, represent not only the tragic plight of the Acadians who eventually settled in Louisiana but also the remarkable determination and religious conviction of the Cajun people, as the settlers came to be known. Yet the tree itself belongs to a dream, a fiction, for Evangeline and Gabriel, thwarted by fate and history, lived and struggled and suffered and wept and died only in a Longfellow poem. And the tears shed beneath the oak's majestic branches are born of a poet's dream.

A short walk away, along the same bank of the Teche, grows another oak, this one watered by actual tears rather than fictive ones. Its leaves shaded a small brick building and kept the burning Louisiana sun at bay for the prisoners inside the St. Martinville jail. The tears shed beneath this tree's branches were grievously real; they were tears born of a people's suffering and fear, and dread. From beneath the branches of this tree behind the courthouse in St. Martinville, blacks were hanged by rope in sentences of death. It was in the shade of this tree, too, that Frederick Francis sought relief from the hot noonday sun while his youngest child, upstairs in the jail, waited for the chair to reach its fatal force.

a short story

We heard a little rumor that somebody across the bayou might have had something to do with this.

—S. J. YONGUE, ST. MARTIN PARISH CORONER

On the morning of November 8, 1944, eighteen months before Willie Francis was sent to the electric chair, newspaper headlines across the country declared that Franklin Delano Roosevelt had soundly defeated New York Governor Thomas Dewey to win a fourth term as president. With World War II raging on both the European and Pacific fronts, Dewey had called FDR a "tired old man" during the election campaign. The president had responded to Dewey's veiled reference to his failing health by urging voters not to "change horses in mid stream" and by promising them that he'd finish the war and win the peace.

In St. Martinville, Louisiana, the headlines were more ordinary. The *Weekly Messenger* reported St. Martin Elementary 4H Club news, as well as the movements and casualties of local servicemen overseas. Elsewhere were listed the names of "colored men" who had been called for pre-induction exams. Another piece quoted Father Maurice Rousseve of the "Notre Dame Catholic Church for the Colored," who was calling for "all the Colored people [to] come and enjoy themselves and help a good cause" at the church fair on the weekend. And the obituary page ran the announcement that Bertrand's half-brother, Francis DeBlanc, fifty-seven, had died in New Iberia and was "survived by Pfc Bertrand DeBlanc, overseas."

Still, all was not right in St. Martinville on the morning of November 8, 1944. By 8:45 a.m., Lucien Bienvenu, who ran a grocery store across from St.-Martin-de-Tours Catholic Church on Main Street, noticed that the pharmacy next door had not yet opened for business. Andrew Thomas, the fifty-three-year-old owner of Thomas's Drug Store, was normally punctual, so Bienvenu tried to reach Thomas at home by telephone. With no answer there, he decided to call Thomas's sister-in-law, Alida Thomas. "Mrs. Zie," as she was known around town, was just leaving to take the children to school when Bienvenu informed her that Andrew had not yet opened the drugstore and wasn't answering the phone at home. "You better go see," Bienvenu told her.

Mrs. Zie took her children to school, then drove to the St. Martinville courthouse to pick up her husband, Rauszelle "Zie" Thomas, Andrew's brother, who was the secretary-treasurer for the St. Martin Parish Police Jury, the governing authority of St. Martin Parish. Zie was unnerved by his brother's absence. Andrew was always very attentive to his business, and normally, if some other commitment demanded his attention, he called upon Zie to watch the drugstore. To simply not show up for work was out of character. Zie and his wife drove to Andrew's house on the outskirts of St. Martinville, across from the Evangeline State Park.

When they pulled into the driveway, they noticed immediately that the garage door was closed. "If the car is still in the garage, there is something wrong," Zie said, but Mrs. Zie had already spotted her brother-in-law lying on the ground, halfway between the garage and the porch steps in the back. She gasped.

Zie bolted from the car and ran to his brother's body. He grabbed Andrew's left wrist. He found no pulse. He clutched his brother's lifeless body in his arms—and surrendered hope. Andrew had been shot in the eye; dried blood stained the ground where his head had rested. "Yes, sure he is dead," Zie said.

With the image of Andrew's broken, bloodied eyeglasses seared in their minds, Mr. and Mrs. Zie Thomas got back in their car and drove to the St. Martin Infirmary on North Main Street. They returned to the house with Dr. A. R. Corne, who lifted Andrew's shirt and discovered additional bullet wounds and more bloodstains. After placing a sheet over the body, Mr. and Mrs. Thomas drove to Elmo Bonin's general merchandise store down the street and called the other Thomas brothers with the tragic news.

Zie Thomas did not have to think very hard about whom to call first. Using Bonin's phone, he telephoned his brother Claude, the St. Martinville chief of police. Claude Thomas, a large man who still patrolled the city proper on horseback, would have given full attention to an apparent murder in St. Martinville under any circumstances. The fact that the victim was his brother added a profoundly felt grief to his investigation.

The first matter of business was to assemble a coroner's jury of five men, and later that day, an inquest was held before Dr. S. J. Yongue, coroner of St. Martin Parish, to officially determine the cause of Andrew Thomas's death. Alvin and Ida Van Brocklin, who were Andrew Thomas's closest neighbors off the highway across from Evangeline State Park, were called to testify before the coroner.

It was close to midnight, they said, and they were asleep when gunshots awakened both of them. "It sounded like an automatic," Alvin said, "just like you pulled a trigger and let it go. You could hardly count it was so fast." Ida agreed. "They came fast, one after the other."

Alvin got up and walked onto his porch. He thought the shots might have been coming from Evangeline State Park, where German prisoners of war were being held at the time. (Guards at the camp also heard the shots.) Ida stayed in bed and looked out the window toward Thomas's house. "There was a car parked in front of Mr. Thomas's house with the lights on," she said. "The car was stopped there. We heard the shots."

"Did you notice how long that car stayed there?" Dr. Yongue asked.

"No, sir," she said. "I was nervous, so I laid down again." The car must have gone the other way, she said, because she did not see the lights pass by her house again.

The Van Brocklins were the only witnesses. They could attest to hearing rapid gunfire; they could attest to seeing a mysterious car parked in front of the Thomas house with its lights on. But they knew nothing more.

●   ●   ●

Andrew I. Thomas was born in St. Martinville on April 4, 1891. His father, Albert Thomas, though English-born, had grown up in St. Martinville, married a Cajun woman, Elmire Broussard, and lived two houses down from the DeBlanc family. Andrew served briefly in the navy during World War I. In 1920, the twenty-nine-year-old Thomas was working as a salesman at Fournet's Drug Store in St. Martinville and living with his mother, Elmire. Three years later, he left St. Martinville to work at a pharmacy in Homer, Louisiana, and by 1930, Andrew Thomas had moved to New Orleans, where he was studying pharmacology at night at Loyola University's College of Pharmacy while sharing an address with his cousin, Howard Thomas, the nineteen-year-old son of his uncle, Hackett. To support himself, Andrew Thomas worked during the day at K & B, the purple-signed drugstore chain headquartered in New Orleans. Also living in New Orleans at the time was another native of St. Martinville, Dr. Earl Eastin, then a thirty-five-year-old dentist. After his studies in New Orleans, Andrew Thomas returned to St. Martinville. There he opened the Thomas Drug Store in the Pavia

Building on Bridge Street in the summer of 1937, but eventually he took over as the pharmacist at his father's drugstore on Main Street. Eastin had also returned to St. Martinville, and on the evening of November 7, 1944, Thomas had been at the house of Dr. Eastin and his wife on Bridge Street until about 11:30 p.m. The dinner was satisfying to Thomas, who was reported to have told his hosts upon leaving, "If I die tonight, I'll die well fed."

Andrew Thomas was a handsome, educated bachelor with his own successful business in St. Martinville. Tall, somewhat stocky, with dark hair and gray eyes, Thomas wore glasses; at work he always wore a dress shirt and tie. "Cordial" and "polite" were words people commonly used to describe him, and according to his obituary in the *Weekly Messenger*, he was "well loved in this community by all who knew him." "No one," the paper added, "can think of an enemy that he ever had."

Shortly before midnight, Thomas drove home from Earl Eastin's house. Playing at the Bienvenu Theater that night was the final film in Paramount's Henry Aldrich series, *Henry Aldrich's Little Secret*. With the theater's marquis fading in his rearview mirror, Andrew Thomas drove north on Main Street to his place outside of town, where he pulled the car into a detached garage behind his house. After turning off the engine, Thomas exited through the front of the garage and closed the door behind him. He had taken just a few steps toward his house when a figure emerged from behind the cistern near the rear stairs. Thomas was jumped, police would later say, and a "terrific struggle" ensued. The druggist got the worst of it as the gunfire that woke the Van Brocklins rang out across the prairie. One bullet struck Thomas an inch under his left armpit; another, six inches below that. Two more bullets struck his right side toward the back. A fifth bullet drove into his right eyeball. All five shots were fired at close range. There was no telling exactly how many shots had been fired, but the coroner stated that the bullets indicated the weapon was a .38 caliber pistol or rifle in the "hands of an unknown party or parties." Any one of the wounds, the coroner concluded, "would have produced death."

The motive appeared to be robbery. As Thomas lay sprawled on the ground near the back steps of his porch, dead or dying, evidently his pockets had been turned out. Police believed his wallet had been taken.

Information from the coroner's report was all that Claude Thomas and Sheriff Resweber had to begin their investigation into the murder of Andrew Thomas. The seemingly random killing meanwhile stunned the sleepy Cajun town on the Bayou Teche. And to the horror of the residents of St. Martinville, the murderer or murderers were still at large.

Word that Andrew Thomas had been shot dead got around town fast, and St. Martinville was whipped quickly into a frenzy of shock, fear, and speculation. On Thursday, November 9, after a "largely attended" funeral was held at St.-Martin-de-Tours Catholic Church, the body of Andrew Thomas was laid to rest at St. Michael's Cemetery just across the bayou. The next day, the *Weekly Messenger* ran the headline:

ANDREW THOMAS KILLED AT HIS HOME
HERE TUESDAY NIGHT

The opening paragraphs of the story included some leads that the police were investigating, but mostly the tone conveyed surprise and confusion.

> Mr. Thomas' death was a shock to the whole community as he was well known and loved by children and adults. His drug store was the hang-out for the younger people here and "Drew," as the kids affectionately called him,

would greet them genially. He is sadly missed by all who knew him.

In the same issue, *Weekly Messenger* editor Marcel "Blackie" Bienvenu, whose musings were a staple of the newspaper, wrote a front-page editorial lamenting Thomas's "so sudden death."

In the days and weeks that followed, the people of St. Martinville were deathly afraid to leave their homes at night. State Representative Sydney Mae Durand, who was a child at the time, remembered how "adults talked about it in whispers. In front of the children, they talked in French. There was a killer at large and everyone was terrified." A white couple who had a social engagement one evening asked a trusted black woman in town to watch after their children; but the black woman, too, was gripped by the terror and refused to venture out unless her teenage son accompanied her. The woman was Miss Louise Taylor Francis, and accompanied by her fifteen-year-old son, Willie, she did watch the couple's children.

The town's expressions of sentiment for the sadly deceased pharmacist soon yielded to gossip and rumor. With no suspects yet in custody, speculation centered on a romantic relationship that might have gone bad and thus led to the death of the druggist. A lifelong bachelor, bright and charming, Andrew Thomas had had a reputation as a bit of a "ladies' man," and rumors began circulating that he'd possibly been killed by either the jealous husband or boyfriend of a woman he'd been seeing. Romance and revenge supplanted robbery as the motive for Thomas's murder in the court of public opinion. The gossip was so widespread in St. Martinville that Dr. Yongue himself began to suspect a motive other than robbery. He recalled Thomas's neighbor, Alvin Van Brocklin, to testify before the coroner's jury.

"We would like to have a little more information," Yongue began. "You are still under oath. We heard a little rumor that somebody across the bayou might have had something to do with this. Do you know of any associations that he might have had with anybody across the bayou?"

Van Brocklin reported what many in town had observed and gossiped about in St. Martinville long before Thomas was murdered. "I saw his car at a lady's house out there several times."

"Do you know the name of this lady?" Yongue wanted to know.

"Nassans, I think," he replied. "Mrs. Louis Nassans, that's all I know about that."

"Where do they live?" Yongue asked.

"Right near Pine Grove somewhere," Van Brocklin replied. "And another place he went to was a Mrs. Duplantis right in front of Pine Grove."

Both husbands, Louis Nassans and Homer Duplantis, worked in the oil business, and both their jobs kept them away from home for long stretches of time. Such circumstances no doubt fueled many of the rumors that involved Andrew Thomas with married women and, more specifically, with Bea Nassans and Henrietta Duplantis.

"Did you ever see any of these ladies at his house?" Yongue asked.

"No, sir. Never have."

"Do you know anything more about the associations of Mr. Thomas, and any other women associates?" Yongue asked.

"No, sir," Van Brocklin replied. "That's all I know."

The five St. Martinville men who had been called and sworn in to witness Dr. Yongue's examination of the body were also present for Van Brocklin's testimony. The fifth member of the jury, Francis Fuselier, was the younger brother of August Fuselier—the deputy sheriff of St. Martinville.

Even though ordinary citizens were cementing their own theories about the murder as the months dragged on, Police Chief Claude Thomas, once a foreman in a sugar refinery, and Leonard Resweber, now the sheriff but formerly the tax collector in town, still had very little physical evidence to advance the investigation. Chief Thomas was also an auxiliary deputy, who therefore had to defer to the judgment of Resweber. This was the first murder case for both men, and neither had had any training in homicide investigations. They had recovered bullets at the scene of the crime, but no murder weapon was retrieved. Nor had they discovered any fingerprints inside or outside the victim's house. Thomas's car, apparently untouched, was still in the garage. They had not found any witnesses to the actual murder, and interrogations around town had turned up nothing. Louis Nassans and Homer Duplantis had been questioned, but despite rumors of a revenge killing, Resweber could find no evidence linking either man to Thomas's death. Both the sheriff's department and the police department in St. Martinville had already logged hundreds of hours on the case, to no avail.

In each issue of the *Weekly Messenger*, an announcement offering a $500 reward by Sheriff Resweber and the Thomas family "for information leading to the arrest and conviction of the person or persons who committed the murder of Andrew I. Thomas at 12:05 A.M. on November 8th, 1944" was surrounded by the usual 4-H Club news and servicemen's discharge notices. A November 24 story in the *Weekly Messenger* stated that there were "new clues found in [the] Thomas murder case," but they were not revealed. Sheriff Resweber assured the community that, in his untiring work on the case, "nothing is being overlooked" and that his men "will not let up in their effort until the case has been solved."

The gossip continued into the new year and throughout the summer of 1945, but it was looking more and more as if the murder of Andrew Thomas might go unsolved. The fact that no further incidents of violent robberies had occurred in St. Martinville in the seven months following Thomas's murder seemed to support the theory that either a spurned lover or jealous husband had sought his revenge on the ladies' man Thomas.

By July of 1945, nearly nine months after the murder of his brother Andrew, Claude Thomas and his men had exhausted all their leads. Sheriff Resweber was beginning to think, though not to admit, that they had reached a dead end. Because both men took tremendous pride in keeping St. Martinville free from all but the pettiest of crimes, an unsolved murder rankled them beyond measure. During a meeting on an unrelated police matter with the Port Arthur, Texas, chief of police Claude W. Goldsmith, Resweber spoke of the murder case that had left St. Martinville's law enforcement totally baffled. According to Resweber's own testimony before the Louisiana Pardons Board, the desperate and frustrated sheriff asked Goldsmith to "try to apprehend any man" from St. Martinville found in Port Arthur, "because so far they had been unable to get the right man."

Port Arthur, Texas, sits adjacent to the Louisiana border about 150 miles west of St. Martinville. A blue-collar, industrial city on the northwest shore of Lake Sabine, Port Arthur had become home to several major oil refineries and, along with the Texas cities of Beaumont and Orange, one of the points in an area known as the Golden Triangle.

On the evening of August 3, 1945, Claude Goldsmith and Detective Edmund Oster were staking out the Port Arthur train station at Seventh Street and Austin in the hope of arresting a suspected drug dealer who was believed to be arriving at the depot. They watched as a suspicious-looking man with a suitcase stepped off the train. They followed their suspect in their cruiser until he began to run. On foot the two policemen then gave chase, but the man easily eluded them and vanished into the dark Texas night.

Just a few blocks away from the train station, Willie Francis had stepped out of his sister Lucille's house at 339 West Tenth Street to get a breath of fresh air before dinner. He was taking a quick walk around the block when he spotted two white policemen running his way in their pursuit of a man with a suitcase. Instinctively, he ducked behind a tree as the man ran by. Goldsmith spotted Willie and mistook him for an accomplice of the suspect they were pursuing. Detective Edmund Oster noted that Willie was stuttering, that he seemed to be nervous, shifty, like he was looking for a chance to run. They cuffed Willie, put him into the police car, and took him to the police station for questioning.

Once in custody, Willie was able to successfully convince Chief Goldsmith that he had nothing to do with the man they were after, and the police dropped the drug charges. Nonetheless, Goldsmith detained Willie for questioning in regard to some other recent crimes in the area; for example, on July 14, an elderly man named William Smith had been robbed and assaulted in an alley off Procter Street. The interrogation unnerved Willie, and he responded to Goldsmith's questions with more and more of a stutter, which the police interpreted as the symptom of a guilty conscience.

They soon learned that Willie was not from Port Arthur—that he had been visiting his sister Lucille during the summer and that, in fact, he lived in St. Martinville, Louisiana. Recalling his meeting with Sheriff Resweber just two weeks earlier, Goldsmith took a closer look at the wallet Willie was carrying. According to Goldsmith, he pulled an identification card out of it, and a jolt shot through him. The card bore the name Andrew Thomas.

According to Goldsmith, who did not keep any notes or records of the interrogation, Willie confessed to the St. Martinville murder in a matter of minutes, as well as to the Port Arthur robbery of Smith. Detective Oster claimed that he later searched the home of Willie's sister Lucille and discovered there a wallet containing a Social Security card issued to William Smith, along with other papers belonging to the victim.

Goldsmith asked Willie if he could read and write. Willie replied that he could, and the police asked if Willie "had any objection to reducing the statement to writing." Willie answered that he did not. Goldsmith claimed that Willie admitted to both the Thomas murder and the Smith robbery in a signed statement, but there is no mention of the Smith robbery in the Port Arthur statement presented at Willie's trial. (Eight days after the botched execution, Goldsmith sent a warrant to Resweber for the arrest of Willie Francis on a charge of robbery by assault, as well as a letter stating, "Sheriff, if this Negro is not executed on the present Murder charge that you have against him and for any reason he should be considered for a release, since the execution failed, please hold him for us.") Whether or not Willie Francis was guilty of the robbery and assault charges in Port Arthur, Texas, in July of 1945 has never been determined.

Goldsmith prefaced Willie's confession with a paragraph in legal language that absolved the Port Arthur police department of coercion. Clearly not written by Willie, it read:

> I, Willie Francis, being in the custody of Claude W. Goldsmith, Chief of Police of the City of Port Arthur, Jefferson County, Texas and having been warned by E. L. Canada, Justice of the Peace, Jefferson County, Texas, the person to whom the hereinafter set out statement is made by me, that I do not have to make any statement at all, and that any statement made by me may be used in evidence against me on my trial for the offense concerning which this statement is made, do hereby make the following voluntary statement to the said E. L. Canada, to wit:

Written in childlike cursive script beneath the above typewritten paragraph, Willie's statement followed in a string of random, disjointed thoughts.

> I Willie Francis now 16 years old I stole the gun from Mr.
> Ogise at St. Martinville La. and kill Andrew Thmas No-
> vember 9, 1944 or about that time at St. Martinville, La.
> it was a secret about me and him. I took a black purse
> with card 1280182 in it four dollars in it. I all so took a
> watch on him and sell it in new Iberia La. That all I am
> said I throw gun away .38 Pistol.

The statement was signed "Willie Francis" and witnessed by Goldsmith and Canada, whose signatures appear at the bottom of the page.

Without a formal request from the State of Louisiana, Chief Goldsmith arranged for Willie Francis's extradition back to St. Martinville, where he would eventually be charged with murder. Sheriff Resweber, along with Captain K. H. Wright and Sgt. H. P. Viator of the state police, simply drove to Port Arthur the following day and placed Willie in the backseat of a police car for the long ride home. They told Goldsmith the murder case had been "almost clueless" until Willie's apprehension, in that much of the material evidence had been destroyed by curious onlookers who had "thronged the site of the crime before police officers could investigate." On the trip back to St. Martinville, sitting between two law enforcement escorts, Willie made another "voluntary and complete confession" to the murder of Andrew Thomas. He scrawled a short note on a small piece of notepaper:

> Yes Willie Francis confess that he kill Andrew Thmas on
> November 8, 1944 i went to his house about 11:30 PM. i
> hide backing his gorage about a half hour, When he came
> out the gorage i shot him five times, that all i remember a
> short story
> Sinarely Willie Francis

News of Willie Francis's detention traveled around St. Martinville quickly, and when the August 6, 1945, issue of the *Weekly Messenger* appeared, hardly anyone in town paid attention to the other story making news that day—the American B–29 bomber, the *Enola Gay*, had dropped an atomic bomb over Hiroshima, Japan, and killed more than 200,000 civilians—for at the top of the front page ran the headline:

ANDREW THOMAS' MURDERER FOUND

Not once in the story did the *Weekly Messenger* refer to Willie Francis as "the accused" or use the word "allegedly" to qualify the actions ascribed to him. Instead, Francis was referred to as "the prisoner," and the news stated, without attribution to any source, that "the Negro admitted selling the watch he had stolen from Mr. Thomas in New Iberia." The *Louisiana Weekly* would later editorialize: "The crime had been an embarrassing mystery to the community; however, Francis' 'confession' cleared the situation."

Willie was detained on the basis of his two confessions. According to the St. Martinville police, Willie told them where he had thrown the weapon after the murder, and at this location, near the Selon Canal, a .38 caliber pistol had indeed been recovered. The pistol belonged to Deputy Sheriff August Fuselier.

Police also claimed that Willie later showed them a culvert near the railroad tracks behind the house of Andrew Thomas where, he said, he had discarded the pistol holster, and there, indeed, the police found it.

Sixteen-year-old Willie Francis had no legal counsel present during any of these proceedings.

The people of St. Martinville had spent the last nine months in fear and shock over the murder of Andrew Thomas. With the accused killer in police custody, their emotions were now turning to rage. Andrew Thomas was Cajun, and the accused was black. There were legitimate concerns for Willie's safety. For one thing, virtually anyone (white) could easily enter the St. Martinville jail if he wanted to. For another, the simple brick building was not designed to hold inmates for any length of time, let alone a local Negro responsible for murdering one of the town's most prominent and beloved white businessmen. So St. Martin Parish District Attorney L. O. Pecot had reason to be concerned about what he termed the "unpleasant" reality of Willie's situation when he stated, "We have repeatedly known in the past, unfortunately, of lynchings going on when crimes are committed."

Indeed, Sheriff Resweber later acknowledged, in a letter to M. E. Culligan, the assistant attorney general in New Orleans, that "due to the fact that our jail is easily accessable [sic] from the outside, . . . we thought it best to have him incarcerated in the Iberia Parish Jail."

To ensure against a lynching by an angry crowd, St. Martin Parish District Attorney L. O. Pecot removed Willie to the New Iberia Parish jail. Fully aware that Willie's family could not afford the services of a lawyer, Sheriff E. L. Resweber did not formally indict Willie until a month after his arrest—a strategy that prevented Willie from obtaining court-appointed legal counsel during the period that he was incarcerated and "participating" with the ongoing investigation. Detentions such as Willie's were in direct violation of a state statute, but they were "the custom throughout Louisiana for generation upon generation."

The first time Willie saw a lawyer was at his indictment on September 6, 1945, less than a week before the start of his trial for first-degree murder, a charge that in the event of conviction carried a mandatory sentence of death in the electric chair. By the time Willie's case came to trial, though, the die had already been cast. The fate of Willie Francis lay in the hands of a fourth-generation judge from St. Martinville, twelve Cajun jurors, and two court-appointed attorneys ill disposed to do anything substantive to defend the youth in court. The trial was a mere formality.

those slips will happen

There wasn't any lynching. There were just six or eight men who were going about their business.

—SHERIFF J. L. BROCK,
WASHINGTON PARISH, LOUISIANA

Late in the evening of August 6, 1945, Willie Francis found himself dressed in prison grays and locked up in a small, dirty cell in the jail above the New Iberia courthouse. He'd never been inside a jail before, never been in any trouble with the law before, but he'd walked past the jail back home in St. Martinville often enough to know that it was a place where he didn't want to be. The cries and shouts of prisoners inside the redbrick building behind the St. Martinville courthouse echoed across the bayou both day and night. Inmates sometimes pleaded with children who passed by beneath the camphor trees on St. Martin Street to gather up cigarette butts, which the kids would attach to long sticks to slip them through the bars of the prison windows.

Willie no doubt knew why he wasn't staying in the St. Martinville jail: because the doors had no locks on them and people could get in at night. The people of Louisiana had a history—for as long as they'd had a history—of meting out their own style of justice before the state had a chance to try a case or impose a sentence. On May

74

18, 1882, a story out of St. Martinville made it into the pages of the *New York Times* when Joseph E. Jenkins, a black inmate, was pulled from the jail by a mob of three hundred men and taken to the scene of the murder for which he stood accused. Along the way, the mob happened across another black man, so they hanged him, too, on the same tree.

From the Reconstruction period following the Civil War through 1930, some 283 men were lynched in Louisiana, the majority of them black men hanged by white mobs, mostly before the turn of the twentieth century. In many of these incidents, lynch mobs broke into jails at night and abducted blacks who'd been convicted of, or in some cases just accused of, crimes against whites: Often times, too, and as recently as World War II, law enforcement officers simply released black prisoners into the custody of white mobs. On August 10, 1934, a mob of three thousand stormed the Morehouse Parish jail in Bastrop, Louisiana, and dragged out Andrew McCloud, a twenty-six-year-old black man accused of assaulting a white girl. A story in the October 30, 1935, issue of the *Nation* describes the mob's treatment of McCloud:

> With blood gushing from a knife wound in his neck, his body crumpled from a beating, his inert form was hoisted to the top of an automobile in the public square, a rope was tied around his neck, and the car was driven from under. The jail was undefended. Chief of Police B. C. Walton was "out of town." Sheriff Carpenter failed to recognize any of the mob.

A little more than a year earlier, the deputy sheriff of Labadieville, a Cajun town in southern Louisiana, had led a mob in the lynchings of Freddie Moore and Norman Thibodeaux, who were charged with murdering a white girl. Moore was killed, but

Thibodeaux became one of the few Negroes to escape a lynching when two railway workers cut him down from the tree on which he'd been hanged next to Moore. Thibodeaux managed to drag his battered body to a hospital, where he waited for days in fear that the mob would find him. By then, however, the murdered girl's step-father had confessed to the killing.

And in January of 1935, a gang of eight white men entered the Washington Parish, Louisiana, jail to bring justice to Jerome Wilson, a successful black farmer who had been convicted in the shooting of the town sheriff. (A mob had gathered outside the courthouse and was threatening and howling at the jury constantly throughout the trial.) The eight "lynchers" began sawing through the lock of his cell, and when the terrified Wilson screamed for help, the men proceeded to riddle him with bullets and beat him over the head with a hammer until he was dead. Sheriff J. L. Brock would later state, "There wasn't any lynching. There were just six or eight men who were going about their business."

News of the Washington Parish lynching caused a storm of protest, and telegrams expressing outrage were sent to then Senator Huey Long from around the country. Roy Wilkins, editor of *The Crisis*, a magazine founded in 1910 by the NAACP, managed to interview Long about the Costigan-Wagner federal antilynching bill (which Long opposed, arguing that Louisiana could prevent lynchings on its own), as well as the Jerome Wilson incident in Washington Parish. Wilkins documented the following conversation with Long in his story in *The Crisis*:

> "How about lynching, Senator? About the Costigan-Wagner bill in congress and that lynching down there yesterday in Franklinton . . . "
>
> He ducked the Costigan-Wagner bill, but of course, everyone knows he is against it. He cut me off on the

Franklinton lynching and hastened in with his "pat" explanation:

"You mean down in Washington parish (county)? Oh, that? That one slipped up on us. Too bad, but those slips will happen. You know while I was governor there were no lynchings and since this man (Governor Allen) has been in he hasn't had any. (There have been 7 lynchings in Louisiana in the last two years.) This one slipped up. I can't do nothing about it. No sir. Can't do the dead nigra no good. Why, if I tried to go after those lynchers it might cause a hundred more niggers to be killed. You wouldn't want that, would you?"

"But you control Louisiana," I persisted, "you could . . . "

"Yeah, but it's not that simple. I told you there are some things even Huey Long can't get away with. We'll just have to watch out for the next one. Anyway that nigger was guilty of coldblooded murder."

"But your own supreme court had just granted him a new trial."

"Sure we got a law which allows a reversal on technical points. This nigger got hold of a smart lawyer somewhere and proved a technicality. He was guilty as hell. But we'll catch the next lynching."

At the time of Willie Francis's arrest, District Attorney Pecot was undoubtedly aware of such pervasive permissiveness regarding lynching and was understandably concerned that an angry white mob might storm the St. Martinville jail, throw a rope around Willie's neck, and hang him from the bridge over the Bayou Teche. He was so worried, in fact, that he had Willie moved to a jail nine miles away from St. Martinville. Sheriff Resweber and his deputies may even have told Willie they were doing him a favor by jailing him above the courthouse in New Iberia, because there he'd be in a safer facility—a rock-solid municipal building that did not allow for easy access after hours. In return, they were also sure to tell him, they expected Willie's full cooperation in their investigation.

Just sixteen years old, Willie was certainly frightened, as he had been since the moment he was picked up by the police in Port Arthur, Texas, three nights earlier. His father had been unable to afford a lawyer, and bail was out of the question; so Willie, still uncharged, was forced to sit in jail and do the bidding of his jailers. Had he been officially charged, the court would have been required to provide him with legal counsel. But Sheriff Resweber was in no hurry to get Willie a lawyer. He'd gotten a confession from the youth, but he still needed physical evidence to link Willie to the murder of Andrew Thomas. By holding off on the indictment, Resweber was able to isolate his suspect in a cell and build the murder case against him without any interference or objection from a lawyer.

Resweber may have had yet another motive for keeping Willie Francis locked up in New Iberia. There, Willie would be in the unprotected custody of a sheriff and his deputies whose treatment of blacks had become so frighteningly violent that J. Edgar Hoover had personally ordered a civil rights investigation by the Department of Justice. If Resweber lacked the stomach for an interrogation that might require threats, intimidation, or violence to make a case for first-degree murder, there was a sheriff just nine miles away who had proven himself up to the task—a sheriff who had organized a powerful and unrestrained group of Klan-like vigilantes to terrorize not only blacks but sympathetic whites as well.

And the sheriff's deputy—who, the FBI believed, was a serial killer—ruled the blacks in New Iberia with "an iron hand."

So Sheriff Resweber put Willie in a sedan and drove him to New Iberia, where a dark, rancid cell and the likes of Sheriff Gilbert Ozenne and Deputy Gus "Killer" Walker awaited him.

the abysmal darkness

*Was there not a great many rumors flying fast and thick,
day and night, which you were trying to run down?*

—St. Martin Parish District Attorney
L. O. Pecot

On September 6, 1945, more than a month after his arrest, Willie
Francis was formally indicted by a grand jury for the murder of Andrew Thomas. It was the first of several trips to the St. Martinville
courthouse he made that month, each time in "drab prison grays,"
sandwiched between Ozenne and a deputy in the backseat of the
sedan. At the end of the proceedings, they'd drive Willie back,
cuffed and shackled, to the jail in New Iberia, only to return him,
cuffed and shackled again, to the St. Martinville court in the morning. Frederick Francis, sitting behind his son in court, helplessly
watched the proceedings.

Judge James Dudley Simon, born in 1897, had attended Tulane
University and was admitted to the bar in 1918. Simon, who could
trace his French and Belgian ancestors back to the Middle Ages,
came more immediately from a long line of St. Martinville residents
who had become judges, including Simon's grandfather, Edward Simon. Edward Simon was also the lawyer that represented Louis
Michel, the condemned man who professed his innocence and put a

curse on St. Martinville as he was being hanged. While studying at Harvard in the 1840s, James Simon's great grandfather, Emile Edouard Simon, had intrigued one of his instructors with the tragic tale of Acadian lovers who promised to meet under a giant oak along the Bayou Teche back in the small Louisiana town he had come from. The instructor was Henry Wadsworth Longfellow.

In 1925, after serving four years as a state senator, James D. Simon assumed his judgeship in St. Martinville. In 1929, when filmmakers from Hollywood came to Louisiana to shoot the movie *Evangeline*, Judge Simon was photographed outside St.-Martin-de-Tours Church with the film's star, Delores Del Rio, at his side. In 1953, eight years after the Willie Francis trial, Simon was elected to the supreme court of Louisiana, but in 1959 he was indicted on four counts of failing to file federal income tax returns, from 1954 to 1957, on more than thirty-six thousand dollars in gross income. The charges were dropped as part of a plea bargain, but not before Judge Simon was forced to resign in disgrace.

When Willie Francis appeared before him in September 1945, Judge Simon, after considering "the impecunious condition of the accused," appointed two lawyers to represent the young Negro. It was at his arraignment that Willie first met James Randlett Parkerson and Otto J. Mestayer, the two attorneys responsible for his defense. Mestayer, fifty-three, had attended law school at both Tulane and Loyola universities. Admitted to the bar in 1926, he had been practicing law in the Sixteenth Judicial District (comprising St. Martin, St. Mary, and Iberia parishes) for twenty years. The prosecution would later say Mestayer "has an unblemished reputation for honesty and decency." Parkerson, at sixty-six a veteran criminal lawyer, had been admitted to the bar in 1900. A graduate of Tulane University, he came to Willie's case with nearly half a century of experience in Louisiana's courts. He was, according to the prosecution, "a keen legal mind, alert and aggressive."

Yet the defense that these two esteemed attorneys and prominent members of their respective white communities mounted on behalf of their client, sixteen-year-old Willie Francis, would later be described by authors Arthur S. Miller and Jeffrey H. Bowman in their book, *Death by Installments* as "singularly inadequate." Bertrand De-Blanc would be more blunt. He described the trial as "a farce and a travesty of justice" comparable to *Powell v. Alabama*, which prompted the U.S. Supreme Court to rule in 1932 that, in capital cases, defense lawyers must provide *effective counsel*.

Despite the fact that the victim was a well-known citizen of St. Martinville, defense counsel made no motion for a change of venue. Nor did Willie's defense team attack the indictment. The very first action taken by the defense counsel occurred immediately after Willie pleaded not guilty to the charge of murder before Judge Simon. Mestayer and Parkerson "requested the Court the right to withdraw its plea of 'not guilty'"—a mind-boggling tactic since the Louisiana Code of Criminal Law and Procedure (Article 740–30), on the books in 1945, required a mandatory death penalty for a person convicted on a charge of murder. Withdrawing a not guilty plea would have been the surest and fastest way to arrange Willie's trip to the electric chair. As it turned out, Mestayer and Parkerson never did change Willie's plea to guilty, but their "less than spirited defense" did very little to slow the march of their client toward his date with death.

After accepting Willie's plea of not guilty, Simon set a trial date—September 12, 1945. Parkerson and Mestayer posed no objection. District Attorney L. O. Pecot would later state that defense "counsel had ample time for preparation and trial." In case #2161, the *State of Louisiana v. Willie Francis*, ample time totaled less than six days.

On the morning of September 12, 1945, thirty-seven days after an atomic bomb was dropped on Hiroshima, the Japanese officially surrendered, bringing an end to World War II in the Pacific. It had also been thirty-seven days since Willie Francis had been detained for the murder of Andrew Thomas, and he was now being taken from his cell in New Iberia to begin the trial for his life. Just before 10:00 a.m. in the Sixteenth Judicial Court, Parish of St. Martin, Willie was led into the whitewashed courthouse in St. Martinville. A Greek Revival structure of brick coated with cement, its four Ionic columns fronting Main Street, the courthouse had been built by slave labor in 1859. It stood just blocks from the house where Willie had grown up and less than two miles from the scene of the murder he was standing trial for.

Willie was led up the stairs to a large, stately courtroom on the second floor. There were wooden benches for spectators, but the dark, windowless room offered little relief from the afternoon heat. No stenographic record was taken, so the only record of the trial consists of minutes taken by the deputy clerk of court, Mina G. Willis, and these minutes are brief. Evidently, the prosecution did not even request that the clerk summarize in the minutes the details of its case against Willie Francis at the outset of the proceedings. Nor did the defense request any record of the proceedings. In his brief to the U.S. Supreme Court, Bertrand DeBlanc would later call attention to "the abysmal darkness which shrouds the trial of Willie Francis."

The first entry in the trial minutes introduces Parkerson and Mestayer as counsel for the accused, who "announced their readiness for the trial." Given the near total lack of a defense on behalf of their client, it is difficult to surmise why they needed even six days to prepare. With the temperature approaching one hundred degrees, Judge Simon made sure no time was wasted on the first day of the trial. He ordered the sheriff to summon forty men for jury service and to "report into Court at Two (2:00) o'clock, P.M." At that time, names of each of these forty white men were "written on separate slips of paper, placed in an envelope, sealed and delivered to the Clerk of Court." After all challenges for cause and peremptory challenges were exhausted (presumably none were significant), the jury was sworn in for trial. Twelve white men would decide the fate of Willie Francis, with one white male, Felix Pellerin, to serve as alternate juror in view of "the possibility of a protracted trial." Pellerin's service would hardly be required.

District Attorney L. O. Pecot would later testify, under oath, before the Louisiana Pardons Board, "not one man on that jury came from St. Martin—they all came from other parishes away from St. Martin, who did not know Andrew Thomas and knew nothing about this case." He would add, "I had in mind to get the most competent jurors to give this man a fair and competent trial. Now I want to say there was not a loophole in that case—not one."

In fact, at least three of the jury members—Moise Ambroise Theriot, Patrick H. Maraist, and the jury foreman, Edwin Rees, were living in St. Martinville at the time of the 1930 U.S. Census. Theriot had lived in St. Martinville his whole life and was working as a watchman at St. John Plantation, a local sugar mill, at the time of Thomas's murder. It would have been impossible for him not to know about the murder of Andrew Thomas. (Just two years after the Francis case, Theriot called in sick one night when he was unable to work at the mill. On that night, a twenty-one-year-old Negro named Clarence Joseph Jr. killed Theriot's replacement, Louis Barras. Joseph would ultimately be convicted and electrocuted in St. Martinville, in the same chair that failed to kill Willie Francis on May 3, 1946.) Another juror, Maraist, was also living in St. Martinville at the time, and locals recalled that the Francis trial was briefly interrupted when Maraist was informed that his son, Patrick Jr., had been killed overseas in the war.

Several of the other white men on the jury were from Breaux Bridge, a neighboring town in St. Martin Parish. And jurors Anasta

Patin, Remi Meche, Moise LeBlanc Jr., L. C. Domingues, J. H. Naquin, Edwin Webre, Jerry Guidry, and Lloyd Guidry all bore surnames that appeared on Judge Simon's family tree. As did that of the twelfth juror: Michel Simon. Pecot's notion that the State had effectively accomplished a change of venue by seating jurors from "parishes away from St. Martin," even if it had been true, would have been of little value to Willie Francis. The rigidly enforced social and cultural boundaries that Cajuns maintained between themselves and other ethnic groups, particularly blacks, were rooted in generations of the region's history and stretched well beyond town limits.

Mestayer and Parkerson voiced no objection to the jury's composition, despite the fact that Willie Francis would not be tried by a jury of his peers. Once the jury had been selected, Judge Simon ordered the sheriff to read the names of the witnesses summoned by the State. Aside from Dr. Yongue, the coroner, and Dr. Corne, the physician who had arrived at the murder scene with Mr. and Mrs. R. L. Thomas, the majority of those named on the State's witness list were law enforcement officials who would testify that Willie's confessions were made voluntarily. There were no actual witnesses to the murder of Andrew Thomas. Missing conspicuously from the witness list was Mr. Rivere of Rivere's Jewelry Store, who would, according to Pecot, have been able to testify that Willie had sold the jeweler a watch with Andrew Thomas's initials on its casing. Presumably, with Rivere not appearing in court, Simon allowed law enforcement officials to testify about the watch on his behalf. Either defense counsel did not object to this use of hearsay, or else Simon overruled.

Also missing were the murder weapon and the bullets that had been recovered from the crime scene. Pecot would later explain that Resweber arranged to send the gun, along with a bullet taken from the body of Andrew Thomas, "to Washington to Hoover and the pistol was lost in transportation." In his report, Coroner Yongue was only able to state, without certainty, that the bullets that struck Andrew Thomas were "fired from a gun or rifle type of about a .38 caliber bullet." Ballistic tests on the "lost" evidence would, of course, have been able to show whether the bullets taken from the body of Andrew Thomas had come from the same Smith and Wesson pistol that had belonged to August Fuselier, Resweber's deputy, until it was allegedly stolen. No fingerprints had been lifted from the gun. Without the alleged murder weapon, bullets, fingerprints, or the wristwatch as evidence, the bulk of district attorney Pecot's case rested exclusively on confessions obtained by police while the teenaged Willie Francis was in custody and without legal counsel.

With the remainder of the petit jury panel dismissed and the polling of the jury complete, the district attorney read the indictment that had been returned by the grand jury, and when he finished, he laid out the case against Willie Francis in his opening statement. The wheels of Louisiana justice were now in motion. In response, Mestayer and Parkerson "waived the right of their opening statement but reserved the privilege of making such statement at the conclusion of State's case." Such statement in defense of Willie Francis was never made.

The State presented witnesses until 10:15 p.m., when Simon instructed the jury and remanded them into the custody of the sheriff. He adjourned court until the following morning at 10:00 a.m. Willie was returned to his cell in New Iberia. Frederick Francis, who attended the trial, had every reason to wonder exactly what Willie's lawyers were going to do on his son's behalf.

The following morning, on Thursday, September 13, 1945, Willie again appeared in court with lawyers Mestayer and Parkerson beside him. Again, the temperature approached one hundred degrees as Willie listened to the remainder of the State's case against him. In not a single instance, according to the minutes of the trial, did the defense cross-examine a witness or object to testimony. In fact, it appears that the prosecution was able to present its case against Willie Francis without any interruption whatever. Once the State "announced that it rested its case subject to rebuttal," Willie might have reasonably expected an elegant and spirited defense from the highly educated and experienced lawyers at his table, unless he had already given up hope by then. Either way, Willie didn't need a background in law to realize the implications of his lawyers' next move: "Counsel for the Defense announced to the Court that it had no evidence to offer on behalf of the accused and rested its case."

Resting their case without offering one whit of evidence on be-half of the accused, Mestayer and Parkerson thus neglected to in-form the jury that the alleged murder weapon—a .38 caliber handgun that was believed to be the property of August Fuselier, one of Sheriff Resweber's deputies—had been "lost" along with sev-eral bullets recovered from the body of Andrew Thomas, and there-fore had not been presented to the court. They did not inform the jury that the coroner's report had concluded that Thomas was "shot by an unknown party or parties" and that bullets from more than one gun may have produced the fatal wounds. The esteemed attor-neys for the defense likewise failed to inform the jury that Willie's fingerprints had not been found on the gun because the police had indeed neglected to check the gun for any prints whatever. Nor did defense counsel take the time to lay out for the court the inconsis-tencies and errors in Willie's differing confessions. In his Port Arthur, Texas, confession, Willie admitted to killing Andrew Thomas on November 9, 1944, yet while in the custody of Sheriff Resweber, he confessed to killing Thomas on November 8. Andrew Thomas was murdered on the night of November 7.

The language in Willie's two confessions is also confusing. Both of them include phrases that read as if they had been dictated to the sixteen-year-old. The first line in his Port Arthur confession, for example, reads: "I Willie Francis now 16 years old." Likewise, in the next sentence the use of the qualifying phrase "or about the time" hardly sounds natural for Willie.

Furthermore, one sentence in the Port Arthur confession appears to have been added after Willie had signed it, as the words "I throw gun away, '38 Pistol" are squeezed between his last sentence—"That all I am said"—and his signature, as if he had been prompted by the sheriff to add more details of the crime.

Then, too, in his handwritten Louisiana confession, Willie begins, "Yes Willie Francis confess that *he* kill Andrew Thomas," but in another sentence, he writes, "*i* shot him." According to Sheriff Resweber, Willie stated that he had had two accomplices to the crime, then "changed his mind" and said only he was responsible.

Finally, there is one sentence in Willie's Port Arthur confession that could not have been written under coercion or dictated to Willie by law enforcement officials eager to close a murder case. Its eight mysterious, unchallenged words contradict the State's claim that Thomas was the victim of a random "stickup" by Willie and perfectly define what Bertrand DeBlanc called "the abysmal darkness which shrouds the trial of Willie Francis." Willie wrote: "it was a secret about me and him."

The defense also rested its case without calling a single witness, not even Andrew Thomas's neighbor, Ida Van Brocklin, whose testimony before the coroner's jury clearly provided Willie's lawyers an opportunity to exploit the weakest link in the prosecution's case. Ida Van Brocklin stated that she saw a car with its lights on, parked in front of the Thomas house, after she'd been awakened by gunshots. If that car belonged to Andrew Thomas, Van Brocklin's eyewitness account did not jibe with what Willie had written in his confession—that Andrew Thomas's car had already been parked in the garage before any gunshots were fired. Willie wrote, "i hide backing his gorage about a half hour, When he come out the gorage I shot him five times." Nor was Van Brocklin's account corroborated by Sheriff Resweber, who testified that Thomas's car was indeed parked in the garage—testimony that squared with Mrs. Zie Thomas's account that when she first arrived on the scene and noticed her brother-in-law's body, his car was in the garage. And if the car Ida Van Brocklin saw did not belong to Andrew Thomas, then someone other than Willie was present at the crime scene. If Andrew Thomas had already parked his car in the garage (and presumably turned off the headlights) when he was fatally shot, whose car with its lights on did Mrs. Van Brocklin see parked in front of Thomas's house immediately *after she was awakened by gunshots*? Fifteen-year-old Willie Francis did not own or drive a car, and police never disputed his claim that he had walked toward the railroad tracks, away from the highway, after the murder. For obvious reasons, prosecutors did not call Ida Van Brocklin to the stand. It is less obvious why Willie's defense team failed to call her as a witness.

For the prosecution to convict in Louisiana, the district attorney is required to disprove every reasonable hypothesis of innocence. Yet the prosecution barely considered—and the defense did not raise—the issue of the rumored jealous husband or lover who might have killed Andrew Thomas. The rumors had been so rampant around St. Martinville that the coroner, Dr. Yongue, had eventually suspected foul play and recalled Alvin Van Brocklin for further testimony before the coroner's jury. District Attorney Pecot later acknowledged the rumors in questioning Sheriff Resweber before the Pardons Board, when he asked, "Was there not a great many rumors flying fast and thick, day and night, which you were trying to run down?" Resweber responded, "Yes, Sir. It kept us busy for eight months. Night and day." But the defense at Willie's trial said nothing.

Is it possible that, as Dr. Yongue may have suspected, Andrew Thomas had been followed home on the evening of November 7, 1944, to become the victim of foul play? Were there other motives, aside from robbery, that led to the death of the amicable pharmacist? And how did Willie become involved, if he was involved? Exactly how did he manage to steal a gun from one of Sheriff Resweber's deputies? Why did he confess to having accomplices, only to change his mind later? Surely in these questions lie reasonable hypotheses of innocence and reasonable doubts as to Willie's guilt. But the defense said nothing.

The New Orleans black newspaper *Louisiana Weekly* reported that many St. Martinville residents believed Willie was "merely the goat and that many other persons were involved in the killing." This was borne out, townspeople believed, by the fact that Willie had walked the streets of St. Martinville for nearly a year after the murder, but is "supposed to have readily admitted his guilt."

Nor had Willie's admission and arrest quelled the rumors about Andrew Thomas. Some whites in town found it hard to believe that Willie Francis, whose stammer they equated with feeble-mindedness, could have managed to steal a deputy sheriff's gun and fire it so accurately during the course of a robbery. And cordial as he was, Andrew Thomas had always been something of a mystery to many in town. A lifelong bachelor, educated and well mannered, Thomas had chosen to live by himself just outside the town's limits, in a rural stretch across from Evangeline Park, when he could have lived anywhere. He wasn't a farmer, so many assumed he just wanted privacy, that he wanted to lead his life away from the center of town—away from the eyes of the town. Nonetheless, as Alvin Van Brocklin noted in his testimony, people had seen Thomas's car out near Pine Grove, at the houses of two married women whose husbands were often gone for long periods of time. Thomas had long been, and continued to be, a topic of gossip among the whites of St. Martinville.

Many blacks were convinced that Willie had been framed—while at a job delivering groceries, they postulated, he'd been tricked into accepting the wallet of Andrew Thomas—and that the confessions of the scared sixteen-year-old Negro in the custody of white law enforcement agents with no lawyer present had been coerced. Bertrand DeBlanc's files include a summary of a conversation he had with Willie's "very spirited" sister, Emily Branch, in which DeBlanc notes, "She believe [sic] he was coerced or forced to do it."

Other white lifelong St. Martinville residents, such as Margaret Bonin, who lived just a stone's throw from the jail, grew up amidst rumors that "a man paid Willie to kill Andrew." Nolan "Cabbie" Charles, a justice of the peace and the first black elected public official in St. Martin Parish, at one time had lived four houses away from the Francises on Washington Street. He knew Willie and was convinced of his innocence. "Willie didn't kill no one," he said, echoing the sentiments of many in town. "He didn't know how to fire a gun. Where would he learn to shoot Andrew Thomas and hit him five times?" Charles recalled a conversation he overheard while washing dishes for a wealthy white family in town shortly after Thomas's murder; it concerned two white men who were supposedly responsible for Thomas's death. When Charles told his mother what he'd heard, she hit him hard: "I got knocked out for that," Charles said, adding that his mother had made him promise never to mention that conversation again—"They're gonna kill you," she'd told him. Up until his death in 2006, Charles would not mention the men by name, but he maintained that their names can be found on the first page of Willie's murder indictment.

The first page of Willie's indictment includes a list of State's witnesses, most of whom are law enforcement officials. August Fuselier is the eleventh name on the indictment. It was his gun that was the murder weapon and had been recovered nearby the scene of the crime. And did the "secret" in Willie's confession involve him? Willie wrote, "I Willie Francis now 16 years old I stole the gun from Mr. Ogise at St. Martinville La and kill Andrew Thomas November 9, 1944 or about that time at St. Martinville La. It was a secret about me and him." Did Willie mean to say, "it was a secret *between* me and him," the *him* being Fuselier? Did August Fuselier have reason to want Andrew Thomas dead?

The secret that Willie Francis alluded to under interrogation in Port Arthur, Texas, was never mentioned again in any testimony, trial minutes, correspondence, or newspaper accounts of the case.

Neither did Mestayer and Parkerson pursue the ambiguity in the one statement Willie apparently voluntarily made when he placed it in his confession. Nor did they broach the matter of coercion. The President's Committee on Civil Rights Report in 1947 had found widespread "violent physical attacks by police officers on members of minority groups, the use of third degree methods to extort confessions and brutality against prisoners." If the defense had shown that Willie's confessions, obtained without defense counsel present, had been made involuntarily, they would not have been allowed into evidence, and without them the case against Willie Francis would have collapsed since the State of Louisiana could not base a conviction on coerced confessions. By the time of Willie Francis's trial, too, the United States Supreme Court had consistently thrown out convictions in Southern courts where confessions had been coerced. Mestayer and Parkerson never questioned the circumstances under which Willie confessed. They rested their case instead.

In the early 1940s handguns made up a very small percentage of firearms sold in the United States. Rare and expensive, a pistol would have been hard for a poor black teenager in Louisiana to come by, as would ammunition. Smith & Wesson .38 caliber pistols available at the time had a capacity for five rounds. According to Willie's confession, he fired five shots at Andrew Thomas. Apparently, all five bullets struck the victim—one in the right eye, two on the left side, and two in the back. Furthermore the St. Martinville *Weekly Messenger* noted that police described "a terrific struggle before the shooting"; so presumably, Willie Francis, without any training or practice with a .38

caliber pistol, managed to fatally hit his target five times while at the same time struggling with his victim in the course of a robbery.

Some time after the murder, Thomas's relatives put the pharmacist's house on the market. It was purchased by Luther Perkins, and his daughter, Ione Guirard, continues to live there today. Although her father had the garage torn down and replaced with a larger one years ago, Guirard vividly recalls two bullet holes that completely penetrated the side of the detached garage facing the house. Bullet holes, her father told her, from the night Andrew Thomas was killed. According to the coroner, all five bullets that struck Thomas had inflicted wounds significant enough to "have produced death." If Willie Francis was in fact the only attacker and none of the bullets he fired missed or grazed Andrew Thomas—for Willie nowhere mentioned that he stole or purchased additional bullets—then two bullets would have had to have fatally penetrated Thomas and then continued on their trajectory with enough force to pierce the wall of the wooden garage. To do so, they would have had to have struck Andrew Thomas while he was still standing. Willie's public defenders did not attempt to square any of the ballistic evidence with the jury. On the matter of the gun, as with everything else, Mestayer and Parkerson remained silent.

●   ●   ●

The killing of a prominent white man by a poor black was not unprecedented in St. Martinville. On June 25, 1937, Fernest Jones, a Negro tenant farmer who lived on the outskirts of town, drove up to St.-Martin-de-Tours Church with the body of white architect and master builder Louis Peeters in the backseat of his car. Peeters's uncle, Joseph "Pere" Peeters, was then the pastor at the church and Jones wanted to let him, and the town, know not just that he had killed Peeters, but that he had done so in self-defense. Immediately taken into custody on the charge of murder, he spent nearly four months in the St. Martinville jail. On October 6, Jones appeared before Judge James D. Simon; a grand jury returned a true bill for manslaughter, and Jones was held without bail. Simon appointed a young, local attorney to represent Jones—St. Martinville resident Edwin Willis, who would later be elected to the United States House of Representatives.

The killing was lodged in a property dispute. Forty-year-old Louis J. Peeters had built a beautiful house near Coteau Holmes, but he felt the house, to be aesthetically appreciated, needed a larger tract of land. The land adjacent to the Belgian Peeters's tract was being planted by Fernest Jones under a tenancy agreement; an arrangement that did not sit well with the architect. It sat even less well when pigs from Jones's farm wandered onto Peeters's property. The architect strode over to Jones's house with a .410 shotgun to settle matters and to "force that nigger to get off the property." With the barrel of his gun trained on the "old darkey," Peeters confronted Jones in his potato field. The two argued and scuffled until Jones "hit Peeters over the head with the cutting part of a heavy cane hoe killing him instantly."

Willis managed to convince a white jury that Fernest Jones had been acting in self-defense when he'd killed "Louis Pete," and on October 17, 1937, the six Cajun jurors returned a not guilty verdict. Judge Simon released the Negro.

Edwin Willis's chances for an acquittal were probably not impeded by the fact that Louis Pete was mostly despised around St. Martinville. His uncle, "Pere Pete" was an "irremovable pastor," which meant that his tenure at St.-Martin-de-Tours was granted in perpetuity. The nephew, however, had taken it upon himself to manage the church finances for the pastor; he had also raised the community's eyebrows when during the lean Depression years, he had managed to build such a magnificent home for himself. "Mr. Peeters," the *Weekly Messenger* noted, "had amassed quite a fortune during his stay here. He owned five farms in this section and was active in money lending." There was, no doubt, little sympathy for Louis Pete among the six Catholic jurors, but Willis, to be safe, persuaded Fernest Jones that he should leave town after his acquittal. Jones moved to Texas.

Rather than being emboldened by the Jones case—knowing that it was possible for an all-white jury in St. Martinville to find a black man not guilty—the counsel for Willie's defense rested its case. At this point the State began its closing argument in the matter of the *State of Louisiana v. Willie Francis*. Presumably, District Attorney Pecot laid out the case before the jurors, in the event that any doubt remained in their minds. Willie Francis was caught in Port Arthur, Texas. In his possession was the wallet of the victim, Andrew Thomas. The accused had signed two confessions to the acts of robbery and murder, which the State had introduced into evidence. The defendant's own lawyers were not challenging any of the State's evidence. The jury's task at hand was clear as day.

Counsel did produce a closing argument for the defense, but what Parkerson or Mestayer argued on Willie's defense does not appear in the record. In any event, it was not persuasive. The minutes state only that Judge Simon then "proceeded to duly instruct the Jury on their duties and the law." The jury of twelve white men retired to their room for lunch and "after only 15 minutes deliberation," according to Claude Goldsmith, the Port Arthur, Texas, chief of police who attended the trial and testified for the State, they had reached a verdict. The sheriff in charge of the petit jury informed the court that the jury had "announced its readiness to report its verdict," and Judge Simon ordered the sheriff to escort the jurors into the courtroom.

After counsel both for the State and for the accused waived the polling of the jury, Judge Simon asked the jury foreman, Edwin Rees, whether they had arrived at a verdict. Rees responded affirmatively, and Judge Simon instructed him to hand the indictment and verdict to the sheriff. When Judge Simon received the verdict, he announced the words written in cursive script on the indictment: "Guilty as charged. Edwin Rees, Foreman."

Mestayer and Parkerson requested that the jury be polled individually "to determine whether the Verdict so announced was their respective Verdict." Each juror concurred and the verdict was recorded. Judge Simon then ordered Willie to be remanded to the parish jail "to await sentence of the Court."

Willie Francis returned to court the following morning at 10:00 a.m. for sentencing. Standing before Judge Simon, he heard the following words: "I now sentence you Willie Francis to suffer death in the manner provided by law."

Simon then ordered the sheriff to "adjourn court without date," and Willie was driven back to his cell, where he would spend the next six months waiting for his death warrant to be issued. Usually during this waiting period attorneys for the condemned are engaged in desperate, last-minute legal maneuvers to save their client. Willie Francis never saw or heard from his lawyers again.

For Willie to appeal the verdict, his attorneys would have had to have reserved a Bill of Exception, an objection to a point of law that must be put on the record before the trial is completed and the verdict announced. According to the minutes, "no Bill of Exception was reserved by the accused through his Counsel during the entire course of the trial, and that following the imposition of the death sentence upon the accused by the court, no motion was filed by the Accused of [sic] through his Counsel, seeking an appeal from the death sentence as imposed."

Locked in his cell in New Iberia, Willie was completely unaware of his right to appeal his death sentence. Mestayer and Parkerson had quickly moved on. Perhaps they felt that they had already done more than they should do for Willie and they could ill afford to continue

with time-consuming legal motions on behalf of their in forma pauperis client. Or perhaps they feared rankling further the courts and
the white communities where they earned their livelihood. Regardless, they let crucial deadlines pass while Willie sat in jail, waiting to
be told the date when he would be sent to the electric chair.

The very last words in the trial minutes regarding case #2161, the
State of Louisiana v. Willie Francis, state that the right of Willie Francis to appeal his conviction and sentence "has thus expired by mandate of law."

On March 29, 1946, more than six months after Willie Francis
was found guilty in the murder of Andrew Thomas, the State issued
a death warrant. Governor Jimmie Davis, "the Singing Governor,"
who, before entering politics in Louisiana, had ensured his fame as a
country musician with his hit song "You Are My Sunshine," set the
date of May 3, 1946, for Sheriff E. L. Resweber to carry out the execution "until said Willie Francis is dead."

we do not have any bad negroes here any more

*These pecks down in Louisiana fear no government
agency as they do the Department of Justice.*

—A. P. TUREAUD,
ATTORNEY FOR THE NAACP

In the spring of 1946, seven months after the trial, while Willie was locked in a New Iberia prison cell following his conviction for murder and awaiting his May 3 execution date, the writer Alden Stevens was traveling around the country documenting life in small-town America for the *Nation*. Stevens's travels brought him to St. Martinville, where he met and became intrigued with Father Maurice Rousseve, a well-educated Catholic priest who was essentially doing missionary work in the town.

When Stevens asked about the black veterans who were returning from the war, Rousseve hesitated. "A few of them come back to visit," he said. "But they aren't going to stay. They've had a taste of freedom and a taste of justice, and they're through with the South forever." Rousseve explained further: "The whites don't think of us as human beings. When there is a concert in town, for instance, it simply doesn't occur to them that we might like to hear it, too. They have no sense of responsibility toward us, of one human being for another. Our schools, our health are not their problems."

Stevens told Rousseve about the "better opportunities" for Negroes that he had observed in other parts of the South, where, for example, the growth of cooperatives had led to political progress. "We have no cooperative here," Rousseve said, "mostly because of the extreme ignorance of the people. And as for progress, it doesn't start in places like this. It moves out from the cities to the country. It will be many years before things are any different here."

Maurice Louis Rousseve, born in New Orleans in 1906 to Barthelemy and Valentine Mansion Rousseve, was one of eight children who grew up on Columbus Street in a racially mixed section of the city. His father, a postal worker, loved music and played the clarinet; he and his wife, Valentine, an accomplished piano player, ensured that music played a prominent role in the upbringing of their children. Indeed, the tightly knit family was known for the classical music concerts it would play impromptu, outside, for their neighbors. Devoutly Roman Catholic, Valentine would gather her family together each evening, after dinners of gumbo and other Creole dishes, to recite prayers in French. In addition to instilling a love of music into their children and nurturing their religious faith, Barthelemy and Valentine continually stressed the importance of education to them.

By all accounts, the parents of Maurice Rousseve were highly successful in the indoctrination of their children. Their first son, Charles, a pianist, received his master's degree from Xavier University and his PhD from the University of Chicago. His book, *The Negro in Louisiana*, was published in 1938 by the Xavier University Press, where he was a full professor for many years, as was Charles's younger brother Numa, who played the cornet. Ferdinand, a clarinet player and the second Rousseve son, attended the Massachusetts Institute of Technology and eventually became an architect.

Twin daughters Leonie, another pianist, and Leona, a cellist, both became teachers. Their brother Rene, a clarinetist, dedicated himself to social work, and the youngest piano-playing Rousseve—Mary—took vows as Sister Mary Theresa Vincent, a nun in New Orleans.

Maurice, too, played the piano, and after attending Xavier Preparatory School for two years, he left New Orleans at the age of fourteen to begin study at the Society of the Divine Word in Greenville, Mississippi. In 1934, he was ordained a priest at the society's St. Augustine Seminary in Bay St. Louis, Mississippi; an occasion that marked the first time a group of American blacks—four in this case—were ordained to the Catholic priesthood. At the time, the seminary in Bay St. Louis was, in fact, the only institution of its kind that accepted blacks, and it had begun hosting young men from Central America and the West Indies as well. After a brief appointment as an assistant at a Lafayette, Louisiana, church, Rousseve was transferred in 1938 to the Notre Dame de Perpetuel Secours Church in St. Martinville, where he became pastor in 1941. His fluency in French was surely a factor in this appointment, as it was the primary language spoken by the mostly poor blacks in his parish. In St. Martinville, Father Rousseve also achieved another first when he took on a white priest to be his assistant in the church.

While in St. Martinville, Father Rousseve built a convent for the nuns, the Sisters of the Blessed Sacrament, and with them attempted to do for his parish what his father had done for him. Tirelessly he stressed the importance of education in the community he served. But it was a difficult task. Unlike in New Orleans, the educational opportunities for blacks in St. Martinville were severely restricted, for black families had been subsisting on plantation labor for generations. They had no use for books in the fields.

Stevens asked the Creole cleric—"a slender man with a finely chiseled, sensitive face"—about the parochial school connected to the church, which he "had heard was unusual and excellent." Rousseve shook his head sadly. "The people here in St. Martin Parish," Rousseve began, "are the most illiterate in Louisiana. Some years ago someone found that three-fifths of them had had less than one year of school. It isn't much better now. We only go to the eighth grade, and until recently we only went to the sixth. We're working up gradually, but it's hard because we have four hundred pupils and only five teachers." Rousseve went on to explain that St. Martinville had no high school for Negroes. "Many of the whites around here don't want Negroes to be educated. They want them to work on the plantations."

Rousseve had something else to tell Stevens. He led the writer into his office, closed the door, and then told Stevens about a series of violent episodes involving law enforcement officials in New Iberia two years before—incidents that were instigated by the very men who were now holding Willie Francis.

"A doctor and a lawyer and two other Negro professional men in New Iberia started a branch of the NAACP there a couple of years ago," Rousseve told Stevens. "They also tried to get a good school. They were beaten and run out of town. One of them was beaten unconscious right in the courthouse. They lost everything they had. I don't know what happened to them finally, but they had to go somewhere else."

Father Rousseve clearly knew what many in the black community, the Catholic Church in New Iberia, and the FBI knew at the time— that Sheriff Gilbert Ozenne and his deputies were behind the beatings and terrorization of the Negro professionals who had finally been run out of town at gunpoint. Whether Rousseve told Alden Stevens as much is not known. What is known is that Stevens left St. Martinville stunned by his meeting with Rousseve, stunned by the hopelessness of life for blacks in rural southern Louisiana. Later he wrote, "After we left Father Rousseve we drove without speaking

along the gravel road running northward out of the Teche country."
If Stevens had stayed on in St. Martinville and inquired further, he
would have learned exactly why Father Rousseve would have had
good reason to fear for Willie's safety despite the strong locks in the
jail above the rock-solid New Iberia courthouse.

In the spring of 1944, just a few months before Andrew Thomas
was murdered, the city of New Iberia, with a population of fifteen
thousand (roughly 35 percent black), had been teetering on the edge
of racial conflict. The local chapter of the NAACP had recently
elected J. Leo Hardy, a former insurance agent, as branch president.
One of Hardy's first initiatives was to champion the right of blacks
to vote. Hardy's reputation as a gambler and his somewhat militant
stance on black enfranchisement rankled some old-time NAACP
members in New Iberia, who argued that "the time was not ripe" to
secure the ballot. Hardy persisted. The brash new branch president
caused whites in New Iberia to take notice, but it was Hardy's next
initiative that inflamed them most.

In early 1944 southern Louisiana's economy was booming,
mostly due to increased oil output during the war. It was estimated
at the time that the Standard Oil complex in Baton Rouge produced
the fuel for one out of every fifteen planes flown during the war.
Blacks wanted a stake in this economic windfall, but whites were reluctant to share the gain.

The NAACP put pressure on the Louisiana Department of Education to fund a welding school for blacks so that they, too, could
work in skilled labor positions in shipyards. Despite a shortage of
welders, white unions colluded with management to keep blacks
from securing these jobs. Blacks, it was reasoned, were needed in
the fields and farms of New Iberia. Hardy managed to persuade the
New Iberia branch of the NAACP to pressure the state government
into funding a welding school for blacks, and Lloyd G. Porter, the
white superintendent of the Iberia Parish schools, was given the task

of running this training program. On May 7, 1944, the welding school opened, in a white neighborhood, and attendance was scarce. Hardy had lobbied for night classes so that blacks who worked days in the cane fields and salt mines could learn a better-paying trade. Convinced the school's location and hours represented a deliberate attempt by Porter to discourage and deter blacks from enrolling, Hardy wrote letters of protest to both the NAACP and the Federal Employment Practice Committee. Those letters sealed J. Leo Hardy's fate.

On May 15, Hardy was the only man to attend the welding class, except for two New Iberia sheriff's deputies who showed up at the school that afternoon. They put Hardy in a car and drove him to the sheriff's office, where Sheriff Gilbert Ozenne and Superintendent Porter confronted Hardy. According to Hardy's account to the FBI, Ozenne began to "browbeat" Hardy, so much so that the NAACP branch president, terrified, began apologizing to both Porter and the sheriff. Hardy was so frightened that he was uttering "yassuh" after every one of his sentences. The locution infuriated Porter. "You yellow son of a bitch," Porter shouted. "You are saying 'yes sir,' but deep down in your heart you would cut my throat." Porter then informed Hardy that he would run the welding school however he chose to, and "not even the President of the United States could make him do otherwise." Ozenne gave Hardy until the next morning to gather his belongings and leave town.

When Hardy was spotted the next evening speaking with friends on the steps of the Negro entrance to Old Tom's Saloon, where he worked as a bartender and card dealer, a black sedan pulled up, and deputy sheriffs Gus Walker, Otto LeBlanc, and Ferd Porciau ordered him into a car and drove him back to Ozenne's office at the New Iberia courthouse. Ozenne, a rugged and meticulous man who was often seen around town in a white suit, white fedora, and black and white spectator shoes, proceeded to kick and beat Hardy senseless while his deputies held the recalcitrant black man down. They then threw him into a jail cell on the fourth floor so that he could ponder his future should he decide to stick around New Iberia. After about an hour, they dragged Hardy back to the car and drove him out of town, where they again beat him before dumping him on the side of a road. As the bloodied NAACP branch president shambled away from New Iberia, one of the deputies fired a pistol in Hardy's direction—his final warning not to return.

Ozenne and his deputies had not finished terrorizing prominent members of the local NAACP branch in New Iberia, however. Dr. Luins H. Williams and Dr. Howard Scoggins were both well-respected physicians who treated patients in one of the state's best public health clinics. It was located in the New Iberia courthouse itself, and the black doctors served alongside white staff—a circumstance that was "setting white tongues wagging," according to historian Adam Fairclough in his book *Race and Democracy: The Civil Rights Struggle in Louisiana, 1915–1972.* Williams had recently begun entering the clinic through the front door rather than through the Negro entrance, and was also hanging his coat on the rack used by white people. The two physicians, in addition to a dentist, Ima A. Pierson, and a schoolteacher, Herman Joseph Faulk, were prominent members of the New Iberia branch of the NAACP, and in the opinion of Ozenne, they had all made the same mistake. At the Negro Congregational Church in New Iberia, they had attended a "very radical talk" by Hardy, in which the new branch president promised to see "that Negroes got the right to vote" and that they would "have the same privileges as white people." Hardy told the congregation that the United States had, in Franklin D. Roosevelt, the "first honest president since Abraham Lincoln" as well as the first honest Supreme Court "since right after the Civil War." Hardy received many "Amens" during his talk and much applause after it.

The NAACP meetings infuriated white officials in New Iberia, and Mayor William Lourd, along with Sheriff Ozenne, called a meeting with the NAACP's board of directors to "discourage organization."

Lourd later said, "I did this, but they organized anyhow. The law enforcement officers and I agreed to meet whenever anything came up on this, and decide together what we should do."

The June 3, 1944, edition of the *Louisiana Weekly*, a black newspaper in New Orleans, reported that the "white fathers" of New Iberia had endeavored to "organize a counter-organization to the NAACP" and that there was a general edict "for all professional Negroes and their families to get out of town." Mayor Lourd, however, denied that he knew anything about white officials holding such countermeetings. Ozenne, meanwhile, had been warning the black men that they would be "personally held responsible for anything that may happen in New Iberia."

In the evenings following Hardy's expulsion, Ozenne's deputies, impersonating FBI agents, rounded up at gunpoint several NAACP members, including Faulk, Dr. Pierson, and Dr. Williams. All three were pistol-whipped, clubbed, and stomped, then threatened with death and dumped at roadsides out of town. The FBI reports on these cases name Deputy Gus "Killer" or "Rough House" Walker as one of the officers from Ozenne's department responsible for the beatings.

According to Faulk's account, Walker and another deputy stuck a gun in his back and made him walk. "Get in that damn car, nigger, before something happens to you," Walker told him. "Knowing Gus Walker has a very itchy trigger finger," Faulk told the FBI, "I thought it best that I get in the car." But before he got in, Walker began slapping him, while another deputy pinned him to the Plymouth sedan. "You are a damn smart nigger, eh?" Walker shouted. "You are one of those niggers going around telling other niggers they will be voting soon. We are going to beat the hell out of you for the first ballot you cast."

Echoing the testimony of Faulk, Dr. Williams told the FBI that Walker, while punching him in the head, called him a "smart darky" and blamed him for organizing the "poor ignorant bastards" who had been living in New Iberia "peacefully for the last hundred years."

Suffering a similar fate as his colleagues, Dr. Pierson moved to Texas. His expulsion from New Iberia deprived him of sleep for weeks, and when he was asked later to provide a statement to the FBI, he was so nervous he "was signing his initials like a three-year-old child."

On the morning of May 18, 1944, another Negro doctor and member of the NAACP, Dr. E. L. Dorsey of New Iberia, drove to Lafayette, Louisiana, where he talked with the men who had been beaten by Ozenne's deputies. Faulk told Dr. Dorsey that Gus Walker had a list of blacks to be run out of town, and that Dorsey's name was on it. Dr. Dorsey then contacted Sheriff Ozenne to confirm "whether or not it was desired that he leave town," to which Ozenne replied that he "did not want to say too much at that time." Dr. Dorsey immediately moved to Fort Worth, Texas.

That Gus "Killer" Walker, the stout and balding former undertaker, had a hand in the brutalization of the NAACP board of directors came as no surprise to the FBI once they began investigating his background. An FBI report by Agent Cover Mendenhall dated June 20, 1944, includes this chilling sentence: "It will be noted that Walker has killed two negroes since the middle of 1943 but no charges have been made against him." Witnesses, the report states, claimed that Walker had killed as many as seven blacks in the New Iberia area. One of the confirmed victims was Roosevelt Theodule, a twenty-eight-year-old "colored male" who died, according to the Iberia Parish coroner's report, from "gunshot wounds inflicted by one Gus Walker."

Appearing at the coroner's inquest, Albert Theodule, the father of the victim, stated that Deputy Sheriff Gus Walker came to his house in nearby Olivier, Louisiana, with a shotgun in hand at 5:00

a.m. on the morning of May 31, 1941, and asked if Roosevelt was there. Albert woke his son, who put on overalls and walked out the door with Walker. A few minutes later, Albert heard a blast. When he went out in the yard, he found his son, shot dead. According to the FBI report, "Albert would not discuss this case further," and "it was quite obvious that he was afraid to make any comment concerning Gus Walker's activities in Olivier, or in Iberia Parish."

Mrs. Cyrus Broussard, a white woman in Olivier who had known Gus Walker for some time, told the FBI that it was generally rumored about town that Walker's teenage stepdaughter, Edith Walker, "had been slipping out at night and going out with Roosevelt Theodule." Gus Walker, she claimed, had gone out looking for Edith that night, to no avail, so when she returned, Walker "forced her" to tell him where she'd been and with whom. Just hours later, Roosevelt Theodule lay dead, buckshot in his heart. The five jury members of the coroner's inquest concluded "that this was a justifiable homicide, and accordingly exonerated Gus Walker." Most likely, Walker was exonerated by virtue of his own testimony as well as that of Edith Walker, who appeared before Sheriff Ozenne and the jury.

In June of 1944, two writers from *PM*, the leftist New York newspaper bankrolled by Chicago millionaire Marshall Field III, interviewed Sheriff Ozenne about the "Gestapo tactics" that had been used to drive New Iberia's NAACP members out of town. Ozenne, a "short, beefy, red-faced man with an air of importance about him," denied that such an expulsion had occurred in his town, and when he was informed that the victims had given signed affidavits to the Department of Justice, Ozenne replied, "Well, I don't know nothing about that. But I know that my deputies didn't believe the niggers. It just isn't true."

In May and June of 1944, both A. P. Tureaud and Thurgood Marshall contacted the Civil Rights Section of the Justice Department and pressed them to take action against Ozenne and his men. J. Edgar Hoover ordered a preliminary investigation; upon reviewing the field reports, he urged presentation to a grand jury at "the earliest possible moment." When FBI agents interviewed Ozenne, the sheriff complained that blacks were insubordinate, and he showed one agent how he'd deal with them should they get out of hand: his gun vault contained Thompson machine guns, shotguns, rifles, and tear gas. "It seems about time that several Negroes resisted arrest," Ozenne said, flaunting before the FBI agent his deadly collection and insinuating that it provided just the answer for any insubordination. "Then they will quiet down for a while." Still, the New Iberia sheriff again denied that any expulsions had taken place, despite growing evidence of a conspiracy among the "white fathers" of New Iberia.

FBI Special Agent William F. York interviewed New Iberia Chief of Police Albert Darby, who acknowledged that he had advised the sheriff's department to use some "strong methods against some of the local negroes." Darby believed that the Negroes were "becoming very sassy" and that he "had to keep them in order." Darby also told Special Agent York that "this was for his own information, and that he, Darby, would deny any knowledge whatsoever of this incident at any future time."

Mayor William Lourd described for the *PM* article a sheriff's department that operated independently of and virtually unchecked by any other local authority, like the police department in New Iberia. The following exchange appeared in the June 18, 1944, edition of *PM*:

> "The only people who have any check on the sheriff, then, must be State authorities?"
> "No, not even they have," he [Lourd] answered.
> "Then nobody has," I said.
> "That's right," he stated emphatically.

The newspaper reports on the expulsions prompted outrage in black communities nationwide. Among the many letters of protest was this one, sent in July 1944 to President Franklin D. Roosevelt by Cpl. Carlton J. Roy, the brother-in-law of one of the victims, Herman Faulk:

Dear Mr. President,

I am a Cpl. in the U.S. Army. I have been in the Army for 17 months and in England for 11 months. I am a Negro with an American heart and has been doing my Duties as an American Soldier. I consider myself as one of the best. I have never had a punishment. I have been awarded the "good Conduct medal," "good driving medal" and sharp shooting with a 30–30 rifle and combine and a key man with a 50 caliber machine gun.

I was sent some papers from the states a few days ago and I read where Colored people in my home city, New Iberia, La were being beaten up and chased out of town. Included in them my sister's husband, Herman Faulk who is a teacher in a local school. He was the chairman of a war bond drive and raised over $5,000 from the colored people in that city . . . so they could help build the tanks and ships we need so badly.

They forced them to leave their homes and also beat up the colored doctors and ran them out of town. The colored people that remains behind is without Medical Care and my family is there. God knows what will happen to them.

I thought we were fighting to make this world a better place to live in. But it seems as though us Colored boys are fighting in vain and that offers little encouragement to me. I am giving the U.S.A. all I got and would even die. But I think my people should be protected. I am asking you Sir, to do all in your power to bring those people to justice and punish the guilty ones.

I remain Humbly Yours,
Cpl. Carlton J. Roy

The beatings and intimidations served their purpose. The targeted professionals left town, as did other members of New Iberia's scant black middle class who feared they might be next. Operating under the false impression that the NAACP was stockpiling ammunition in New Iberia for an armed confrontation, Ozenne had also planned a raid on black saloons to confiscate weapons. Ultimately, he'd decided against it. After consulting with Judge James D. Simon in St. Martinville (the judge who would later preside over the trial of Willie Francis), he had come to the conclusion with the judge that maybe the black community had been intimidated enough. A raid, they reasoned, might cause a Negro exodus that, in turn, "would not leave any colored help for the merchants and planters."

Ozenne's reign of terror in New Iberia was not limited to blacks alone. Father Joseph P. Lonergan, a member of the Holy Ghost Fathers at St. Edward's Church in New Iberia (whose fellow priest and mentor, Father Charles Hannigan, would comfort Willie Francis in his cell two years later), told the FBI that he was convinced Ozenne had personally facilitated the expulsions but that he doubted the former highway patrolman and newly elected sheriff would have instigated the actions, "inasmuch as the Sheriff was an ignorant man who had apparently been put into office by one Paulin Daug [J. Paulin Duhe] a wealthy oil man of New Iberia." Lonergan stated that he was also "very much afraid of Sheriff Gilbert Ozenne, and his deputies, because of the Gestapo methods" they employed.

The fact that Lonergan had nearly six hundred black members in his church, he felt, had prompted Ozenne to call him on the phone one night with the warning that, "from that time on, he would not be considered a Priest by the officials of Iberia Parish" and would be treated like any other citizen. The sheriff, he said, was abusive, and at the end of the conversation, Ozenne had threatened him with the words of his own faith: "May God have mercy on your soul." Lonergan told the FBI that Walker particularly frightened him and that he did not want to get involved because "he could be liquidated by the Sheriff's office without too much difficulty."

As the reach of the civil rights case expanded, however, witnesses to the beatings and expulsions in New Iberia grew increasingly more reluctant to go on record in naming Ozenne and his deputies as the parties responsible for the actions against the black professionals. Their fear that their testimony might result in them being "found dead in a gutter somewhere" was not entirely unjustified.

In the end, the Justice Department's case collapsed because a federal grand jury in New Orleans refused to return any indictments. Leo Hardy died a year after the beating he took at the hands of Ozenne and his deputies. In a report to Attorney General Francis Biddle, Assistant Attorney General Tom C. Clark noted that Hardy "was proved to be an unsavory character, who had been a gambler and bartender in a saloon of dubious reputation in New Iberia and who made his living by gambling. He was a positive detriment to the case throughout and it was not possible to eliminate him." But however detrimental Hardy's character proved to be in the minds of the grand jurors, his rhetoric would be echoed by black leaders years later during the civil rights movement in the United States. Tom C. Clark, who would be appointed by President Truman to the U.S. Supreme Court in 1949, would later vote to end racial segregation by siding with the majority in landmark cases like *Brown v. Board of Education*. (Ironically, Truman, who went on to order the bombings of Hiroshima and Nagasaki, would later say, "Tom Clark was my biggest mistake," then add, by way of explanation, "It isn't so much that he's a *bad* man. It's just that he's such a dumb son of a bitch.")

With the departures of so many from New Iberia, the welding school for blacks closed down, and the doctors never returned. Sheriff Gilbert Ozenne, just weeks after the expulsions, was elected to the post of vice president by the Louisiana Sheriffs Association— a reward, A. P. Tureaud believed, for Ozenne's "excellent work in the handling of the negro situation in New Iberia."

Certainly, Ozenne and his deputies had targeted and expelled blacks from New Iberia with "clinical efficiency," thereby preventing an exodus of "colored help" that might have disrupted the local economy. Judge S. O. Landry of the 16th Judicial District of Louisiana told FBI agents that the "job done by the Sheriff was a job expertly done," and stated further that "we do not have any bad negroes here any more."

Tom C. Clark's report to Attorney General Biddle on January 20, 1945, stated that there was "probably no doubt in the mind of anyone who heard the testimony given to the grand jury that there was in fact such a conspiracy directed from the sheriff's office." Clark concluded that the "basic cause of the failure to obtain an indictment is undoubtedly that the community is not yet quite prepared to penalize this type of activity."

Just a few months after learning they would not be indicted on the 1945 federal civil rights charges for the beating and intimidation of several prominent Negroes, Sheriff Gilbert Ozenne and Gus "Killer" Walker were still working at the New Iberia courthouse, and at the jail above it. In August they were asked to make room for a Negro boy from St. Martinville who had been accused of murdering a white man. Sheriff E. L. Resweber was hopeful that he could build a case against his suspect in New Iberia, where, with the help of Sheriff Gilbert Ozenne and his deputies, he could interrogate

Willie Francis, alone in a cell on the fourth floor, without a lawyer present. Willie was likely shown the trapdoor beneath the chair of jailer Clemarie Norris in the booking area, and if he looked up, he could see the ring suspended from the ceiling. Odds are, he was also told the fate of the condemned New Iberian, Honore Migues, who, on July 19, 1940, dropped through the trapdoor when he was hanged by the sheriff and his deputies, just paces away from Willie's cell on the fourth floor.

As Willie's interrogation proceeded over the course of the next few months in the New Iberia jail, he was—according to later testimony before the Louisiana Pardons Board—exceptionally cooperative. Sheriff Resweber even noted that Willie "has been a good prisoner and has given no trouble whatever." Sometimes they'd take Willie for a ride—to a jewelry store on Main Street, or to the Selon Canal near the house of Andrew Thomas—in the hope of tracking down evidence that linked Willie to the crime. Exactly how Sheriffs Resweber and Ozenne, along with deputy Gus Walker, managed to extract information from Willie was never documented, but District Attorney L. O. Pecot was confident that he had all the evidence he needed to convict Willie Francis of murder.

On one of these evidence-gathering excursions, Resweber said, Willie led law enforcement to two areas near the railroad tracks on the north side of town. It had to do with the murder weapon, a .38 caliber pistol, which belonged to August Fuselier, one of Sheriff Resweber's deputies; supposedly, he'd reported that the Smith & Wesson gun had been stolen from his car before the Thomas murder. In the confession that Willie wrote in Port Arthur, he admitted to stealing the gun from a "Mr. Ogise," a locution that reflects the formal manner in which blacks often referred to whites in the South, "Ogise" being Willie's phonetic spelling of the Cajun French pronunciation of "August." Fuselier had stated that the gun's holster had a "leafy design" and that threads at the bottom had been cut to accommodate the length of the pistol; a holster found in a culvert area underneath the railroad right-of-way matched Fuselier's description. Willie allegedly also told the police where he had disposed of the murder weapon—in an area near the Selon Canal—the very place where a town worker had discovered a .38 caliber pistol in a clump of grass shortly after the Thomas murder.

On yet another ride, this time in New Iberia, according to Sheriff Resweber, Willie took Resweber and his deputies to the Rivere Jewelry Store, where Willie pointed to a watchcase and said to the owner of the store, Mr. Rivere, "I sold you that watch for $5.00." Rivere did not remember Willie, but his cashbook indeed indicated a purchase of $5.00, and the Elgin watchcase bore the initials "A. T." (The movement of the Elgin watch, a popular, mid-priced brand, had been removed and put in a different case.)

During one of the interrogations in the New Iberia Parish jail, with Resweber present, Willie broke down and told them that he had two accomplices to the murder. He gave Resweber the names of "two colored boys and told me where they lived—who they were and where I could find them." Resweber, who claimed to know everyone in St. Martinville "by their first name, their nickname and all," visited the mothers of the supposed accomplices Willie had named. One of the mothers said that her son had a different name and was "away at the time" in the "armed service." Concluding that Willie had given him fictitious names, Resweber decided that Willie "was just fooling" and was "the only one committed that murder." The St. Martin Parish sheriff, when he later appeared before the Louisiana Pardons Board, was asked about Willie's admission to having accomplices. "I checked that," Resweber said, "and was satisfied to just forget about it."

The false confession did not please Ozenne and his deputies. They circled the boy, then circled him again, because such discrepancies cast doubt on each previous incarnation of the confession.

Willie had told them once that *it was a secret about me and him*, but he wasn't going to bring it up again. It was safer to tell them what they wanted to hear.

"I took a black purse with $4 in it and a watch," Willie said.

"It was a stickup," they surmised.

"Andrew Thomas is dead. Murder by Willie. Murder at Mid Night. A short story."

But it wasn't the whole story. Only hours after Willie walked away from Gruesome Gertie, a reporter would ask him why he did it, and Willie would reveal another secret.

"I wasn't after money."

for heaven's sake he's just a kid

I can say without fear of contradiction that I was one of Andrew's best friends.

— BERTRAND DEBLANC

By the time Frederick Francis left Bertrand DeBlanc's house on Claiborne Street—only a few short hours after his son rose up and walked away from the electric chair—he had found a lawyer to represent Willie. But the young Cajun attorney knew he didn't have much time. Governor Jimmie Davis had set May 9, 1946, as the day for Willie's return to the electric chair. DeBlanc had just four days to block the scheduled execution.

As a first maneuver, he filed a petition for a writ of habeas corpus in Louisiana state district court. The Latin term for "you have the body," a writ of habeas corpus is a judicial mandate to a prison official that orders that a prisoner be taken to court to determine whether the prisoner is being lawfully detained and whether he should be released from custody. The petition must show that officials have made a legal or factual error in the imprisonment of the person detained. In the petition, DeBlanc stated that Willie Francis was "now unlawfully and illegally detained against his will and consent" and that Sheriff E. L. Resweber, by taking custody of the prisoner, was "depriving him of his liberty." DeBlanc asserted that Willie's sentence had been "carried out and through an Act of God your petitioner has lived through said execution." He reasoned that, should Willie Francis be subjected to further electrocution or simply to the threat of a second electrocution attempt, it would be cruel and unusual punishment, which violated Louisiana's constitution.

DeBlanc knew that the possibility of Willie being released from jail was slim. The judge taking DeBlanc's petition under consideration would be Judge Simon himself, who was unlikely to order Willie's release from the New Iberia jail. Just as DeBlanc had expected, only hours after he filed the petition, Simon denied it. But the process of obtaining a stay in the execution of Willie Francis had begun. Anticipating Simon's denial, DeBlanc had also prepared an appeal to be filed with the Louisiana State Supreme Court. He knew the supreme court of Louisiana would not be able to move as quickly as Judge Simon, and he reasoned that the court might grant Willie a reprieve so that it could more carefully consider his case.

DeBlanc also knew he was cutting it close. He did not file the appeal until late Tuesday afternoon, May 7. By noon the following day, with Willie Francis scheduled to return to the electric chair in less than twenty-four hours, the appeal had still not reached any of the justices. Sheriff Resweber told reporters that the chair was now in fine working order and that he was prepared to carry out the death sentence "unless I am enjoined by the courts or other legal means."

DeBlanc told reporters, "I believe that every citizen should have all of his rights, whether he is white or Negro, and I do not believe that a man should be made to go to the electric chair twice."

The days following the failed execution attempt were markedly more exciting for Willie Francis than the months he'd spent awaiting the issuance of his death warrant and subsequent trip to the electric chair. For one, the press had taken a genuine interest in the "Negro Slayer" who had cheated death, and letters of support were pouring in to Willie in care of both Sheriffs Ozenne and Resweber. A nineteen-year-old girl in Fort Wayne, Indiana, pleaded with Sheriff Resweber to "have mercy for this poor boy." An anonymous person from New York argued, "If it had been a white boy around 15 years old you would not had him killed." A writer from Beaumont, Texas, noted, "True it might be that that boy killed that man, but for heavens sake he's just a kid."

Some of the letters were patriotic in tone. A man in Los Angeles wrote, "If this 2nd killing goes thru it will be an American atrocity." Others suggested that a decision to send the youth back to the chair would be uncivilized. After all, one man contended, "He carried out his part of the bargain. It was the state that failed to complete the bargain." But most of the letters—echoing the belief of Reverend R. W. Coleman of New Orleans, who had once survived a "Ku Klux Klan lynching party," that divine intervention was at play—insisted that God Himself had spared the life of Willie Francis. Typical was the assertion by Divine Workers in Montgomery, Alabama, who wrote to Sheriff Resweber: "For it is God's plan that he live. If you and your officials by wicked hands and minds take his life God will punish you and all your families with death, as a token for his life."

According to the New Orleans *Times-Picayune*, Governor Davis's office, too, was "deluged with an unprecedented flood of mail," the majority of it urging clemency for Willie Francis. One writer implied that Davis could expect political consequences should he not commute the death sentence: "Do you really mean to let the world know that Gov. Jimmie Davis is nothing but a sadistic moron?"

Bertrand DeBlanc made his own appeal: "If any lawyer in the country knows of a legal opinion which would be a precedent in this case, I certainly wish that he would get in touch with me."

Just days after the failed execution of Willie Francis, the New Orleans branch of the NAACP began asserting itself into the case, much to the dismay of DeBlanc. NAACP attorney A. P. Tureaud told reporters that he would travel to St. Martinville to petition Judge Simon for writs to stay the execution. Tureaud stated, "We believe Francis has gone through an ordeal that makes it justifiable to have his sentence reduced."

On May 6, Willie's sister Emily Branch had written a letter to the NAACP authorizing the organization to "take complete charge of all legal matters in behalf of my brother and to employ any lawyers they desire to represent him" in all legal proceedings. Seemingly with the Francis family's blessing, then, Tureaud arrived in St. Martinville to prepare the necessary legal papers for Willie's stay of execution. Alexander Pierre Tureaud, a light-skinned man of Creole heritage, was, at one time, the only black lawyer in Louisiana. He used his initials, A. P., professionally so that whites could not address him on a first-name basis—a patronizing characteristic of Jim Crow segregation that he had no tolerance for. He was therefore known to all simply as "Tureaud."

DeBlanc met Tureaud at the courthouse, where he "ordered" the NAACP attorney off the case and demanded that he "stay out of St. Martinville and leave the matter for local handling." DeBlanc resented the "outside interference," but Tureaud told the branch office that he "paid no attention to his [DeBlanc's] orders." The NAACP had filed the stay at the supreme court of Louisiana, Tureaud added, while DeBlanc "was wasting time in St. Martinville."

Louisiana Weekly latched onto Willie's story immediately following the botched execution. Undeniably, the paper also served as a mouthpiece for the New Orleans branch of the NAACP. *Louisiana Weekly* was owned by Tureaud's wife, Lucille Dejoie's family, and Tureaud would often write the stories himself. The tension between DeBlanc and Tureaud can only have been heightened when DeBlanc read editorials in the newspaper that questioned his motives for taking the case: "What sinister circumstances lay behind the murder? Why was Willie Francis ever sentenced to die without a plea of insanity entering the case? Why did Lawyer Bertrand DeBlanc volunteer his service and if he's really interested in the youth's welfare why did not he welcome the aid of an organization as the NAACP?"

Tureaud also attempted, unsuccessfully, to get approval from Frederick Francis to use Willie's signature in a newspaper advertisement designed to rally public support for his cause. More successfully, the NAACP organized letter-writing campaigns on behalf of Willie Francis, as did various church congregations around the country. The *State Times* reported, "One such telegram carried the signatures of more than 200 persons."

Bertrand DeBlanc quickly realized that public sentiment might be a tool he could effectively exploit in his defense of Willie Francis, and he must have been heartened by a telegram he received from Boys Town, Nebraska, from Father E. J. Flanagan, who wired:

DEEPLY INTERESTED IN SAVING THE LIFE OF WILLIE FRANCIS WOULD YOU DEAR MR DEBLANC TRY TO DO EVERYTHING WITHIN YOUR POWER TO HAVE THE DEATH SENTENCE COMMUTED FOR WILLIE FRANCIS PLEASE DO WHAT YOU CAN

Father Flanagan sent a similar telegram to Governor Davis, urging him to "use your power of authority to commute death sentence. May God direct you to do His holy will." And to Willie, Flanagan wrote, "I feel sure that you will be saved from the death chair and with God's help, your imprisonment will bring you much closer to God. Say your prayers well, Willie, and then the peace of light will reign within your heart."

For all the legal scholars, clergy members, and capital punishment opponents such as the singer Marian Anderson and former New York City mayor Fiorello La Guardia, who weighed in on behalf of Willie Francis, however, an equally opinionated but perhaps less vocal contingency resented the outpouring of sympathy for a black youth who had been convicted in the murder of a white man. Nowhere was this antipathy toward Willie more apparent than in

St. Martinville. In the very face of the crime, threatened and still afraid, many in the white community believed only more strongly that blacks had to be made continually aware of the grave consequences of crimes committed against whites.

DeBlanc recognized that he was in a delicate spot. To encourage and facilitate public support for Willie's plight, he would have to be outspoken and vigilant in defense of his client. Not surprisingly, most of the money that was eventually raised for Willie's defense came from out of town, from people and organizations appalled by what they were reading in the news about justice in southern Louisiana. They needed to believe that, in Bertrand DeBlanc, Willie Francis had found an aggressive and passionate advocate on his side. On the other hand, DeBlanc could ill afford to offend and alienate the community where he hoped to raise a family and earn his livelihood. With rumors spreading that DeBlanc might be working alongside two Negro attorneys, Tureaud and Joseph Thornton, to free a confessed murderer, the resentment toward DeBlanc in St. Martinville was becoming palpable. "The city wasn't too happy," says Robert Adams, a longtime friend of DeBlanc's. "St. Martinville didn't like him trying that hard to save that kid." Indeed, Father Rousseve later claimed to have overheard one white man remark that "there should be two chairs, one for Willie Francis and one for Bertrand DeBlanc."

With a second trip to the electric chair looming just days away, Willie was holding up as best as could be expected. He told reporters on May 4 that he did not feel nervous but had slept little the night before, only because he had taken a good rest on the previous night. On the morning of May 8, Willie's name appeared in headlines on the front pages of newspapers around the country as the United Press announced, "Willie Francis Moving Nearer New Execution."

Later that day, a clerk brought DeBlanc's appeal to the attention of Chief Justice Charles O'Neill, who, on that same Wednesday afternoon, received separate writs of *certiorari, mandamus,* and *prohibi-*

tion from attorneys Tureaud and Thornton on behalf of Willie Francis. O'Neill saw at once that it would be impossible for the supreme court of Louisiana to come to a decision before Willie's scheduled execution on the following day.

Jimmie Davis was out of the state, as he frequently was during his first term as governor, either performing at country music venues or appearing in movies like *Louisiana,* the 1947 biographical film in which he played himself. So Justice O'Neill telephoned Lieutenant Governor J. Emile Verret, who was serving as acting governor on behalf of the absent Davis. After a long phone conversation with DeBlanc, Verret recalled and cancelled the death warrant, and granted a thirty-day reprieve for Willie Francis, until noon on June 7, 1946. The reprieve, O'Neill believed, would give the supreme court of Louisiana adequate time to consider the appeal. The court scheduled a hearing for the very next day.

Willie's family received the news "with tears and prayer," according to a United Press story. "The Lord must be with that boy all right," a sister declared.

Meanwhile, Willie took the news in stride. "I was just sittin' here reading my prayer book," he said. That same day, just twelve hours before his scheduled second trip to the chair, Sheriff Ozenne had let reporters back into the jail to talk to Willie. Willie good-naturedly posed for a photograph: His head freshly shaved, his fingers crossed for luck, he's smiling at the camera.

As the criticism directed at the young Cajun lawyer for taking this racially charged case grew, Bertrand DeBlanc wrote a letter to Marcel "Blackie" Bienvenu, the editor of the *Weekly Messenger*:

Dear Blackie:

Although some criticism might be directed against me for having taken the case of Willie Francis, I have no apologies to make for taking the case. That is my profession—to defend people and see that they get all that the law allows them. I do not intend to be false to the oath I took as an attorney.

Willie Francis' father came to see me with tears in his eyes just as any good father would have for his own son no matter what crime he had committed, and he asked me to take the case but he had no money to pay me. I have not received one penny from anyone in this case. But I figure it this way— every man is entitled to his day in Court whether he is rich or poor, black or white. It's not what the Courts decide in this case that is of the greatest importance but the fact that a man is entitled to be heard. Otherwise, we might as well junk our system of law.

I fully realize the tragedy of Andrew's death. I was in France at the time and I was shocked at the news of this brutal murder. I can say without fear of contradiction that I was one of Andrew's best friends. I spent a lot of time going to the drug store just to talk to him. Being neighbors my three children spent most of their time around his store—and he liked them and they liked him.

Willie Francis was tried and convicted of the murder of Andrew Thomas. He was brought to the Parish Jail to be electrocuted. But what happened—the State failed in its attempt to electrocute him. In a nutshell, the question is Can the State electrocute a man twice? My contention is that it cannot. It matters not whether the person involved be Willie Francis or any one else—it might have been any of the 23 persons killed on that same chair. It is a legal matter and not a personal one. It involves our constitutional right of freedom from cruel and unusual punishment. It involves our constitutional right of due process of law and double jeopardy.

He's just a kid

I have not urged and do not now urge that Willie Francis be set free—I merely seek to prevent his being electrocuted a second time and that course I will pursue to the end. It [sic] it means life imprisonment as the alternative then that is what I shall urge.

I have requested and urged the Lieutenant Governor of the State to give my client a stay of execution which he graciously did upon the recommendation of the Supreme Court. He was granted a 30 day stay of execution. Now he will have his day in Court. He will be heard.

I am not associated with any lawyer or firm of lawyers in this case. If any come here they come down on their own.

Therefore, I reiterate, I do not apologize for taking this case. But rather I am proud of having taken this case, because my few critics will soon be dead and buried but the principles involved in this case of freedom from fear of cruel and unusual punishment and that of due process and double jeopardy will live as long as the American flag waves on this continent.

Sincerely yours,
Bertrand De Blanc

DeBlanc knew that A. P. Tureaud was poking around the St. Martinville courthouse and that the Creole attorney was reaching out to Willie's family members. The NAACP, DeBlanc knew, would stir things up in St. Martinville, and DeBlanc could not afford to be associated with the organization's agitating tactics. He also believed that such "outside interference" could only hurt Willie's chances.

When Tureaud returned to New Orleans from St. Martinville, he urged that "the widest publicity be given to this case to bring pressure to bear on the Governor to grant a stay of execution and eventually a commutation of the sentence." Highly motivated by what he had learned in St. Martinville, Tureaud stated in a letter to NAACP executive secretary Walter White that he was told "some other person, presumably white, was connected with this killing and for some unknown reason Francis will not reveal his identity to anyone."

Though of African American ancestry, Walter White had grown up as a blond-haired, blue-eyed boy in Atlanta, Georgia, but later chose to live his life by his bloodline as a black man. Because he could pass as Caucasian, White had spent many years touring the South in the guise of a white reporter so as to investigate lynchings in the communities where they had recently occurred. As the head of the NAACP, White had campaigned to have the federal government pass an antilynching law, but senators in the South had successfully prevented the law from being enacted. White would later reply to Tureaud that "being familiar with the way in which Negroes, and particularly Negro youth, are charged with murder in the South, and considering the kind of defense that is given to them by lawyers assigned by the court, I would like to know the facts. . . . If Francis did kill the druggist, was there any provocation?"

As the factions vying to lead the defense of this boy were each attempting to assert their own authority in the case, the supreme court of Louisiana decreed that six days constituted adequate time to consider Willie's appeal. On May 15, 1946, the seven members of the high court unanimously dismissed all writs filed and refused to grant Willie Francis immunity from a second trip to the electric chair. The court reasoned that, because Willie's trial and sentencing were "entirely regular," it had no authority to set aside the sentence, to release Willie from the sheriff's custody, to pardon him, or to commute his sentence.

"Things look pretty bad, all right," Willie said. "But maybe the Lord will save me again. However, I'm not afraid to die. I've never been afraid to die. When I pray, I don't pray to be saved. I just pray for courage. I think of God as like Jesus Christ—a young, handsome man with a beard. And I know he will forgive me of any sins I have committed."

With time once again running out, DeBlanc chose not to apply for a re-hearing with the supreme court of Louisiana. Although the governor of Louisiana could independently grant a reprieve, he was not empowered to grant pardons or commute sentences without approval from the Louisiana Pardons Board, which included the lieutenant governor, the attorney general, and the presiding judge at the trial of the convicted relater. Keenly aware that he would be appealing once again to Judge James D. Simon, DeBlanc recognized that the Pardons Board also comprised two state officers who might be harboring political ambitions and might therefore be swayed by public opinion.

"My client must not go to the chair," DeBlanc told the press. "Such physical torture would shock the good people of the country."

nothing against the boy

A little wire was loose and the current went back into the ground instead of going into the nigger.

—CAPTAIN EPHIE FOSTER

Bertrand DeBlanc packed his sedan with legal briefs and drove east through Evangeline country, past New Iberia, and through Houma, then across the Mississippi River via the Huey P. Long Bridge. He didn't much like driving. DeBlanc, in suit and tie, could often be spotted walking briskly around St. Martinville, sometimes a good distance from the center of town, and if anyone should pull alongside him in a car to offer a ride, and someone invariably did, De-Blanc would politely refuse. "No, thank you," he'd say. "I'm exercising!" At one point DeBlanc bought a bicycle, which he figured would discourage such offers, but it didn't, for friendly Cajuns around town would insist instead that he throw his bicycle in the back and hop in.

On this day—as he sped down to New Orleans—DeBlanc did not have the option of eschewing automobile travel for his trusty bicycle. The Louisiana Supreme Court building, on Royal Street in the heart of New Orleans's French Quarter, was designed in the beaux arts style and stood four stories high. Faced with Georgian marble on the first two stories and with terra-cotta on the upper two stories, the building's pristine grand exterior offered a stark contrast to the smaller buildings, crowded together with their cast- and wrought-iron balconies on the narrow streets surrounding it.

Making his way down the main entrance hallway, which was flanked monumentally by two-story white marble columns, DeBlanc would no doubt have noticed on the walls the oil portraits of former Louisiana Supreme Court justices, such as St. Martinville's Edward Simon, grandfather of James D. Simon who would be sitting on the Pardons Board on this particular day. DeBlanc may have considered more carefully the portrait of his own grandfather, Jean Alcibiades Maximillian DeBlanc, who served a three-year term on the court beginning in 1876.

After emerging from the elevator onto the fourth floor, DeBlanc passed beneath a Roman arch of oak and entered into the supreme court chamber. The rotunda featured a stained-glass ceiling and ten large windows draped with velvet that overlooked the French Quarter and, to the south, the Mississippi River. Behind the bench was a fasces, its ax protruding from a bundle of willow rods bound with a red strap, this ancient Roman symbol of civil authority a reminder of the origins of modern justice.

It was unusual for a Pardons Board hearing to take place in the supreme court chamber, but senate and other high-profile hearings sometimes made use of its size if the accommodations of the adjacent conference room were deemed inadequate. Such was the case for the Willie Francis hearing, in which a whole procession of witnesses was scheduled to testify.

Aware that he'd undertaken a formidable task in laying the Willie Francis case before the Louisiana Pardons Board, DeBlanc was nonetheless confident he could stop the state from sending the teenage boy to his death a second time. The young Cajun lawyer would be facing St. Martin Parish District Attorney L. O. Pecot, whom the board had called upon to represent the respondent—in this case, Sheriff Resweber. Pecot, who would in testimony claim to have a "wonderful memory" and to have seldom "made notes in cases," had successfully prosecuted Willie Francis in St. Martinville before twelve jurors and Judge Simon.

No doubt realizing the possibility that he might be overwhelmed before the board without a partner or even an associate, DeBlanc ultimately accepted the assistance of A. P. Tureaud, the experienced and competent New Orleans attorney who had filed separate writs to the supreme court of Louisiana on behalf of Willie, much to the initial chagrin of DeBlanc. Tureaud was known for his affiliation with the NAACP in New Orleans, and DeBlanc did not believe the color of Willie's skin was relevant to the task at hand. With so much work to be done on Willie's behalf in such little time, however, DeBlanc could not afford to take on both the State of Louisiana and his more pedigreed, experienced opponents. He needed help, and he consented to share the table with the black Creole lawyer Tureaud and his Negro associate, Joseph A. Thornton.

●　　◆　　●

Alexander Pierre Tureaud was born on February 26, 1899, three years before the U.S. Supreme Court upheld segregation and the constitutionality of the "separate but equal" doctrine in the landmark case of *Plessy v. Ferguson*. Homer A. Plessy was a black Creole activist and shoemaker who was jailed and found guilty of sitting in a "white" car of the East Louisiana Railroad. Plessy, an "octaroon" in nineteenth-century racial parlance (only one-eighth black—he had to inform the conductor that he was not white so as to be arrested), appealed his case to the supreme court of Louisiana and the U.S. Supreme Court, both of which upheld the guilty verdict. As a result of the decision, the "separate but equal" doctrine was quickly extended into other areas of public life, including public schools, restaurants, and bathrooms. Two years after the *Plessy* decision, the Louisiana Constitution stripped blacks of many of the social and economic gains they had made after the Civil War, and their political influence was eradicated under Jim Crow laws that reduced the number of black voters from 130,344 to 5,320. By 1904, after the poll tax was enacted (the tax ensured that only sufficiently wealthy citizens would vote), there were just 1,342 black voters in Louisiana. By the time A. P. Tureaud had come into the world, then, blacks had no political power base to effectively challenge white supremacy in Louisiana. Tureaud, however, would spend a lifetime in the Louisiana courts, attempting to undo the damage of the *Plessy* decision and the Jim Crow laws under which he lived.

One of eleven children born to Louis and Eugenie Tureaud, Alexander Pierre's childhood home on Kerlerec Street in the 7th Ward—an area of New Orleans heavily populated by black Creoles—was just blocks from where a young Father Maurice Rousseve was living at the time. Like the Rousseves, the Tureauds were highly educated and deeply Roman Catholic. They attended St. Augustine Catholic Church, which had been founded by slaves and free people of color in 1841, but when the sanctuary was crowded, the Tureauds and other black Creoles were forced to stand in the back, as pews were reserved for white Catholics. Young Alexander Pierre was eventually too humiliated to attend church at all. And with no high schools for blacks in the city, Tureaud set out, much to his family's disapproval, for Chicago, where he took a job laying track on the Illinois Central rail lines.

By 1919, he was in New York washing dishes and performing in Harlem theaters as an actor in bit parts. Directionless yet ever aware of the need for a higher education, Tureaud became intrigued by the black activism he witnessed in New York, but not until his score on a civil service exam helped land him a job in the library of the Department of Justice in Washington, DC, did his interest in law blossom.

(He took particular interest in the Constitution's Fourteenth and Fifteenth amendments with regard to race in the United States, both of which had been passed during Reconstruction.) Tureaud was inspired to finish secondary school and then enroll in a two-year legal program at Howard University Law School in the evenings.

With a law degree from the university that had turned out three-quarters of the black attorneys in the country, Tureaud returned to New Orleans. Aspiring to "right the wrongs" that *Plessy* had imposed on his race, he first had to make a living, and in the mid-1920s, even blacks did not want to hire Negro lawyers, whom they feared were incompetent. It took years for Tureaud just to become certified as a notary. When he did finally make it into a courtroom, the indignities suffered by black attorneys painfully reminded him that he was practicing law in a world that the Negro could still only hope to penetrate. One state judge commented in open court, "I didn't know they let you coons practice law."

Five feet six inches tall, barrel-chested, and with "'good' hair (not nappy)," Tureaud spoke deliberately and politely in a slow, rich Creole accent. Always politely; he was never one of the NAACP's more radical crusaders. Rather than offer social ultimatums or invite polemics, Tureaud preferred to make his points in the court of law. Unwaveringly well mannered, he was noted for his patience and perseverance. When he was pressured to take "more extreme measures," Tureaud would commonly respond that he and his ilk were being "as aggressive as the times permitted."

In 1931 Tureaud married Lucille Dejoie, who came from an old New Orleans black Creole family. Lucille had a degree in pharmacy from Howard University, and the Tureauds were one of few two-income couples starting their lives together in the 7th Ward of New Orleans. Eventually, the couple raised six children, who ranged in color from "the soft caramel of A. P., Jr., to the white-like-her-father of Elise." Tureaud would cook country breakfasts for them each morning before they hopped into the back of the city's street-cars and busses to travel to the segregated public schools of New Orleans. Family vacation trips always began before sunrise so that the Tureauds could drive out of the South and not have to face at the end of the day the uncomfortable task of finding sleeping accommodations for blacks. On those occasions when they were forced to find hotels south of the Mason-Dixon Line, the Tureaud children would later recall, their father would shout, "Hide the brown kids!" as he pulled the car into the hotel's entrance.

In the 1930s, a new breed of civil rights lawyer was emerging. Activist attorneys were becoming more aggressive in their strategies to eliminate Jim Crow. The strategist in Tureaud was convinced that the road toward equality had to begin in the field of education. He was particularly incensed that black teachers in the South's public schools received less than half the wages of white teachers. Discriminatory practices in private business were one thing, but, Tureaud believed, government payrolls "ought to be color blind." Working alongside Thurgood Marshall in parish courts across Louisiana, Tureaud began to file lawsuits arguing for salary equalization under the "equal protection of the laws" clause that was guaranteed under the Constitution's Fourteenth Amendment. He filed suits against school boards in sixteen parishes, all of which hired lawyers and went to trial against Tureaud. His toil was barely rewarded, as the fees for his work were nominal and the NAACP, in Tureaud's opinion, did not do enough to ensure he received his due and appropriate compensation. Yet Tureaud never allowed his personal difficulties to get in the way of his goals, and by 1942 he had won equal pay throughout Louisiana, a measure that forced the state legislature to appropriate the necessary funds in every parish to pay black teachers the same salaries paid to whites.

As a light-skinned man of color, Tureaud "looked like a white man" but chose not to take advantage of the higher social status that "*passablanc*" Creoles could enjoy if they chose to pass. If the lightness of one's skin was a source of controversy and division among blacks in Louisiana, it was also a reminder of the absurdity and hypocrisy of segregation, especially in New Orleans. Certainly if some blacks could avoid the laws of Jim Crow by passing, then white claims of "pure blood" were less legitimate. As Huey Long once noted, "pure whites" in Louisiana could be fed "with a nickel's worth of red beans and a dime's worth of rice."

By the time he appeared alongside DeBlanc at the Pardons Board hearing, Tureaud was living on North Rocheblave Street, just blocks from where he had grown up in New Orleans. He had taken an office at 612 Iberville Street, which had once been an autopsy room for a local hospital, in the Creole section of the French Quarter known as the Vieux Carré. Devoid of books and furniture, the office was only a short walk from the Louisiana Supreme Court. By then, too, given all of his trial experience in Louisiana, A. P. Tureaud was particularly attuned to the dynamics of race in the courts. He had once appeared in court with an opposing lawyer who, unaware of Tureaud's race, suggested that he and Tureaud "have some fun with these niggers."

The Pardons Board, which was composed of Lieutenant Governor J. Emile Verret and Attorney General Fred S. LeBlanc in addition to Willie's trial judge, James D. Simon, convened on the morning of May 31, 1946, and DeBlanc, who just weeks earlier had ordered Tureaud out of the St. Martinville Courthouse, took a seat beside the Creole attorney and his black associate, Joseph Thornton.

The State, in its attempt to demonstrate why Willie Francis should not be pardoned, argued that the electric chair had been in proper working order but that an electrical defect had prevented any current from reaching the convicted party. Willie Francis, the State argued, had been in no way harmed by the execution attempt, and, therefore, any argument as to cruel and unusual punishment bore no merit.

The State's first witness was Warden Dennis J. Bazer, who stated that he normally traveled to the Louisiana parishes with the electric chair for executions; however, he'd had to remain in Angola because he was meeting with Governor Davis on the day of Willie Francis's botched execution. In Bazer's words before the board:

> On this occasion I did not go—it would have made no difference if I did or did not but I sent Captain Foster in charge. The chair is kept at the penitentiary. Mr. Esnault is our chief electrician and he keeps the chair up and whenever he takes the chair out to the one that is carrying it I sent the electrician along with him. I sent this time Vincent Venezia, who is an inmate, with Captain Foster. The electrocutioner, who lives in Shreveport, has nothing to do with that—all he does is apply the switch and the chair is supposed to be checked out when it leaves the penitentiary in good shape and, of course, if something goes wrong with the wiring or anything on the way—of course—I am not enough electrician to explain that. Anyhow, that is how it is handled whether it is proper or improper I don't know.

Bazer then introduced a letter sent to him by D. W. Stakes from the Texas Prison System in Huntsville, Texas. The letter stated that a prisoner, John W. Vaughn, at the state penitentiary in Huntsville was led to the execution chamber on the morning of April 22, 1938, and strapped into the electric chair. For some reason, the electrical appliances failed to function, and after several attempts, the warden advised the governor of Texas of the problem. The governor granted the condemned man a seven-day stay of execution. Vaughn, the letter stated, was duly executed in the electric chair a week later, when prison officials were of the opinion "that the matter was all clear."

Bazer told the board that only in St. Martinville did the state of Louisiana's portable electric chair fail to operate, "and it has operated since then."

Next to testify for the State was S. D. Yongue, coroner of St. Martin Parish, who had been in the St. Martinville jail on May 3, 1946. Yongue informed the board that he had watched as Willie Francis was strapped in the chair, and when the switch was thrown, "nothing special happened right away. Then I saw the chair move around two or three times. Something seemed to go wrong." Yongue stated that he had then noticed that Foster "threw the switch off and waited a minute" and then threw it back on. "Directly the chair swinged around a little bit and the blindfold slipped on his face and he says, 'take this off I cannot breathe,' and I heard somebody say, 'you are not supposed to breathe.'"

Yongue had also heard Willie cry out to Foster, "I am not dying," and then, Yongue said, the switch was thrown off and the officers escorted the youth back to a cell. "As coroner of the Parish I supposed it was my duty to examine him afterwards," Yongue stated, "which I did and found nothing wrong with him except that his pulse was a little bit fast—I took my stethoscope and examined his chest—I listened to his heart beat, which was perfectly normal except a little bit accelerated, which could easily have been from the apprehension or being excited, but I found no serious impairment. I then left."

The board questioned Yongue about any physical damage Willie might have received: "Doctor, did you find any marks showing any burns?" Yongue replied that he did not: "I examined his forehead and his chest and I saw his legs. Neither did I smell an odor of burned flesh." Yongue elaborated on the absence of burn marks: "I watched that when they took the strap off his legs and did not see any. I did not examine the back part of his leg but the front part had no marks. If there had been any marks, I probably would have seen them, yes."

Yongue noted, too, that Willie did not complain to him about any pains and, in fact, did not speak to the coroner at all. Asked if, after the attempted execution, he could gauge Willie's mental or physical condition, the coroner replied that, when he "followed him into the room where they had carried him, somebody else was talking to him. I stopped—examined his chest—examined him with my stethoscope so as to be able to report to your Excellency what I had discovered, but he did not talk to me, neither did I talk to him."

The State next called Captain Ephie Foster. "Will you tell us just what happened?" the board asked.

"We set the chair up and it worked perfect," Foster replied, "and when you throwed the main switch on there the needle went back to zero. There was a shortage—a little wire was loose and the current went back into the ground instead of going into the nigger."

The bluntness of the Angola prison captain before the board cannot have come as a surprise to Tureaud. Having spent considerable time over the years interviewing suspects and witnesses to violence against blacks throughout Louisiana, the NAACP attorney had encountered his fair share of men like Foster. Foster continued by declaring that, although he was no electrician, he was of the opinion that no electricity had gone through Willie Francis because, contrary to what he'd observed in other executions, he had seen no evidence of burns on Willie's head and legs. Tureaud then asked Foster if he could be absolutely sure that no electricity had reached Willie's body, to which Foster admitted that he could not say so for sure.

The State then called Vincent Venezia, the inmate trusty who worked as an assistant to the chief electrician at the Louisiana State Penitentiary. Venezia described for the board how he and Foster had set up the electric chair on the morning of May 3, 1946. "We started about 8:30 to unload," he said. "I hung it all up and go downstairs and stopped my engine and made my test and set the voltage at 2500 and test my ampmeters—A.C. and D.C.—and see that they all work perfectly. Then I run it for about five or ten minutes and see about my engine and generator and see if it is working good and turn it off. Left it until about ten minutes to twelve." Venezia stated that, after he had inspected the wires and run his tests, he'd stayed with the truck and had not observed anyone tampering with the equipment.

The board wanted to know why Captain Foster had signaled to Venezia during Willie's execution. "Well," Venezia began, "Captain Foster, after he threw the switch on the machine, signaled to me to give him more gas—that is, more power on the engine so he could raise the voltage, to run it up to 2500 volts, and I done so but he hollered to me and told me it would not work, so I shut the engine down and go upstairs and checked over it and checked it thoroughly and found one of the wires broke loose, and I just figured it hit the ground. From the switchboard to the outside to the ground had broke aloose and it all went back into the ground."

"Are you prepared to state, as electrician, that no current whatever passed through the body of Willie Francis?" the board asked.

"Yes, I would say that no current went through the body of Willie Francis—if it had he would not have been able to walk to his cell. Anytime electricity hits you you are going to be weak or fainted. You are going to be too weak."

"In other words," the board continued, "it produces a certain amount of shock."

"Yes, sir," Venezia replied. "I was the one who took the strap off him. I said, 'how do you feel,' so I walked pretty near to the door with him and I asked him, 'did you get shock at all.' He said 'no, sir.'"

"Did he claim that the current tickled him?" the board asked.

"No, sir," Venezia said. "I asked him how he felt when I unbuckled him and I asked him 'were you hurt,' and he said 'no, sir.' I then took my board down."

"Did you take occasion to examine his left leg and head?"

"He was not burned," Venezia replied.

"In previous executions, were there evidence of burns on the head and leg?"

"If it hits them," Venezia replied, "you can tell it. You can see the rim of the cap which touches him. We put gauze dipped in salt water and shoot the electricity through—it dries it up and when it dries it shows a real burn."

"Did you do that in this case?"

"Yes, sir," Venezia said. "The gauze was not dry at all either on the leg or head."

So it was that in the opinions of both Captain Foster, who was not an electrician, and Vincent Venezia, who was not present in the room during the botched execution, the electric current could not have passed, and indeed did not pass, through the body of Willie Francis. U. J. Esnault, chief electrician at the Louisiana State Penitentiary, then testified that the chair had been tested and found to be in good working order before it left Angola. He noted further that the chair had been used the following week at Leesville, where it had worked satisfactorily. (Eighteen-year-old George Edwards Jr. was executed on May 9, 1946, in the Vernon Parish jail after being convicted of killing a farmer and robbing him of five dollars. As he was being strapped to the chair, he smiled and told witnesses, "I'll see you up there.")

The State's next witness was Sheriff Resweber. After he recalled how Willie had "squirmed around a little bit" when the switch was thrown, and how he had "rocked the chair," the sheriff then reiterated the State's case against Willie Francis. His testimony must thus have sounded eerily similar to the steady, uninterrupted flow of the evidence presented at Willie's criminal trial, not by witnesses but by law enforcement officials.

"You know the defendant, Willie Francis, fairly well, don't you?" the board asked.

"Very well," Resweber answered.

"Did you have any conversation with him after the attempted electrocution?"

"On his way out," Resweber said. "I asked him what happened."

"What did he say?"

"He said, 'The Lord was with me that time.'"

"Did he complain of any pain?" the board asked.

"No, he did not," Resweber said.

"Was he walking alright?"

"Apparently alright."

"Sheriff, are you familiar with the arrest of Willie Francis and the incidents thereafter which occurred in connection with any confession he may have made to any official?" Judge Simon asked.

"You mean in Texas, Judge," Resweber inquired.

"In Texas and Louisiana."

"He admitted assaulting and robbing a white man in Port Arthur, Texas," Resweber said. According to Port Arthur Chief of Police Claude Goldsmith, Willie confessed to following Smith down an alley and hitting the man over the head with an empty wine bottle before robbing him. Both the bottle and a bloody quilt on which the victim was lying were recovered from the scene.

"Is there an outstanding warrant for him?" Judge Simon asked.

"I have a warrant right now to hold him in case he should be let free," Resweber replied.

Resweber then described how he had driven to Port Arthur to bring Willie back to St. Martinville.

"Did he make a confession to you either on your way back, in Texas, or after you got back to Louisiana?" Judge Simon asked.

"On my way back to Louisiana. Yes, sir."

"Did he, in that confession, admit the killing, or murdering, of Thomas?"

"Yes, sir," Resweber said. "He showed us where he threw the gun away—where we had already found the gun—showed us where he had thrown the holster away in the culvert back of the railroad tracks back of the Thomas place."

"Did he say where he obtained the pistol and holster with which he killed Thomas?"

"He stole that gun from one of my deputy's car," Resweber said.

"Did he admit stealing it?"

"Yes, sir."

"How many times did he admit shooting Thomas?" Judge Simon asked.

"How many times he shot him? Five times, I think it was."

"Did he explain just how he went about shooting Mr. Thomas? Tell us about that."

"He went to Thomas's home pretty early," Resweber said. "Mr. Thomas went home early. He was not long—"

"You are taking this from his confession?" Judge Simon interrupted.

"Yes. He was waiting behind his garage for three hours. When Mr. Thomas came in and was closing the door of his garage he shot him."

"Tell how he shot him—was he shot standing?"

"He said standing, yes, sir."

"Did he say, after he shot Thomas one time, that Mr. Thomas fell to the ground?" Judge Simon asked.

"He did not say," Resweber said. "He said he was standing all the time."

"Did he tell you that after he shot Thomas he took his wallet and watch?"

"By the way," Resweber offered without answering Judge Simon's question. "We recovered that same watch at Rivere Jewelry Store in New Iberia. Willie Francis showed us—took us to the jewelry store to the man—the man was not so sure about buying such a watch but he looked up his cashbook and found where he had made a purchase of $5.00."

"How long ago was that?" Judge Simon asked.

"That was soon after we brought him from Texas," Resweber said. "That was about eight months after. Mr. Rivere did not remember him at all but Willie Francis said, 'I sold you that watch for $5.00,' and several days after, Mr. Rivere found the watchcase that had initials on the back. We could not have made a mistake as to the identity of that watch." Resweber explained to the board that Mr. Rivere had removed the movement of the watch and placed it in a new case, since watches were "hard to get" during the war.

"What we would like to know, Sheriff," Judge Simon said, "is after this defendant made the confession, did you take it at face value or check it?"

"I checked every angle of the confession and it checked out," Resweber answered.

"Did you take him with you to the place he sold the watch?"

"Yes, sir."

"What about the holster?"

"The holster also—the holster, gun and watch."

"What about the wallet?

"They found the wallet on his person in Texas that he admitted taking from Thomas," Resweber said.

"Did he ascribe any reason as to why he shot Thomas?" Judge Simon asked.

"He told us he had had a little trouble with Thomas and then later on he said he had no trouble with Thomas—that Thomas was a fine fellow but that he did not know why he did it."

"Has he ever denied his guilt?"

"He never did," Resweber said.

"Did he appear as repentful or sorry for his deed after you had him?" Judge Simon asked.

"No, sir."

"What was his general attitude?"

"He did not care."

"Sheriff, there is some testimony here about a fifteen-year-old boy," Judge Simon said. "For the benefit of the record, what is the physical makeup of this Willie Francis as far as physical development is concerned?"

"He is fully developed. He is about five feet eight or nine inches tall, weighs about one hundred fifty or one hundred fifty-five pounds, is a well built boy."

"What would you, not knowing his age, give him from all appearances?"

"About nineteen or twenty—maybe twenty-one," Resweber said.

"You conclude that from his physical appearance?"

"Yes, sir."

A. P. Tureaud must have harbored more than a little doubt as to the validity of testimony presented by a white sheriff in the Deep South who maintained that a young black man accused of murder had, without reluctance or qualm, proffered him a full confession. Tureaud's first questions struck an almost incredulous tone. "You did not have to use any force to get a statement from him?" Tureaud asked.

"Everything he told me was voluntary," Resweber replied.

"Voluntary?"

"He showed no nervousness."

Tureaud was familiar with the circumstances of enough lynchings to know that police participation in brutality against black suspects in police custody was commonplace across the South. His own investigation into the activities of Sheriff Gilbert Ozenne and Gus "Killer" Walker—the very men guarding Willie Francis in New Iberia—told him everything he needed to know about law enforcement, coercion, and violence. J. Edgar Hoover, in his testimony before President Truman's Committee on Civil Rights, referred to a particular jail where "it was seldom that a Negro man or woman was incarcerated who was not given a severe beating, which started off with a pistol whipping and ended with a rubber hose." Allan B. Durand, who worked in the St. Martinville sheriff's department and later served as the town's interim sheriff when Sheriff Charles R. Fuselier (the son of August Fuselier) died in office, confirmed that the St. Martinville jail matched the type of southern jail described by Hoover. Durand told his son, "If you were black and they wanted you to confess, you confessed." Father Maurice Rousseve, too, believed that Resweber's jail fit the common southern mold. "St. Martinville was always prejudiced," Rousseve would say years later. "You know, southern town. People said, St. Martinville, they used to whip those Negro prisoners at night till you could hear it."

Continuing with Sheriff Resweber, Tureaud shifted his line of questioning in regard to Willie: "Does he act like a man who is a killer?"

"That is the first killer I have had in my custody," Resweber replied. "He looks absolutely normal to me. I am not saying that for any reason—I have nothing against the boy."

Tureaud then stated, "You were surprised when you heard he was fifteen years old."

"I was surprised," Resweber said. "I went so far as to get a baptismal certificate on him."

L. O. Pecot also had some questions for Resweber. Recognizing some of the weaker elements of Resweber's case against Willie Francis, District Attorney Pecot was clearly making a point of getting certain facts on the record.

"Sheriff, does he read and write?"

"He does read and write," Resweber replied.

"Is not it a fact that, after Andrew Thomas was murdered, the whole town was astir over this happening?" Pecot asked. "Was not there a great many rumors flying fast and thick, day and night, which you were trying to run down—you and the State Police?"

"Yes, sir. It kept us busy for eight months, night and day."

"Is it not a fact that that boy, who had killed and murdered Thomas on November 8th, 1944, remained in the town of St. Martinville, passing in front of your home while working for Bullot?" "Bullot" was most likely a misspelling in the hearing's transcript of "Bulliard"—a reference to Edmond Bulliard's Evangeline Pepper and Food Products Company, located across the bridge over the Bayou Teche and not far from Sheriff Resweber's house.

"Yes, sir," Resweber replied.

"Is it not a further fact," Pecot asked, "that he only left to go to Texas about the month of February or the early part of March 1945, when matters had sort of calmed down and you were still working on the case?"

"I would not be able to tell you the exact time he left," Resweber said, "but I know it was a few months after the murder was committed."

"Was there any other statement made by Willie Francis implicating any other person when he was in your custody?"

"I believe he was in Iberia Parish jail when he made that statement," Resweber replied.

"Was that statement made to you?" Pecot asked.

"Yes, sir. He gave me names of two colored boys and told me where they lived—who they were and where I would find them," Resweber said. "I run that down and he gave me some fictitious names. There was nobody by those names and after, finally [he] said that he was just fooling that he was the only one committed that murder."

"Did any of his statements made to you involve the life or well-being of other people?" Pecot asked. "In other words, did he make any statements to you involving other people?"

"No, not to me," Resweber replied. "It was said—it was rumored—but so many rumors were going around that 99 $^1/_2$ percent of them were not true. Just rumors. He did not make any such statement to me."

When Resweber was finished, the board called Sheriff Gilbert Ozenne and established that he was sheriff of Iberia Parish.

"What do you know about Willie Francis's case, Sheriff?"

"What I know is that I am keeping him for Sheriff Resweber, in New Iberia, and I happened to take him to St. Martinville the day of the electrocution," Ozenne replied.

"You did not have him before that day?"

"Yes, he had been in jail five or six months."

"Did you find any difference in his general attitude since the attempted execution?" Ozenne was asked.

"No, sir," he replied.

"Does he appear repentant and sorry for his deed?"

"He is about the same," Ozenne said. "He was a little nervous for a day or two after the date of the execution."

The board inquired more specifically about Willie's behavior during the time he spent in the Iberia Parish jail, perhaps in an effort to stem growing sentiment in the black community that the State of Louisiana was attempting to re-execute a mentally deficient youth. "Sheriff, tell us whether or not, in your opinion, this defendant, Willie Francis, appears to be normal—do you think he is normal?"

"The only trouble with him—his speech is very bad," Ozenne said. "He stutters."

"Is not that known with other individuals who are perfectly sane? Aside from the fact that he stutters, is there anything else to make you believe that he is mentally weak?"

"No, sir."

At the time of the Louisiana Pardons Board hearings in New Orleans, articles in the black press had been questioning the sanity of Willie Francis. The *Philadelphia Tribune*, for one, ran a story beneath the headline: "Willie Francis, Death Cell Principal, Called In-

sane on Eve of Re-execution." The article stated that "an investigation by 'Scoop' Jones, star reporter for the *Louisiana Weekly* found
much evidence for insanity. Both Mr. and Mrs. Frederick Francis,
parents of the youth, who is the youngest of fourteen children, admit that Willie Francis has never had the tendencies of a normal
child. Neighbors, friends and other members of the community tell
of harmless pranks that he has played from childhood that gives in-
dications of insanity." The story also quoted Father Maurice Rousseve as saying that Willie did not show signs of a "bright child."
Likewise, stories in the *Chicago Defender* referred to the youth as
"mentally unbalanced" and "mentally subnormal." A. P. Tureaud
himself asked Willie's sister, Emily Branch, about Willie's mentality,
and she "expressed the belief that her brother is not quite normal."

A study published in the *Journal of Criminal Law and Criminology*
(2005) cited nearly 200 instances in the United States between 1989
and 1993 in which an individual convicted of murder was later
found to be innocent and was ultimately exonerated. Twenty-one
percent of these murder convictions were based on false confessions. The study also found that, of the total 340 exonerations for
serious felonies (mostly rape and murder) in that same time frame,
44 percent of the convicted juveniles (persons under the age of
eighteen at the time of the crime) had falsely confessed. Among the
twelve- to fifteen-year-olds, eight of the twelve juveniles charged
with serious felonies and later exonerated had given false confessions to police. According to the same study, a significant 69 percent
of mentally disabled people who were exonerated had falsely confessed to the crimes for which they were convicted, often because
they had an "excessive desire to please" the authority figures questioning them. The report concludes: "False confessions also played
a large role in the murder convictions that led to exonerations, pri-
marily among two particularly vulnerable groups of innocent defendants: juveniles, and those who are mentally retarded or mentally ill.

Almost all the juvenile exonerees who falsely confessed are African American."

Willie Francis, an African American in the Jim Crow South, whose mental abilities were questioned not only by Father Rousseve but also by many residents in St. Martinville as well as his own family, was just fifteen years old at the time of Andrew Thomas's death and only sixteen nine months later when he "voluntarily" confessed to murder.

murder at midnight

The allegation further has it that after the altercation, and murder seemed eminent [sic], that this white person offered the services of his gun. Further rumor has it, that there was a hidden motive behind the move that probably will never be told.

—JESSYL TAYLOR

"The consensus of opinion," said the *Philadelphia Tribune* in its story on Willie's imminent re-execution, "is that Willie Francis should have never been sentenced to die. When Francis was brought to trial, the story is told that he never seemed actually aware that he was on trial for his life. He appeared to be cocky and acting like a kid who was playing a game. Some offer the idea that he was merely a pawn in an intrigue of revengeful murder. That if he did kill the druggist, there is more (and probably other parties) involved. There is much speculation on this angle."

Jessyl Taylor, a writer from Dallas, Texas, working on a story for the black newspaper the *World's Messenger*, spent time with the Francis family and visited Willie in jail at the time of the hearing. She wrote, "The writer expected to meet a bitter young man who talked out of the side of his mouth and snarled in the process.

Instead I found a co-operative fellow who seemed delighted when told we were working on a petition for life. The picture of health, Willie is an intelligent lad. He is soft spoken and very modest."

Taylor added, "An interesting side light on the story might well be discerned from a current rumor, that is quite widespread in these parts. It is alleged that the gun used in the murder case has been proved to be the gun of a white person. The allegation further has it that after the altercation, and murder seemed eminent [sic], that this white person offered the services of his gun. Further rumor has it, that there was a hidden motive behind the move that probably will never be told."

Turning its attention to another of Willie's confessions—this one supposedly written by Willie on the wall of his cell in the Iberia Parish jail—the board continued questioning Sheriff Ozenne, who had, by this time, become used to taking questions from boards and investigators.

"Did he [Willie] ever indicate to you at any time that perhaps he had not committed this crime?" the board asked.

"He never denied it to me, no sir," Ozenne replied.

"Did he ever admit it to you?"

"Yes, sir."

"Have you ever seen anything in writing from him to indicate that he still maintains that position?"

"Not in writing—no, sir," Ozenne said, then added, "Do you mean in writing, any kind of writing? He had in print the cell where he is at that he did kill Andrew Thomas."

"Written where?" the board asked.

"In his cell on the wall in print," Ozenne replied.

"Was that before or since the attempted execution?"

"No, sir. It was before."

"Do you recall what is written on the wall?"

"Yes, sir," Ozenne replied. "He says 'I kill Andrew Thomas and today he is lying in a grave and I am not a killer but I wonder where I am going to be laying and in what kind of grave I don't know.'"

"Is that written on the wall?" the board asked.

"Yes, sir, on the wall."

In 1984, the legal scholar Arthur S. Miller would write of Willie's case, "No one other than Ozenne is known to have seen the scrawl. If, in fact, Willie had written it, it would be some sort of confession (but not admissible as such in court)." Nevertheless, Ozenne—aware, perhaps, that his account of this confession would not be challenged or contradicted—managed to inject the confession into sworn testimony before the Louisiana Pardons Board.

The scrawl, however, has not been entirely lost. On May 3, 1946, the evening of the botched execution, when Sheriff Ozenne let reporters and photographers into the jail, a photographer captured on film an image of the newly bald teenager standing before the north wall of his jail cell. There is writing on the wall, in large, dark letters, that appears to match Willie's hand (Willie misspells "Thmas" consistently in all of his writings), and the words are similar to the "confession" Ozenne either paraphrased or read from notes in his testimony before the Louisiana Pardons Board.

Similar, but not the same.

The words Willie may well have written on his cell wall are by no means precisely the words ascribed to him by Sheriff Ozenne, and they certainly do not constitute an admission to first-degree murder. In fact, if Willie Francis was indeed the author of the words on the wall of his cell, and if he wrote them free from any duress, Sheriff Ozenne either carelessly mischaracterized the meaning of Willie's "confession" or else intentionally lied under oath. Even if the latter was the case, the combination of a confession obtained without a lawyer present and perjury on the part of a sheriff would still stand as evidence against a defendant, especially a black defendant, in Louisiana in 1946. The photograph clearly shows these words written on the north wall of Willie's cell:

PRACTICALLY I KILLED ANDREW

BY ACCIDENT. IT WILL HAPPEN

ONCE IN A LIFE TIME

LOOK WHERE ANDREW IS

TODAY HE'S IN IS LONELY COLDLY GRAVE

Further along the wall, on the other side of Willie's body, which obstructs some of the words in the photograph, the following phrases can be clearly read:

OF COURSE I AM NOT A KILLER

MORRIS IS A SON OF A BIT

ANDREW THMAS IS

MURDER BY WILLIE

MURDER AT MID NIGHT

WILLIE FRANCIS

800 WASHINGTON STREET

SAIT MARTINVILLE LA

SORRY AT MYSELF

("Morris" could be a misspelled reference to the New Iberia jailer, Clemarie Norris, who was once photographed bringing Willie bundles of mail and who stated for a newspaper that Willie was, for the most part, well behaved in jail. "He got sassy only once," Norris said.)

What the actual words on the jail cell wall suggest, then, is that Willie had an encounter of some sort with Andrew Thomas, or "Andrew" as Willie also refers to him, at the time of the murder or "accident." What sort of encounter was never explored during the murder trial that sent Willie to the electric chair, nor was it mentioned in any of the hearings or testimony thereafter.

Not surprisingly, Tureaud had a few questions for Sheriff Ozenne. Tureaud, no doubt remembering that the New Iberia sheriff had been investigated by the FBI just a year earlier, got right into it with Ozenne about what Willie may have experienced in the chair. "In your opinion, did he or did he not get a shock?"

"I could not tell that," Ozenne said defensively, before asking, "What would you think?"

"I would not know but I know he was tickled," Tureaud replied, unfazed. "You attended the electrocution. At the time of the electrocution did not the chair move around? Was it your opinion or not that he got a shock?"

"It was something that must have made him move," Ozenne admitted.

Tureaud wanted to return to the facts of the trial and Willie's confession. He, too, had heard the rumors and must have found it unsettling that Willie had attempted to admit to having accomplices. "Long before the trial," Tureaud asked, "did he make any statement that there was someone else in St. Martinville who was connected with this crime? Did he ever make that statement?"

"Not to me, no sir," Ozenne said.

"Before the trial, now, did he ever make the statement that someone else was connected with this crime?"

"At one time," Ozenne admitted, "he said that but we checked and could not find it."

When Tureaud had finished questioning Ozenne, District Attorney Pecot addressed the board. Summarizing the events that had led up to the trial of Willie Francis, he stated that Willie "had stolen that pistol from Mr. August Fuselier, a very prominent citizen of St. Martin, while his car was on the street one night." When the board asked if Fuselier was a deputy sheriff, Pecot replied in the positive and added that Fuselier had even "notified the Sheriff's office of the pistol being stolen in the month of September, while court was going on and before this killing. I remember him coming up and saying his pistol had been stolen."

Despite the fact that the gun used to kill Andrew Thomas had been lost before the trial and thus never presented as evidence, there appeared to be little doubt that it belonged to Mr. August Fuselier. Still, there is nothing, other than Pecot's recollection, to document that Fuselier had reported the theft of his gun in September of 1944.

August Fuselier was born in 1890, and his family, whose ancestor Gabriel Fuselier had founded the original Poste des Attakapas settlement along the banks of the Teche more than two centuries before, ran a prosperous plantation in St. Martinville. Fuselier grew cotton, pepper, potatoes, okra, and snap beans, largely through the benefit of sharecropping agreements with black families who lived on his land and worked his fields from sunup to sundown. On occasion, Fuselier might bail a black man out of jail and have him work in the Fuselier fields until his debt was paid. If the man didn't hold up his end of the bargain, Fuselier, who kept a pistol tucked into his belt, would either personally deliver a beating or he'd leave it up to "Dob," the large, black overseer who saw to the cattle on the farm and to any disciplinary problems that might arise.

"Fuselier was mean to blacks," another woman would say. "He didn't like them." Mean enough, as a townsman recalls, that he'd force blacks to remove their clothes, then run them at gunpoint through the cane fields so that their skin would be cut to ribbons by the razor-sharp stalks.

Father Maurice Rousseve believed that Fuselier was essentially a "bad man." Once, encountering a black man who "had quit Mr. Fuselier's employ and gone to work for another white man," according to Rousseve, Fuselier simply beat the man right there on the road. By all accounts, rarely did Fuselier hesitate to resort to violence at any affront.

Aside from having a strong opinion about Fuselier, Rousseve also believed that Andrew Thomas was an adulterer, "with women black and white, married and single," and that many men in town, in Rousseve's estimation, wanted to see him dead. August Fuselier was one of them. Reportedly, he walked into Andrew Thomas's drugstore one night and warned Thomas to stay away from his wife "or he wouldn't live long." Variations on this story suggest that Fuselier may have been threatening Thomas to stay away from a common girlfriend rather than his wife.

Word around town at the time of the murder was that Fuselier, though married and in his fifties, was seeing more than a few women on the side. Among them—and it was no secret—was thirty-nine-year-old Lena Foti, who ran a saloon off Main Street. Fuselier's car was parked there on the evening that Willie Francis was said to have stolen Fuselier's gun—the gun that would end the life of Andrew Thomas and become fodder for enough rumor and speculation to keep Resweber "busy for eight months, night and day."

●   ◆   ●

After the board had questioned L. O. Pecot, the St. Martin Parish district attorney concluded by reiterating that the panel should not lose sight of the fact that Willie Francis was a murderer, and a murderer should not be entitled to escape justice because of an electrical mishap.

> Gentlemen, it seems to me this case is a question as to whether or not this board is going to follow the judgment of the jury of twelve men who listened most carefully to the evidence before bringing in their verdict, or whether

or not, because of an unfortunate happening due to no fault of anyone, but just a mechanical defect, this board is going to say "for that reason we are going to extend this man an extra portion of mercy—we are going to send him to the penitentiary for life instead of making him pay to society for the terrible crime he committed in the Parish of St. Martin."

Pecot then stressed the importance of respecting the jury's decision. Otherwise, he reasoned, "How can we expect them to convict men to pay their debts to society when, afterwards, what they have done is undone by another authority of law having the power to do so? This is what has happened in this case."

Pecot offered a dire warning. In Louisiana, lynchings have often followed crimes like Willie's, he said, and "the only way and safest way to keep that from happening is to bring to justice and punish, according to each case, the guilty party." Perhaps to preempt any emotional appeal that Bertrand DeBlanc might plan to deliver to the board, Pecot pled: "Society looks to us to do our duty and I know that you gentlemen are not going to be carried away by sentiment in this case and that you are going to carry the law as far as it is possible to do so."

Pecot had closed, but he was not finished. A. P. Tureaud had some points he wished to discuss with him. In a series of questions to Pecot, Tureaud deftly exposed to the board some of the weaknesses in the State's murder case against Willie Francis, significant among them the fact that none of the witnesses brought in to testify against Willie had seen him commit the crime.

"Is it not a fact," Tureaud asked, "that the only testimony against Willie Francis in this case was the alleged confession of Willie Francis?"

"That was the principal part of the testimony—his admission—in addition to these other facts and circumstances," Pecot said, "such as the finding of the pistol. The jury convicted him on the evidence they heard."

"Were there any witnesses who testified in behalf of Willie Francis?"

"As I understand it, there were none," Pecot said. "I don't remember anyone."

Tureaud then asked Pecot about the testimony of Andrew Thomas's neighbor, Mrs. Van Brocklin, at the coroner's inquest. She had stated that she awoke to the sound of several gunshots, and when she looked out her window, she saw a car parked in front of Thomas's house with its lights on.

"She looked outside," Pecot admitted, "and, according to the testimony at the coroner's inquest, saw this car outside with the lights on. I don't know if it was his car. She saw a car."

"Was she ever brought in to testify?" Tureaud asked.

"No."

Once he'd gotten Pecot to admit that the State had produced no witnesses to Willie's commission of the crime, Tureaud raised the issue of the missing murder weapon. Pecot tried to explain that the gun had been lost in transit to the FBI in Washington for ballistic tests, but he did not bother to explain why such tests were even necessary, given that Willie had proffered a complete confession. Pecot said only, "We have never heard from that pistol since."

Tureaud had just two more questions for Pecot.

"How long did the trial last, Mr. Pecot?"

"Two days."

"Were there any bills of exception taken during the trial?

"The judge overruled almost every exception that was made," Pecot replied.

What Tureaud was no doubt striving to get on record in his questions to Pecot and his cohorts in local law enforcement was that Willie, at one time, had admitted to having accomplices in the murder of Andrew Thomas. Certainly his confession to Resweber contained ambiguous language on this point, as when Willie wrote "*he* kill" and "*I* shot."

Since five bullets had struck and killed Andrew Thomas, Tureaud may have believed that bullets from two different guns might have been fired on the night of November 7, 1944. If Willie Francis had been the only shooter, and given that Pecot had both a confession from him and corroboration from a sheriff's deputy as to the gun's ownership, why would Pecot and Resweber bother sending the gun and bullets to Washington, DC, for analysis? Perhaps the intent was, in fact, to lose the ballistics evidence at the behest of someone in St. Martinville who had the ability, motivation, and opportunity to arrange its disappearance, thus leaving a poor, uneducated black youth and his hapless (or worse, complicit) public defenders in the awkward position of having to convince twelve white jurors and Judge Simon that the law enforcement officials in their town were corrupt and incompetent.

By raising the issue of the lost gun and bullets, Tureaud may have been attempting to lay the groundwork for an appeal to a higher court or for a special investigation by getting certain elements of the prosecution's case on record, elements that earlier court transcripts did not contain. At the same time, Tureaud was clearly implying a much larger and more insidious conspiracy in the town of St. Martinville.

a boy on the threshold
of eternity

How long does the State of Louisiana take to kill a man?

—BERTRAND DeBLANC

Between them, A. P. Tureaud and his associate, Joseph A. Thornton, dealt with the cross-examination of all the State's witnesses at the hearing of the Louisiana Pardons Board. In his questioning of St. Martin Parish District Attorney L. O. Pecot, Tureaud hinted at the lack of "effective counsel" on behalf of the convicted youth. He was attempting to link Willie's case with that of the "Scottsboro Boys" (*Powell v. Alabama*), wherein eight black youths were wrongfully accused of raping two white women. The U.S. Supreme Court in 1932 had overturned their convictions by ruling that the poor performance of their attorneys deprived the youths of the Sixth Amendment right to effective counsel.

Bertrand DeBlanc, however, had no interest in rehashing the facts of the State's case against Willie Francis. He knew that the Louisiana Pardons Board was not likely to be receptive to any points raised about the fairness of Willie's trial, especially with Judge Simon on the board. Instead, DeBlanc focused on the torture that Willie Francis had suffered at the hands of the State. When he stood to address the Pardons Board, he hoped to affect them not by arguing the rule of law but by appealing to their sense of fairness and justice—much the way Huey Long had in his campaign speech for the governorship beneath the Evangeline Oak back in St. Martinville. He was, in effect, asking for mercy on behalf of Willie Francis on the grounds that it would be cruel and unusual punishment to send the boy to the electric chair a second time.

However, before he could appeal to the board's sentiments, which, as Pecot had argued, were irrelevant in the face of law and duty, DeBlanc had to rebut the State's contention that no electricity had reached the body of Willie Francis during the execution on May 3. DeBlanc produced six affidavits from official witnesses to the failed execution. Among them was that of Father Maurice Rousseve, who observed that, after Captain Foster threw the switch, Willie's "lips puffed out and his body squirmed and tensed and he jumped so that the chair rocked on the floor." In a similar vein, Ignace Doucet stated that he saw Willie's body go tense and, in his opinion, "this boy really got a shock when they turned that machine on." Doucet added that he also heard the executioner tell Willie that, "although he did not kill him that time, the next time he would kill him if he had to use an iron bar to do it." Like Father Rousseve, Sidney Dupois, the barber in St. Martinville, noted that the moment the switch was turned on, "Willie Francis's lips puffed out and he grunted and made the chair jump." Dupois added that Francis yelled, "Take it off. Let me breathe."

Other witnesses appeared. Indeed, "a parade of witnesses and negro preachers trouped before the board," among them, Reverend L. L. Haynes of New Orleans who declared, "In the name of more than 13,000,000 negroes who have given their bit in carrying on for American democracy, I plead with the pardon board to offer Willie Francis clemency." Certainly, DeBlanc had roused public sentiment in support of the cause of Willie Francis, and he demonstrated it in the face of the board's public officials.

DeBlanc then argued that the State's decision to send Willie back to the chair would constitute double jeopardy, as Willie had already suffered the tortures of death for the same crime. "Everything was done to electrocute this boy up to and including the pulling of the switch and the passing of electricity into his body," DeBlanc said. "He died mentally, his body still exists but through no fault of his." De-Blanc reminded the board, too, that the State of Louisiana had never in its history imposed a death sentence on a fifteen-year-old boy.

> The main point which I wish to stress, gentlemen, is that no man should go to the chair twice. No man should suffer impending death twice. The voice of humanity and justice cries out against such an outrage. You men who compose this honorable body are just and sincere and I know that you will be guided only by the hand of justice. I am not asking that this boy be set free. I am only asking that his sentence be commuted from death to life imprisonment in the state penitentiary. Is that too much to ask for a boy who has gone through the mental and physical torture that he has?

Then, invoking instances of divine intervention behind failed executions in biblical times, DeBlanc cited the story of the three men who emerged from King Nebuchadnezzar's fiery furnace untouched—their hair not singed, their skin not burned—as well as the story of Daniel in the lion's den, in which God shut the mouths of the lions so Daniel would come to no harm. DeBlanc believed, as Willie did, that the hand of God had prevented the accomplishment of the black youth's execution on the day of May 3, 1946. "There is the law of the Bible," he told the board. "Isn't that law good enough for us here?"

DeBlanc proceeded by reciting a history of failed executions, one by one, that resulted in the condemned man's sentence being reduced.

He began with the case of Englishman John Lee, who was sent to the gallows at Exeter jail on February 23, 1885, after being convicted in the vicious murder of Miss Emma Ann Keyse. A white bag was placed over Lee's head, and as he stepped onto a trapdoor, a noose was placed around his neck. When the sheriff gave the signal, the hangman removed the bolt to release the trapdoor so that Lee would drop through the floor and thereby be strangled to death. But the trapdoor failed to open. The hangman had Lee step aside; he tested the trapdoor. It worked perfectly. But when Lee again stood in place on the trapdoor and again the hangman pulled the bolt, the door again failed to open. They repeated the process several times, each time with the same result. Frustrated, the sheriff had Lee returned to his cell. Ultimately, the House of Commons debated the failed execution, and Lee's sentence was commuted to life in prison. (Ironically, the gallows had supposedly been built by a convict serving a life sentence himself, and he, legend has it, designed the trapdoor so that it would not open during an actual execution because the chaplain would be standing on a board that jammed the trap. Whatever the truth to this part of the story, prison labor was never again used to construct a gallows in England.)

Then there was the strange case of nineteen-year-old Will Purvis in Mississippi who, in 1894, was scheduled to hang for the murder of his neighbor, Will Buckley, a member of the White Caps, a clandestine organization similar to the Ku Klux Klan. Buckley had been outraged to discover that some fellow members of the White Caps had flogged one of his Negro servants, and he'd threatened to expose the group and its covert activities. Out one evening in the company of his brother and the servant, Buckley was shot dead in an ambush. Buckley's brother, who survived along with the servant, became the prosecution's chief witness, and he fingered Will Purvis as the assassin. Despite the fact that he had an alibi, Purvis was found guilty and sentenced to hang.

On the day of his execution, the three thousand spectators who had gathered around the gallows fully expected to hear Purvis make a last-minute confession. Once the noose had been placed around his neck, Purvis surprised everyone by shouting, "You are taking the life of an innocent man!" A moment before the hangman lowered his ax to sever the stay rope supporting the trap door, a preacher shouted, "God save this innocent boy!" The ax fell, the trapdoor opened, Purvis descended. But the hangman's knot had come undone, and Purvis hit the ground. Furious, he jumped to his feet and shouted, "Let's get this over with!" The hangman was ready to try again, but the crowd of spectators, convinced that Purvis had been saved by divine intervention, opposed a second attempt. They voted to spare the life of Will Purvis, so Sheriff J. O. Magee obliged (under threat) and returned Purvis to the jail. (The Mississippi Supreme Court, however, re-sentenced Purvis to death, although to no avail because Purvis was rescued by a mob and hidden by friends. Essentially a fugitive, he became a farmer and raised a family of eleven children. In 1920 another man confessed to the murder of Will Buckley, and the governor of Mississippi pardoned Purvis, who was later given $5,000 as compensation for his troubles.)

Bertrand DeBlanc next called attention to the case of Lonnie Eaton, a black man from Monroe, Louisiana. Convicted of murdering a white man, Eaton was sentenced to hang on February 4, 1921. Luckily for him, that day came and went with the condemned man waiting silently in his cell for the executioner. The parish sheriff later wrote Governor John Milliken Parker a letter stating that he had been "so rushed with work that he forgot to hang Eaton." Eaton's sentence was ultimately commuted to life imprisonment.

DeBlanc pleaded with the board and, on the basis of the Eaton case, argued that there was precedent in the state of Louisiana. "Surely the case of Willie Francis, who sat in the electric chair, and had the current go through his body and lived through it, is infinitely stronger than a case where the sheriff forgot to hang the condemned man."

In a conciliatory tone, DeBlanc informed the board of Willie's excellent prison record and stated, "I'd stake my reputation that he would make a model convict at the State Penitentiary." From the looks on their faces, DeBlanc sensed that the board was unmoved by his biblical tales, legal oddities, and predictions. He'd been hoping for a sympathetic nod or smile somewhere along the way, but LeBlanc, Verret, and Simon sat stone-faced before him.

At this point, Tureaud no doubt thought that DeBlanc was grasping at straws in the hope of appealing to the emotions and sympathies of southern white males for a poor Negro convicted of murder, in the same way that DeBlanc might have earlier believed that Tureaud would get nowhere by arguing the facts of Willie's case before the board.

In any event, DeBlanc had prepared for stone faces. From his briefcase, he pulled out an eight-by-ten-inch black-and-white photograph. It was the photo taken by Father Maurice Rousseve at Willie's execution. Just a moment before Captain Ephie Foster had pulled the switch, Rousseve had slipped his head under the velvet hood on his view camera and captured an image of Willie seated in the lap of Gruesome Gertie. He'd made a print of the image and given it to DeBlanc, who was now holding it high in the air.

> I show you a picture of Willie Francis sitting on the electric chair awaiting death. Look at him strapped to the chair of death, the chair that had already claimed 23 victims, the chair that was later to claim another victim. What chance did he think he had of surviving? Look at him, gentlemen, a beaten animal, do you think there was any hope within that brain? Here you see the picture of a human being facing death, a boy on the threshold of eternity, a picture that speaks a thousand words.

Confident that he now had their attention, DeBlanc challenged the board to look at the photograph. Bertrand DeBlanc wanted the Louisiana Pardons Board to realize, to feel, the horror of electrocution: If they could send young men to the electric chair, they should witness it as well.

> Here is a boy, who, were it not for a quirk of fate, was about to plunge headlong into the dark abyss of death. What thoughts ran through his mind? Is there any belligerency in that bowed head? Is there anything but humility in those dark features? Is this not a picture of a boy ready and willing to carry out his part of the bargain? Yet the State failed and failed miserably. For this there can be no excuse. The State is to blame and they must shoulder it. Must this boy go through this again? Must he again be strapped to this chair and go through the agony of death for a second time?

The photograph got the board's attention. "When they saw it they shook," DeBlanc would say later. Pacing before the raised oak and marble bench where his grandfather, Alcibiades DeBlanc, once sat, the young Cajun lawyer recognized an opening, and mixing the theatrics of Clarence Darrow with the passion of Huey Long, he summoned all the anger he could muster at the horrors and cruelty that a powerful majority could impose on a helpless minority. Perhaps he saw the face of his grandfather before him, perhaps he was railing at his own family's past. Regardless, DeBlanc had the board back on its heels. His eyes welled with tears as he spoke:

> What assurance, gentlemen, does this boy have that he will go to his death in a humane manner, quickly and painlessly? Supposing that the chair doesn't work a second time? Suppose it doesn't work the third time? That

could happen, it's happened once and it could happen again. What is this going to be? An experiment in electricity? An experiment in modern forms of torture? An experiment in cruelty? Is the State of Louisiana trying to outdo the Caesars, the Hitlers, the Tojos, the Nazis, the Gestapo in torture? How long does the State of Louisiana take to kill a man? If we want to make it cruel, let's do it right, let's boil him in oil. Why not burn him at the stake? Or put him on the rack. Then we would be sure that by sundown he would be dead.

Gentlemen, the whole system of capital punishment which is the policy of this state is in jeopardy because of the inhumane method in which it is being inflicted. I say, without equivocation, that unless this board sees fit to say that this boy will not suffer the torture of death again, the critics of our method of execution shall have ample ground to condemn as a whole our system of punishment.

Gentlemen, I have traveled throughout southern Louisiana since the attempted electrocution on May 3rd, and I can say with certainty that public opinion is against this boy being electrocuted again. If this boy goes back to the chair, they will say that the one and only reason is to satisfy the bestial lust for blood, to satisfy this cry for revenge. If he goes back to the chair, they will say that it is nothing short of murder.

People all over America have written to me expressing their sincere belief that it was the hand of God that stopped the electrocution. They have expressed their horror and disgust at a second attempt. I say in all sincerity that I believe that Willie Francis was not killed because it was not meant that he should be killed, that there was some reason, perhaps not explainable now, but still there was a reason in the design of Fate that this boy should live. Fate acts in strange ways. I, for one, would want no part in his re-execution. When I meet my God face to face, I would not want the stain of his blood on my hands.

DeBlanc paused for a moment to determine what effect his words might be having on the board. He had observed Lieutenant Governor Verret shifting in his chair, and Attorney General LeBlanc was avoiding eye contact while nervously shuffling the papers in his hands. DeBlanc did not look at Simon, who must surely have been simmering at this point. If DeBlanc's reference to meeting God with the stain of a boy's blood on your hands was directed at anyone, it was directed at Judge Simon. Impassioned, unabashed, Bertrand DeBlanc wanted the board to feel, if nothing else, uncomfortable. He wanted to force Simon, Verret, and LeBlanc into thinking about Willie Francis as a human being when they voted to decide his fate. DeBlanc lowered his voice and spoke solemnly:

You, gentlemen, are the heart and soul of the State of Louisiana in this case. Men and women everywhere are asking: What will Louisiana do in this case? Will they return this boy to the chair? Will Louisiana be fair to the Negro? A boy's life is in your hands. I have done my duty. All remedies have been exhausted—the case is in your hands. And may God be your judge.

•   •   •

Tureaud and Thornton were impressed enough with DeBlanc to shake his hand upon completion of his statement. After shaking hands and leaving the courtroom, DeBlanc made the long drive back to St. Martinville by himself. He had time to ruminate over every word and gesture that had been made by both sides in the case throughout the appeal. The two NAACP attorneys would gain them no ground by pointing out weaknesses in the State's case against Willie Francis before the Pardons Board, DeBlanc firmly believed. He did not think that the board could ignore Father Rousseve's picture of the broken, compliant boy just moments before the switch was thrown, however. The photograph of Willie—his head bowed, "a beaten animal"—had provided an effective ploy. The three men on the board had been taken aback by it, and DeBlanc was certain he had jarred them enough to commute Willie's sentence to life imprisonment.

The young lawyer returned to St. Martinville where there was, according to one reporter, an "indescribable tenseness" in the air. The fate of the condemned black youth had taken on a "religious significance" in the heavily Catholic town, which was "tightly bound to the Francis case." There were whispers of the curse and the strange fate of Louis Michel who'd hung for murders he swore he did not commit some fifty years earlier. A story in the *Chicago Defender* noted, "More than a few St. Martinville inhabitants strongly feel that the wrath of God may be visited upon the town if Willie Francis' life is taken."

praying harder than ever

When you go to bed at night, you think of it.

—J. SKELLY WRIGHT

On June 3, 1946, just three days after hearing DeBlanc's appeal for mercy, the Louisiana Pardons Board returned with their decision. Willie Francis would not spend the rest of his days at Angola. He would return to the electric chair. The decision was unanimous, and the board offered no opinions. DeBlanc was stunned. He had felt confident that the growing public support for Willie's cause would influence the board. He'd believed, too, that he had detected some sympathy for Willie on the part of both Verret and LeBlanc when he'd pulled from his briefcase the photograph of Willie strapped in the death chair. "I guess the picture didn't have the results it should have," DeBlanc would later say.

Dr. A. O. Wilson of the African Methodist Episcopal Church in New Orleans, who had pled for Willie's life before the board, told reporters, "It looks as though the last vestige of hope is gone. He is the victim of a bad civilization. The Pardons Board was the last resort."

In fact, DeBlanc's options were now limited to just one. He would have to take the case to the U.S. Supreme Court—a possibility for which he had planned. He'd contacted a high school friend, Paul

Pietri, who worked in legal publishing, and Pietri had recommended that DeBlanc get in touch with an old friend of Pietri's from New Orleans, James Skelly Wright. A former U.S. attorney in Louisiana who, like DeBlanc, was fresh out of military service, Wright was now practicing law in Washington, DC.

J. Skelly Wright, the second of seven children, was born to a poor Irish Catholic family in New Orleans, Louisiana, just six days before Bertrand DeBlanc on January 14, 1911. The son of a housing inspector for plumbing equipment, Wright grew up on Camp Street in one of countless "shotgun camelback" row houses that littered a section of the city, one of the toughest in New Orleans, known as the "Irish Channel." There immigrant Irish, as well as those from northern states in search of work after the Civil War, took backbreaking jobs as seamen and dockworkers and became the "niggers of the time." It was, in fact, these same Irish who built the levees along the lower Mississippi, for they "came cheaper than native blacks for whom high prices had been paid at auction and who were needed to work the cotton fields, not to be wasted on such unskilled work."

Except for an uncle (Joe Skelly), no one in Wright's family had attended college, though his mother, Margaret, was a ward leader and heavily involved in local politics. His older adopted brother Eddie had, at age fourteen, gone to sea to work aboard a merchant ship to support the family, so Wright knew that, if he was going to pursue his interest in higher education and possibly a career in law, family financial resources would be extremely limited. With the benefit of some financial aid and by working during the day, he managed to attend law school at night, and eventually in 1934, he received his degree from the Jesuit-run Loyola University School of Law. During the Depression, unable to find a steady job in the field of law, Wright obtained a teaching certificate and taught English, history, and mathematics at Alcee Fortier High School in New Orleans. At the same time, he set up a small downtown law office that he shared with a friend; after school he'd hurry there to practice what little law was possible in the two hours before the building closed for the evening.

In 1936, to help launch his legal career, Wright turned to his Uncle Joe, who was by then a politically connected Democrat in New Orleans. Uncle Joe, in turn, reached out to the new U.S. senator, Allen J. Ellender, who was able to secure a full-time job for the ambitious twenty-five-year-old Catholic lawyer from the Irish Channel. Skelly Wright became an assistant U.S. attorney for the Eastern District of Louisiana.

After the assassination of Huey Long in 1935, his political successors had, as Liva Baker notes in her book *The Second Battle of New Orleans*, "gone on an orgy of embezzling, kickbacks, influence peddling, vote stealing, and fifty-seven varieties of graft—everything but sex." Indictments flew, and the attorney general's office was working around the clock. Wright, in his late twenties, was gaining some notoriety for prosecuting many of these "Long Machine" cases, as he was sending prominent politicians to jail for their roles in some of Louisiana's most colorful and outrageous scandals.

When the Japanese bombed Pearl Harbor in December 1941, Skelly Wright joined the Coast Guard, in part, he would later say, to avoid the draft. Assigned to the subchaser *Thetis* and based in London, Wright was commissioned as a lieutenant and served on the legal staff of Admiral James Stark. Seasick nearly every time the ship left port, Wright ultimately secured a land-based assignment in New York, and it was there that thirty-one-year-old Skelly Wright met twenty-three-year-old Helen Patton.

At the time, Helen Patton was working as a secretary to one of President Roosevelt's aides. The daughter of Admiral Raymond S. Patton, Helen had grown up in Washington, DC, and had attended the preparatory school at Gunston Hall and, later, Sweet Briar College. She was not, by a long shot, the type of girl Wright might find back home in the Irish Channel. With bright blue eyes, thick reddish hair, and striking features, Helen once caught the eye of the famous sculptor Jacob Epstein while she was running an errand, and the artist convinced her to sit for a study of her head. (The resultant sculpture was later given by Helen to Yale University.)

Skelly and Helen spent an afternoon together visiting the Statue of Liberty, but before any serious romance between them could develop, Skelly found himself transferred back to London in June 1943. Not long afterward, Helen, too, was transferred to London, and when Wright learned that she was working at the American embassy, he ardently pursued her. He hoped a Washington society girl might have a place in her heart for an Irish Channel man who was prone to "N'awlins" locutions such as "Where-yat?" and, "ersters berled in erl." She'd have to get used to being called "Sugah," too.

Skelly Wright courted Helen Patton as World War II raged. The Germans were launching V–1 and V–2 rockets into London, killing thousands, and Helen remembers having to duck into air-raid shelters with Skelly. On one such occasion, she braved the buzzing overhead to collect a piece of shrapnel on the street from a recently exploded "doodle bug" bomb. "Foolish," she later admitted.

On February 1, 1945, Skelly Wright and Helen Patton were married in London. Later that year, when the war ended, the two moved back to Washington, DC. Finding his contacts limited there, Wright decided to make a temporary move back to New Orleans to resume work with the U.S. attorney's office, and for the time being, he left Helen in Washington.

It was upon his return to New Orleans that Wright began to see the South through the prism of the war and his experience in Europe. Although he had noticed in his time aboard the *Thetis* that the only blacks he saw were cooks and servants, never officers, the inequity hadn't truly registered with Wright until he began observing the patent and pervasive racial discrimination in New Orleans after the war. Until then, by his own admission, he had been "just another southern boy." He'd never sat in a class with a black boy; he'd never questioned the "Colored" signs on drinking fountains. He'd accepted segregation as a natural component of the world in which he grew up.

Wright himself would later say, "I was as southern as anybody else was around there. I saw what was going on down there. While I didn't embrace it, it didn't repel me." Upon returning home after the war, however, it did. Like Bertrand DeBlanc in St. Martinville, Skelly Wright, too, was moving toward a new consciousness about race. "The Negro went to war like the white person did," Wright would say. "He fought like the white person. We saw this, those of us who were in the service—we saw this."

Wright's new, ambiguous feelings about race crystallized in a matter of minutes on Christmas Eve in 1945. That night, while a sixteen-year-old boy he had never heard of by the name of Willie Francis was sitting in a jail cell some 135 miles west in Cajun country, waiting for Governor Jimmie Davis to sign a death warrant, the U.S. attorney's office was having its annual Christmas party off Lafayette Square. Across the street at the New Orleans headquarters of the Lighthouse for the Blind—a two-story building attached to a four-story stucco lighthouse—another Christmas party was under way, and Wright watched as the sightless guests arrived. Then, before his eyes, a curious scene unfolded. As they were greeted by their hosts, the blind whites were escorted to a large room at the front of the house, whereas the blind Negroes were taken to the rear, where they stayed. Separated. Transfixed, Wright had to look twice before it dawned on him: "They couldn't see to segregate themselves," Helen would recall him saying incredulously.

The absurdity of this scene, played out on Christmas Eve in his hometown of New Orleans, was one that Wright would never forget.

"When you go to bed at night," Wright would say, "you think of it. That was the beginning really."

By early June of 1946, Wright was back in Washington. He'd located an old friend from the Coast Guard, and with a few other young lawyers, they'd rented office space together and tried to make a go of things in the nation's capital. Retainers from Standard Fruit as well as some other Louisiana businesses helped, and thanks in part to his maritime law experience in the Coast Guard, Wright also managed to do legal work for a flamboyant New Orleans entrepreneur named Andrew Jackson Higgins. Higgins designed and produced amphibious boats that delivered men and equipment from ship to shore—the same "Higgins boats" that had been used in mass numbers during the Battle of Normandy two years earlier, as well as for every other major amphibious operation in both the European and Pacific theaters. Higgins oversaw the first racially integrated workforce in New Orleans, and his more than 20,000 employees shattered production records. All were paid equal wages according to their responsibilities. President Eisenhower would later say that Higgins "won the war for us."

Still, Skelly Wright had not yet made much of a name for himself when another young lawyer, just back from military service himself, contacted him from the sleepy Cajun town of St. Martinville. Their mutual friend, Paul Pietri, had already spoken with Wright about DeBlanc and his appeal before the Louisiana Pardons Board. If the news was bad, Pietri had told him, Wright could expect to hear from his Cajun friend. On June 3, 1946, DeBlanc wired Wright:

BOARD REFUSED TO COMMUTE SENTENCE.

FILE PETITION AND WIRE ME.

With Willie Francis scheduled to die at noon on June 7, 1946, Wright and DeBlanc had just three days to file a writ of *certiorari*, by which the Court is asked to correct an error made in a lower court, and to obtain a stay of execution. Wright filed the writ with the Supreme Court, and the Court, recognizing that there would be no time to hear the case before Willie's scheduled execution, issued an immediate stay of execution. Governor Davis then issued a reprieve "until further order."

If all went as expected and the Court agreed to hear Willie's case, the stocky Irish native of New Orleans and the fiery young Cajun, both recent veterans of World War II, would be taking potentially the biggest case of their careers to the U.S. Supreme Court. Because the Willie Francis case might prove to be a protracted and expensive legal battle, and because their client was poor and legal funds extremely limited, the two lawyers agreed that they would communicate by mail as much as possible.

On June 10, 1946, however, it looked like the U.S. Post Office might not be getting much business from Wright and DeBlanc. The U.S. Supreme Court handed down a very brief order. Wright immediately wired the news to DeBlanc in St. Martinville.

SUPREME COURT DENIED WRIT
FRANCIS CASE TODAY.

In a letter that followed the telegram, Wright told DeBlanc that he was "consoled by the fact that we did everything in our power to be of assistance."

After receiving the telegram, Bertrand DeBlanc walked a few blocks into the black side of town, to 800 Washington Street, and delivered the bad news to Willie's parents. Although DeBlanc knew he had done all he could for Willie, he found himself apologizing to Frederick and Louise Francis, for DeBlanc had truly thought it was a case they could win together, as he'd told Francis a little over a month ago in his house on Claiborne Street. Now it was over. They had no higher court to turn to. The Francises' youngest son would again be coming back to St. Martinville; again they would have to make arrangements for the coffin and hearse. DeBlanc told the Francises that he would drive to New Iberia and give the news to Willie himself. Once more, he said he was sorry.

DeBlanc returned home, got in his car, and drove to New Iberia. He told Willie all hope was lost; they'd nowhere else to turn. Willie was shocked. Together, the two St. Martinville natives sat silently in Willie's cell, both having been certain that the U.S. Supreme Court would have at least agreed to hear their case. There was little more to say.

Once Willie had regained his composure, he agreed to talk to reporters who had arrived at the jail for a statement. "I'm praying harder than ever," Willie said. "Got myself a new prayer book. All I can do is wait."

Again, reporters filed out of the dark, narrow corridor in the east wing of the New Iberia jail. They said their good-byes to the condemned youth, and Willie Francis faced another long, sleepless night in the queasy awareness that there was nothing Bertrand De-Blanc could do for him anymore.

The following morning, June 11, 1946, Skelly Wright received a telephone call from a horrified clerk at the U.S. Supreme Court. A terrible mistake had been made. Wright was speechless as the clerk labored to explain. There had been a big mix-up; the Willie Francis case had been designated "denied" when it should have been designated "granted."

Wright couldn't believe it. The Court would indeed hear Willie's case. Justice Hugo Black had ordered Willie's execution "stayed pending further order of this Court."

Somehow, the clerk had erred and misread the order. It was a mistake, Barrett Prettyman Jr., author of *Death and the Supreme Court*, noted, that remains "virtually unparalleled" in the history of the Supreme Court.

A stunned but now elated Skelly Wright quickly notified DeBlanc of the strange turn of events, and the Supreme Court clerk contacted Governor Davis's office. DeBlanc immediately drove over to the Francis house on Washington Street and gave the news to Frederick and Louise, who, at this point, must have been more convinced than ever that the hand of God had touched their youngest son. DeBlanc, however, wanted to get the news to Willie himself. The day before, Willie had been crushed, and DeBlanc couldn't help but feel he had let the boy down. Now, he was driving to New Iberia with candy, cigarettes, and magazines. "Every time he comes to see me he brings me candy and magazines," Willie later said. "I quit smoking and told him so, but I guess he forgets because he brings me cigarettes anyway." But the candy was appreciated, and Willie enjoyed the magazines as well. "I guess I like western and romance stories best of all," he said.

Willie was eating a chocolate bar on his cot with DeBlanc when reporters began arriving at the jail. Sheriff Ozenne led them into the east wing. Asked for his reaction, Willie said, "That's funny, sort of. I was expecting good news yesterday, and I got bad. And now when I'm expecting bad news, it's good." Willie smiled. "I feel pretty good."

One reporter asked him if he would be content with his sentence commuted to life imprisonment. "A life in prison would be a lot better than that chair," Willie said.

With Willie beside him, DeBlanc was asked what he thought of the new developments. "I'm tickled to death," he said—the unintentional pun might have struck Willie as odd—then added, "I think there is something of Divine Providence in this case." DeBlanc reiterated his belief that it would be cruel and unusual punishment to kill his client.

"I had to agree with him on that," Willie later said.

In stark contrast to their solemn visit the day before, Willie and DeBlanc sat next to each other on the cot, both of them smiling, eating chocolate, and talking excitedly with reporters.

get to the law

I told Justice Black . . . that I would not stand for any more of his bullying . . .

—JUSTICE ROBERT JACKSON

On April 22, 1946, just two weeks before Willie Francis had been strapped into Louisiana's portable electric chair in a failed attempt to take his life, the U.S. Supreme Court was nearing the end of its first postwar term—a term marked by jealousy, public backbiting, and dysfunction. It was about to get worse. Chief Justice Harlan Fiske Stone, who had just finished voicing his philosophy in regard to judicial restraint, was about to deliver his opinion on a case, when the Court fell silent. Justice Hugo Black sensed something was wrong and gaveled an adjournment. Stone sat slumped, unconscious, on the bench. Black and Justice Stanley Reed helped remove the chief justice from the bench, and he was rushed to the hospital. Stone had suffered a massive cerebral hemorrhage. He died later that afternoon.

Now leaderless, the judiciary that President Roosevelt had filled with his own appointments had for years been mired in philosophical feuds that were eroding public confidence in the nation's highest court. Prior to Stone's death, with Justice Robert Jackson absent because he was serving as the American prosecutor at the Nuremberg War Crimes Trial, the severely divided Court had been besieged by 4–4 decisions and an endless flow of dissenting opinions. Tension among the Supreme Court justices, which had been building for some time, finally reached toxic levels during *Jewell Ridge Coal Corp. v Local Number 6167*, the case known simply as *Jewell Ridge* to legal practitioners that came before the court in 1945.

When Justice Black declined to recuse himself from considering the case—although Black's own former law partner was representing one of the parties to the lawsuit, Local Number 6167 of the United Mine Workers—he prompted the fury of Justice Jackson. To further enflame his peers, Black ended up, or so it appeared, providing the crucial swing vote that brought the Court to rule in his ex-partner's favor.

Justice Stone had suggested at a conference of all the justices that the Court issue an opinion saying that it had no authority to force Black to recuse himself; that it was up to Black himself. Black had approached Jackson in private. If this opinion was issued, he'd said, "it would mean a 'declaration of war.'" Shortly thereafter, Justice Robert Jackson, appalled by what he considered shameless judicial behavior, told Black that he "would not stand for any more of his bullying."

The opinion proved to be as divisive as Black had foretold—a virtual declaration of war. It marked the beginning of a feud that would shake the Court's foundations for years. It would also erupt into the public arena, eventually ruining one man's chance to become chief justice. While subsequent developments would create the impression that it was Black and Jackson who stood most strongly at odds, the battle for the soul of the Court was, in truth, a battle between Justice Felix Frankfurter, the intellectual leader of a conservative movement, and Hugo Black, the man who led the liberal movement within the Court—the side DeBlanc hoped could save Willie from a second electrocution.

In 1946, the year that Willie would file his appeal with the U.S. Supreme Court, Jackson—without relinquishing his seat on the Court—went to Nuremberg to prosecute the war trials, where his lackluster cross-examination of Hermann Goering and subsequent tantrum in open court over his inability to control Goering's responses earned Jackson the ridicule of his fellow justices. Indeed, Justice William O. Douglas, Black's constant intellectual and social companion, pilloried Jackson's performance in a limerick:

> *There was an upstart called Jackson,*
> *Who went to Germany for action,*
> *Not to bring men to justice,*
> *But to feather his nest-ice,*
> *And finally fell on his ass-ton.*

During Jackson's stay in Europe, the friction among the justices at home was steadily increasing so that, when Stone's death left them leaderless, it created not only a vacancy for the position of chief justice but also a critical rift in and beyond the chambers. Roosevelt had promised the post to Jackson before Truman took office, but newspapers were soon reporting that both Black and Douglas had informed President Truman that, if he appointed Jackson as chief justice, they would both resign. The next day, the same newspapers were running a letter in which Jackson excoriated Black and insinuated that Black had attempted to influence contract negotiations during the Jewell Ridge coal strike by proposing to announce the decision without waiting for the opinion and dissent.

Major newspapers, among them the *New York Times*, debated the significance of the breach. Some columnists praised Jackson for his courage in exposing what he felt was an "irregular situation" in the Court, while others commended Black for refusing to engage in a public dispute with Jackson. Senator Scott Lucas of Illinois deplored the "dissention-ridden" Court and called for both their resignations

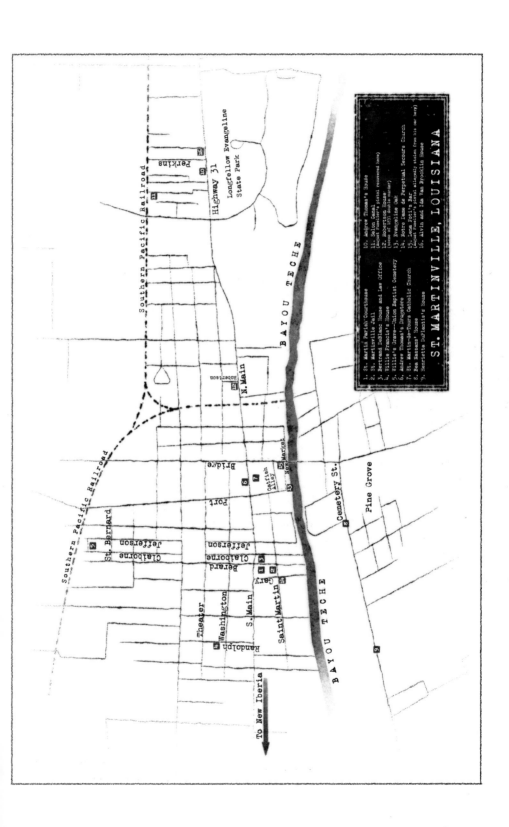

ST. MARTINVILLE, LOUISIANA

1. St. Martin Parish Courthouse
2. St. Martinville Jail
3. Bertrand DeBlanc House and Law Office
4. Willie Francis's House
5. Willie's Grave—Union Baptist Cemetery
6. Andrew Thomas's Drugstore
7. St. Martin-de-Tours Catholic Church
8. Bea Hassan's House
9. Henrietta DuPlantis's House
10. Andrew Thomas's House
11. Sheton Canal pistol recovered here)
12. Robertson House (scene of 1971 double-murder)
13. Evangeline Oak
14. Notre Dame de Perpetual Secours Church
15. Lena Foti's Bar (Andrew Francis's pistol allegedly stolen from his car here)
16. Alvin and Ida Van Brocklin House

In 1941, when the State of Louisiana switched from hanging to electrocution in death sentences, International Harvester was contracted to provide a truck, gasoline engine, and portable electric chair, which the prisoners at the Louisiana State Penitentiary nicknamed "Gruesome Gertie."

Photograph courtesy of the *Advocate*, Baton Rouge, La.

District Attorney L.O. Pecot believed the jail in St. Martinville was not secure, and had Willie moved to New Iberia to prevent the possibility of a lynching. On May 3, 1946, onlookers climbed the trees and fence surrounding jail, hoping to get a look at Willie Francis in the electric chair.

Photograph from the Edith Garland Dupre Library, Special Collections and Archives, Mary Alice Fontenot Riehl Collection, University of Louisiana, Lafayette. Courtesy of the DeBlanc family.

Delores Del Rio came to St. Martinville to make the movie Evangeline *in 1928. Standing in front of St.-Martin-de-Tours Catholic Church, the actress poses for a photograph, with James D. Simon, the judge in the Willie Francis case, to her left.*

Courtesy of the Martin Photo Collection at the Iberia Parish Library in New Iberia, La.

The State of Texas }

County of Jefferson }

August 5, 1945 AD

I, Willie Francis, being in the custody of Claude W. Goldsmith, Chief of
Police of the City of Port Arthur, Jefferson County, Texas and having been
warned by E. L. Canada, Justice of the Peace, Jefferson County, Texas, the
person to whom the hereinafter set out statement is by me made, that I do
not have to make any statement at all, and that any statement made by me may
be used in evidence against me on my trial for the offense concerning which
this statement is made, do here make the following voluntary statement in
writing to the said, E. L. Canada, towit:

*I Willie Francis now 16 years old I stol sthe
the gun from Mr. Ogise at St. Martinville La. and
kill andrew Thomas november 9, 1944
or about the time at St. Martinville La. it was a
secret about me and him: I took a block for
these I will card 12801 82 tin it
four dollars in it I all so took a water on him
and sell it in new Iberia La. that all dum said
I throw my gun away 38 Pistol*

Witnesses to statement **Willie Francis**
E. L. Canada J.P. Prect #2 Jeff Co. Texas
Claude W. Goldsmith - Chief of Police. Port Arthur, Tex

*Willie's handwritten confession in Port Arthur, Texas,
where he wrote, "it was a secret about me and him."*

Willie was interrogated in New Iberia, under the supervision of Sheriff Gilbert Ozenne, who, just two years earlier, was the subject of a civil rights investigation by the Department of Justice. According to the FBI, Ozenne and his deputies assaulted leaders of the local branch of the NAACP and ran them out of town at gunpoint.

Courtesy of the New Iberia Parish Sheriff's Department.

"Lucky" Willie Francis posed for photographers in his cell in New Iberia just hours after he walked away from "the bad chair."

Courtesy of AP/WIDE WORLD PHOTOS.

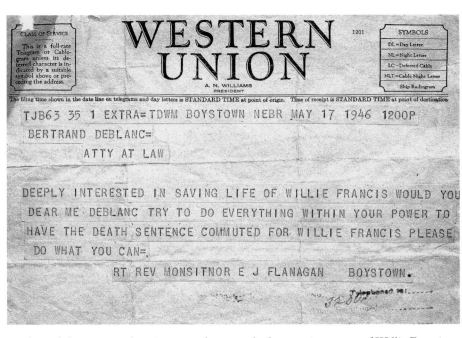

Around the country, Americans sent letters and telegrams in support of Willie Francis and flooded the office of Governor Jimmie Davis with letters of protest. Bertrand DeBlanc received this telegram from Father Flanagan in Boystown.

A. P. Tureaud, the Creole attorney for the NAACP in New Orleans, was often at odds with Bertrand DeBlanc during the Willie Francis case. Tureaud believed the Cajun lawyer was not aggressively attacking the white power structure in St. Martinville.

Courtesy of A. P. Tureaud Jr.

"Dapper" Bertrand DeBlanc. "I like that guy," he said of Willie Francis just before the botched execution. "And I got to liking him more."

Courtesy of the
DeBlanc family.

Jailer Clemarie Norris poses for photographers as he brings the condemned youth some letters of support that arrived daily at the New Iberia jail.

Photograph from the Edith Garland Dupre Library, Special Collections and Archives, Mary Alice Fontenot Riehl Collection, University of Louisiana, Lafayette. Courtesy of the DeBlanc family.

Mother and Father of Willie Francis

Mr. and Mrs. Frederick Francis
. . . The boy was not normal as a child, they said.

Willie was the youngest of thirteen children born to Frederick and Louise Francis. "That child could cook and make a bed as good as womenfolks," Louise said of Willie.

Courtesy of the DeBlanc family.

J. Skelly Wright would later admit to a biographer that Willie Francis "still weighed heavily on his mind." In 1962, President John F. Kennedy ranked Wright as "one of the great judges of America," before appointing the Louisiana native to the court of appeals for the District of Columbia.

Courtesy of Helen Patton Wright.

Felix Frankfurter was deeply troubled by his vote to allow Louisiana to return Willie Francis to the electric chair. He was opposed to the death penalty and felt such an act would be a "serious blot" on the State of Louisiana were she to execute the youth.

Courtesy of the Library of Congress.

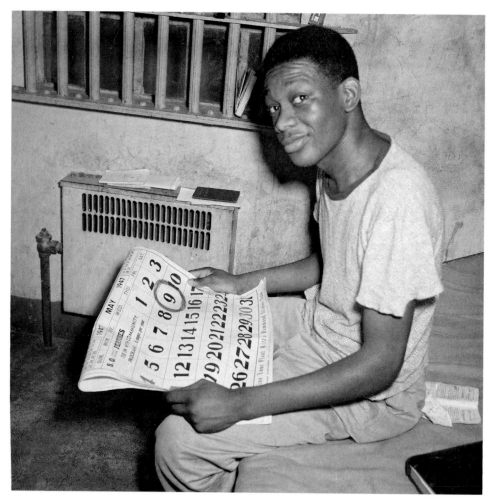

With apparently no hope left, Willie circled May 9 on a calendar—the day he was scheduled to die. DeBlanc would fly to Washington for one last appearance before the U.S. Supreme Court in an attempt to save the youth's life.

Courtesy of AP/WIDE WORLD PHOTOS.

A sign posted on the wall of the Purple Circle Social Club on Thirteenth Street in Baton Rouge, Louisiana.

Standard Oil Collection Photographic Archives, Special Collections Ekstrom Library, University of Louisville.

Willie's case captivated the nation and commanded frontpage headlines as time began to run out for the condemned teen.

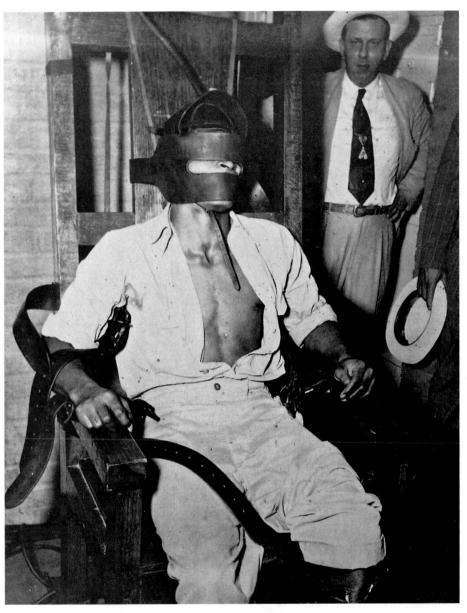

A photograph of Gruesome Gertie after she claimed the life of Clarence Joseph Jr. in St. Martinville in 1949. Officials stated they wanted "no repeat of the Willie Francis incident."

Courtesy of Allan Durand.

A good Catholic to the end, Willie wanted "nothing but fish" for his last meal on the Friday he was scheduled to die.

Photograph from the Edith Garland Dupre Library, Special Collections and Archives, Mary Alice Fontenot Riehl Collection, University of Louisiana, Lafayette. Courtesy of the DeBlanc family.

—WIREPHOTO by The Associated Press.
LAST MEAL—Mrs. Paul Guilbeau, wife of the St. Martinville jailer, is shown with the last meal which she prepared for Willie Francis, condemned Negro slayer who paid with his life Friday in his second seating in the state's portable electric chair. The meal, at Willie's request, consisted of catfish, fried potatoes, pickles and a "coke."

Louisiana's official executioner Grady Jarratt checks over the electric chair. One year earlier, a drunken guard and inmate from Angola botched Willie's execution and the state wanted "no more amateur executioners in Louisiana."

Photograph from the Edith Garland Dupre Library, Special Collections and Archives, Mary Alice Fontenot Riehl Collection, University of Louisiana, Lafayette. Courtesy of the DeBlanc family.

—AP Wirephoto
IT WORKED — THIS TIME — St. Martinville, La., May 9.—An attendant checks Louisiana's portable electric chair, set up in St. Martin parish jail, just a short time before Willie Francis, condemned slayer, died in it today. A year ago it "just tickled" the negro.

Willie is led to a waiting sedan on the morning of May 9, 1947. To his left is St. Martinville jailer Paul Guilbeaux, and to his right is Sheriff Resweber's son, Deputy E. L. "Brother" Resweber. Following behind is Associated Press reporter Elliott Chaze. "I'm wearing my Sunday pants and my Sunday heart to the chair," Willie said. "Ain't going to wear no beat-up pants to see the Lord. Been busy talking my way into heaven for this past year. Them folks expecting me to come in style."

Courtesy of AP/WIDE WORLD PHOTOS.

Nearly 40 years later, DeBlanc returned with reporters to Willie's grave in St. Martinville. "If Willie's appeal was today we'd win," DeBlanc said, brushing away a tear.

Courtesy of the DeBlanc Family.

"for the good of themselves and the good of the country." He added, "There can't be any confidence in this court from here on as a result of this feud."

President Truman determined that under the circumstances he could not appoint Jackson to the post of chief justice. Instead, he chose Frederick M. Vinson, a former judge from Kentucky who had served in the Roosevelt administration. By the time Jackson finally returned to the Court, the rancor and bitterness had reached the point where some of the justices were not even speaking to each other. In addition to, facing a divided court, therefore, Bertrand De-Blanc and Skelly Wright were stepping into a legal minefield as well.

Sixty years later, alleged violations of double jeopardy, cruel and unusual punishment, and due process would constitute unquestionably valid legal strategies for attorneys. But not in 1946. Not once, not twice, but many times, the U.S. Supreme Court had held that the Bill of Rights did not apply to states. Thus, most of the rights in the first ten amendments to the Constitution, rights citizens decades later would take for granted, simply did not exist for litigants in a case originating at the state level—cases like Willie's. In other words, one's right not to be tried twice for the same crime, for instance, could only be invoked if one was being tried in a federal court. In a state court, neither the constitutional prohibition against double jeopardy nor the right to remain silent would apply. In 1937, in fact, the Supreme Court had ruled unequivocally that in a state court a man could be tried twice for the same murder.

Furthermore, in 1908, the Supreme Court had held that the Fifth Amendment—the right regarding self-incrimination—did not apply to state court trials. Prosecutors in state trials could, therefore, contend that a defendant's refusal to testify was a sign of guilt. Not until 1965 did the Supreme Court reverse itself in regard to this position on self-incrimination.

When Skelly Wright and Bertrand DeBlanc argued that in the Willie Francis case both the double-jeopardy clause and the prohibition against cruel and unusual punishment granted by the Eighth Amendment had been violated, they were going out on a legal limb. Not only were they asking the Supreme Court to extend the reach of constitutional rights to state courts, but they were also asking the nation's highest court to reconsider its previous decisions.

The two attorneys believed, however, that they had a powerful ally on the Court: Hugo Black. A former Alabama trial lawyer and prosecutor, Hugo Black had run a masterful campaign as an underdog for the U.S. Senate and won in 1926. His nomination to the Supreme Court had been publicly controversial; Roosevelt had passed Black's nomination to Congress secretly and without preamble or notification of the congressional leaders beforehand, as was customary, probably to rush Black's confirmation through the Senate before opposition could mount. Even so, before the Senate's vote, newspapers revealed that Black had been a member of the Ku Klux Klan. The Senate confirmed Black, nonetheless, and the Alabama native was sworn in quickly, before his confirmation could be recalled.

Such an urgent confirmation did not prevent the NAACP from making a public outcry for Congress to reverse itself, even as allegations swirled that Black was still active in the KKK and that he had indeed accepted a lifetime membership. As a result, Black was forced to reassure the nation in a radio address that he had renounced his KKK membership, and the controversy then died away. (Roosevelt had confided to Black that his address "would do the trick," and it did.)

DeBlanc and Wright had good reason, however, to believe that Hugo Black—a former KKK member—was the best hope for Willie Francis. During his time on the bench, Black had gained a reputation as a fighter for the common man, regardless of race. Much of this reputation stemmed from Black's opinion on the case of *Chambers v. Florida* in 1940. A young and tenacious civil rights lawyer named Thurgood Marshall had argued before the Supreme Court on behalf of three black men who had been convicted for the murder of a white man in Florida. Outrage had overtaken the white community, and the Florida sheriff's investigation had apparently consisted of rounding up thirty to forty black transients and interrogating them relentlessly until one or more of them confessed. The interrogations had continued for an entire week. Speaking in defense of his police procedures, the sheriff said that he had questioned the men only during the days—at night, he said, he was tired.

At Marshall's behest, the Supreme Court threw out the confessions of all three men on the grounds that they had been coerced and were therefore involuntary. The Court further found that the convictions of the three men offended the due process clause of the Constitution. Writing for the majority, Justice Black commented on the Supreme Court's role in righting indignities visited upon the defenseless common man by the high and mighty in a democracy:

> Under our constitutional system, Courts stand against any winds that blow as havens of refuge for those who might otherwise suffer because they are helpless, weak, outnumbered, or because they are non-conforming victims of prejudice and public excitement. . . . No higher duty, no more solemn responsibility, rests upon this Court, than that of translating into living law and maintaining this constitutional shield deliberately planned and inscribed for the benefit of every human being subject to our Constitution—of whatever race, creed or persuasion.

It has been said that Black felt so strongly about this guiding principle that he was unable to read this passage without "tears streaming down his cheeks." Opinions like this one cemented his reputation for color-blind justice and compassion, particularly in cases set in the Deep South.

This reputation might have led DeBlanc and Wright to expect to find in Hugo Black a sympathetic justice. More importantly, perhaps, Black fervently believed that the Bill of Rights should apply to the states, and Willie's two lawyers surely felt that their case offered the justice a perfect vehicle to advance that view. Also, Black led the liberal wing of the court. With three other justices—William O. Douglas, Wiley B. Rutledge, and Frank Murphy—who usually voted with Black on issues fundamental to Willie's case, Wright and De-Blanc could reasonably hope to stop Louisiana from attempting to execute Willie Francis again.

On the other side of the equation stood Felix Frankfurter, who was reputed to lead the Court's conservative wing. An Austrian-born Jewish immigrant who believed fervently in civil liberties, Frankfurter had defended the anarchists Sacco and Venzetti in their controversial robbery-murder trial before becoming a professor at Harvard Law School. (He purportedly maintained the role of "professor" and routinely lectured his colleagues on the Court.) From his post at Harvard, Frankfurter had helped place supporters of the New Deal in Roosevelt's government, and he, like Hugo Black, had been appointed to the Court because of his affiliation with the president's "New Dealers."

Undoubtedly, Roosevelt had hoped to advance liberal views in Supreme Court rulings by putting Frankfurter on the bench. Once Frankfurter became a justice, however, he made it very clear both publicly and privately that he would not allow his liberal views—his sincerest convictions, supposedly—to interfere with his administration of the law. Instead, he would exercise what he called "judicial restraint." While he personally may have believed that the government had the duty to protect small minorities from the popular will, as the Court had said the Constitution required, he was not necessarily going to rule that way if federal law stood contrary to state statutes. Nowhere was Frankfurter's policy of judicial restraint more apparent than in his handling of the 1940 *Gobitis* case, which illuminated his true colors no less than the *Chambers* case demonstrated Black's.

Walter Gobitis and his family—which included two children, Lillian and William, who were sixth and seventh graders in the public school—were Jehovah's Witnesses in the heavily Catholic town of Minersville, Pennsylvania. Inspired by the refusal of Jehovah's Witnesses in Hitler's Germany to join in the required raised-palm salute to Nazi flags, young Lillian and William decided that they would neither salute the American flag nor recite the Pledge of Allegiance in their local school. Their refusal to participate in this daily American classroom ritual created an uproar, and the Minersville School Board passed a compulsory flag-salute law. When the children still refused to salute, they were expelled. Walter Gobitis sued the Minersville School Board, and the case found its way to the Supreme Court after Pennsylvania courts ruled that the flag-salute law comprised an act of religious compulsion and thus violated the Constitution's guarantee to freedom of religion.

Felix Frankfurter—who, as an Austrian-born Jew, would have been especially sensitive to claims of religious persecution at a time when Hitler was extending his reign—surprisingly voted to reverse the holdings of the Philadelphia courts and was assigned the task of writing the majority opinion, his first as a justice. Immensely proud of his hard-won American citizenship, Frankfurter put his judicial stamp indelibly on the opinion. He argued that religious belief did not entitle one to shun one's patriotic responsibilities in general or the saluting of the flag in particular, which he viewed both as an act of obeisance and as an instrument of national security.

Frankfurter had lain out the keystone of his judicial philosophy. Although he might personally believe that the Gobitis family had the right not to salute the flag, it did not lie with him but, rather, with the legislature to decide. The *Gobitis* decision set off a wave of attacks against Jehovah's Witnesses across the country by ardent patriots who had been emboldened by a ruling that, in their minds, equated the refusal to salute the flag with a virtually treasonous act on the part of Nazi sympathizers. Mobs burned halls and assailed meetings of the Witnesses everywhere. One Nebraska Jehovah's

Witness was brutally beaten and castrated. As a result of the wide-spread violence, Frankfurter began receiving angry letters from Jews who were surprised at the insensitivity of his majority opinion. Three years later, the Supreme Court overruled the *Gobitis* case in *West Virginia State Board of Education v. Barnette*, with Justice Robert Jackson writing for the majority. In what is widely considered one of the greatest statements of freedom in American history, Jackson sys-tematically smashed Frankfurter's *Gobitis* opinion to pieces. Consis-tent to the end, Frankfurter filed the lone written dissent.

Wright and DeBlanc, then, were bringing the fate of Willie Fran-cis to the Supreme Court at the very time when Frankfurter and Hugo Black were locked in a fight for its soul. In formulating Willie's legal brief, Wright and DeBlanc knew that their strongest argument—and their best chance for saving Willie's life—lay in the assertion that the punishment was cruel and unusual. The standard for the notion "cruel and unusual" had been laid down more than fifty years earlier in the case *in re Kemmler*, when William Kemmler, convicted of murdering his wife, Tillie Ziegler, became the first man sentenced to death in the electric chair. Kemmler's lawyers ap-pealed the sentence, arguing that such an execution would amount to cruel and unusual punishment, but the New York State Court of Appeals rejected the argument. An appeal to the U.S. Supreme Court affirmed the ruling of the New York State court, and Chief Justice Melville Fuller provided what would become the standard definition of cruel and unusual punishment. Fuller wrote: "Punish-ments are cruel when they involve torture or a lingering death; but the punishment of death is not cruel, within the meaning of the word as used in the constitution. It implies there something inhu-mane and barbarous, something more than the mere extinguish-ment of life."

Unfortunately for Kemmler, and for all subsequent victims of the electric chair, the Supreme Court's ruling on cruel and unusual punishment was handed down ten weeks *before* the Court could evaluate the report on the first execution by electrocution. With his legal options exhausted, Kemmler was strapped into the electric chair at Auburn prison on August 6, 1890, where warden Charles Durston's last words to Kemmler were, "It won't hurt you, Bill. It won't hurt you at all." Moments later, the switch was thrown. After Kemmler absorbed a seventeen-second blast of electrical current, doctors ordered the current turned off, only to discover Kemmler sucking for breath. Officials, wanting no mistake the second time, blasted Kemmler with 1000 volts of current for several minutes, until his coat caught fire and the room began to smell of burnt flesh. One witness fainted, another vomited. The sheriff of Erie County exited the room with tears in his eyes. The gruesomely botched execution was reported in newspapers across the country. One newspaper would describe it as "a disgrace to civilization," and the *New York World* stated, "The first experiment in electricity should be the last."

The challenge for Wright and DeBlanc, therefore, was to make the Supreme Court aware of Willie's ordeal in the electric chair, because no details regarding the attempted execution of Willie Francis stood in the official record that the Court would have before it. The Pardons Board hearings were not part of the appeal, and any information from them was thus technically "outside the record." Wright and DeBlanc would thus have difficulty establishing in their brief for the Supreme Court the enormous pain and torture Willie had undergone when he had been electrocuted, or even showing the general circumstances surrounding the electrocution. Wright and DeBlanc therefore tried to cram into the brief as much grisly detail about the execution as possible. Additionally, and in violation of Supreme Court rules, Wright and DeBlanc appended to the brief the affidavits of witnesses to the execution, which were also outside the record, for they had not been presented to the Louisiana courts when seeking a writ of habeas corpus. In determining whether Louisiana had erred in denying the writ, the Supreme Court was obligated to review only the evidence that had been placed before the Louisiana state courts.

Luckily for Wright and DeBlanc, the Louisiana lawyers arguing against them in the Supreme Court appended the record of the Pardons Board hearings to *their* brief! However elated Wright may have been initially at this discovery, he must have soon been disappointed, for although the Pardons Board hearing testimony helped establish that Willie had indeed suffered during the electrocution, it also enabled the Louisiana prosecutors to introduce their own evidence—most of it derived from the testimony of the executioners Ephie Foster and Vincent Venezia—that Willie survived the execution completely without harm.

Although not climbing the steps of the Supreme Court building with DeBlanc and Wright, the NAACP continued to work behind the scenes on behalf of Willie Francis. The organization's relationship with these two white lawyers was still tenuous at best. Emily Branch had recently written a letter to the NAACP to inquire why the organization had "dropped" her brother's case. Responding to a letter inquiring about the case, Tureaud cited a "great deal of difficulty" with DeBlanc, adding, "Without the aid of the NAACP he [Willie] would have been executed long before now." A few weeks earlier, Tureaud had received a tip that the Supreme Court of Louisiana would honor a writ "based on the fact that no Negroes were in the jury panel." Thurgood Marshall believed, however, that, if such a writ was honored by the court, they would "place a Negro on the jury and lynch him [Willie] anyway."

Bertrand DeBlanc once again drove across the state of Louisiana to the newly built Moisant International Airport in New Orleans, where he boarded a New York–bound Delta DC–3. Two days prior to his appearance before the Supreme Court, DeBlanc showed up unannounced at the New York offices of the NAACP. He was looking for money from the NAACP beyond the individual donations the organization had been forwarding to him; DeBlanc was told he'd have to meet with Robert Carter of the Legal Defense Fund. Carter was not in, and the Cajun lawyer was turned away. The next day he wrote the NAACP a letter stating that he and Wright "have rendered a service to the colored people in general and Willie Francis in particular," and that Willie's father was "greatly disturbed" that DeBlanc's requests for financial help had not been acted upon. DeBlanc had been spending his own money to defend Willie, he wrote, and he'd had to borrow money from his sister to make the trip.

Upon his arrival in Washington, DeBlanc registered at the Hotel Statler, a large, modern hotel at 16th and K streets built during World War II. At the time, another young veteran, John F. Kennedy, who'd recently been elected to Congress, was living at the hotel. Skelly Wright, who had only been back in Washington for a few months at this point, was living with his wife at his mother-in-law's house in nearby Chevy Chase, Maryland.

On the morning of November 18, 1946, the young Irish Channel and Louisiana bayou attorneys entered the classical, Corinthian-styled Supreme Court building through the bronze doors and made their way down the corridor of the Great Hall toward the oak doors of the Court chamber. Helen Wright was also in attendance. At twelve noon, the velvet curtain parted, and the clerk rose.

"Oyez! Oyez! Oyez!" he announced. "All persons having business before the Honorable, the Supreme Court of the United States, are admonished to draw near and give their attention, for the Court is now sitting. God save the United States and this Honorable Court!"

In their customary black robes, the justices entered the chamber and took their seats.

Wright and DeBlanc waited for Willie's case to be called. Several decisions were announced, and two oral arguments were heard. The Court then broke for lunch. Not until 2:30 p.m. was Willie's case finally called before the bar.

"Louisiana ex rel. Francis v. Resweber," said Chief Judge Vinson.

DeBlanc was seated beside Wright at the counsel table before the bench. Without an admission to the bar of the Court, DeBlanc would have to rely on Wright to argue before the justices. The square-jawed, blue-eyed Wright rose and responded with the traditional, "Mr. Chief Justice, may it please the Court," before he began summarizing Willie's case. The first interruption—interruptions during oral argument usually take the form of a judge's question—came from Frankfurter.

With the magisterial air of a law professor questioning a green student, Frankfurter habitually peered down through his spectacles at the lawyers arguing their cases. Doesn't the sheriff, Frankfurter wanted to know, have express authority to electrocute Mr. Francis until he is dead? There is nothing, he noted, in the statute suggesting precisely how or how many times that can occur.

Wright was prepared for this question. Whether the sheriff has an order or not is not at issue, he replied. No order given by the State directing the sheriff or anyone else to violate the constitutional rights of any individual can be valid.

Frankfurter nodded and made a note. Wright, no doubt feeling that he had successfully jumped one small hurdle, quickly moved on. Because oral arguments are limited in time, judges' questions can prevent a lawyer from making important and sometimes critical points in the sixty minutes allotted for certiorari cases.

Wright proceeded with his double-jeopardy argument, and without interruption the justices let him talk—until he began summing up the issue. Wright argued that Willie Francis suffered "anguish of mind" by receiving punishment "up to the last moment," when his head was shaved and he received last rites from Father Maurice Rousseve. "A second execution," Wright said, according to Miller and Bowman in their book *Death by Installments*, "repeats all of the previous punishment up to that point."

Justice Reed jumped in, posing a hypothetical about a man who has been sentenced to ten years in prison and who has served nine before escaping. Wouldn't you then be arguing, Reed asked, that he could not be forced to serve his ten years all over again? The question mocked Wright's double-jeopardy argument. At that point, though, Wright could not know whether Reed's dismissive statement regarding double jeopardy might also signal Reed's rejection of the crucial Eighth Amendment cruel-and-unusual-punishment claim.

During Wright's response to Reed, Burton chimed in, wanting to know just how far this doctrine could be carried. Suppose Resweber had only shaved Willie's head a second time before putting him in the chair again. Would that, Burton wondered, be double punishment? Burton wasn't buying the double-jeopardy argument either.

Next, Frankfurter piled it on: Would the double-jeopardy argument still be valid if a man had been taken from his cell and started toward the chair, only to have his execution postponed? Would that invoke jeopardy?

"Why don't you let him talk?" Helen wondered.

Clearly, Wright was finding his double-jeopardy argument to be rather unwelcomed by the Court, and it was not likely to win Willie's case. Answering as best he could, Wright directed the justices back to the facts in Willie's particular, actual case and away from the hypotheticals, to which it bore little similarity. Whatever conclusions one might draw from the circumstances presented in the hypotheticals, what happened to Willie Francis was wrong, Wright argued. "If the State of Louisiana had a right to execute Willie Francis," said Wright, now couching his double-jeopardy claim in terms of cruel and unusual punishment, "she was bound to make his death as instant and painless as possible. By her failure to do so, she has forfeited the right to his life."

Facing no further questions on the issue of double jeopardy, Wright moved on to his cruel-and-unusual punishment and equal-protection arguments, which the court permitted him to summarize without further interruption. When, however, Wright asserted that, by subjecting Willie to electrocution not once but twice, Louisiana would be submitting him to the cruelest and most severe punishment it had ever meted out, the court intervened.

"Why are these affidavits here?" Vinson asked, as he indicated the affidavits that Wright had improperly affixed to his brief. Wright attempted to defend their inclusion with the legal briefs on the grounds that the Court needed them to determine whether any electric current at all had indeed entered Francis's body—a point in contention before the Court—and, if so, to what effect. Vinson observed that the affidavits did not constitute a part of the record and therefore should not stand before the Court. From the bench, Vinson ordered that the affidavits be stricken from the Supreme Court record and that the justices not consider them.

Improperly or not, Wright wanted the facts before the justices. They had seen the affidavits, and Wright hoped they might not ignore them when considering how to rule on Willie's case. Still, Wright was acutely aware that this tactic might be more effective on a trial jury than on U.S. Supreme Court justices, who will often ignore any matter that is off the official record, just as they will any facts on the record that are inconsistent with the conclusion they desire to reach. But he had at least drawn their attention to the affidavits.

His oral argument completed, Wright sat down, and the State weighed in. The State advanced a twofold argument: whatever the State did, it did properly under Louisiana statutes in accordance with both the federal and the Louisiana constitutions; and Willie Francis suffered no hurt or injury due to the malfunctioning of Louisiana's electric chair during the attempted execution.

Two attorneys were arguing for the State's case: Michael Culligan, of the Louisiana attorney general's office, and L. O. Pecot, the district attorney who had prosecuted Willie Francis. Culligan began much the way he might have down in Louisiana during the opening statement of a criminal trial—by describing, in great detail, the senseless, cold-blooded murder of Andrew Thomas at the hands of a young Negro bent on robbery.

"We know that a terrible crime was committed," Frankfurter barked, according to Miller and Bowman. "We want the law." Plainly, Culligan was trying to appeal to the justices' emotions rather than their reason, and Frankfurter was having none of it. "Get to the law," he ordered.

Culligan, chastened and stunned, complied. He argued, with citations from previous Supreme Court cases, that double jeopardy and the provisions of the federal Constitution prohibiting cruel and unusual punishment did not apply to Louisiana in particular, because they did not apply in general to any of the states. Culligan urged that the Supreme Court thus defer to the ruling of the State of Louisiana in the matter of Willie Francis. No justice questioned or interrupted Culligan. He had taken ten of the sixty minutes allotted the State.

When L. O. Pecot addressed the Court, he argued, as expected, that Willie Francis had been tried fairly and had been accorded due process—until Justice Black interrupted him with a question that might have been pulled from Wright's own brief: "Just how many times," asked Black, "does a man have to go to the chair without being killed to suffer sufficient punishment? Would it be fifteen times, and would he have to be burned each time?"

Pecot's response also echoed Wright. He said that Black's question, a question regarding a "hypothetical," was not before the Court. As to the actual matter being considered, Willie Francis, Pecot asserted, certainly had not suffered cruel and unusual punishment. Pecot finished his argument, which prompted no further questions, and he sat down.

Chief Justice Vinson nodded at counsel, informed them that the case had been submitted, and announced the next case before the Court.

"The Justices seemed unusually subdued, perhaps under the impact of the terrible events which had already befallen Willie and the possibility that those events would be repeated if the Court failed to intervene," wrote Barrett Prettyman Jr. in *Death and the Supreme Court.* "The spirit of the Court was almost sullen, and the Justices, straight-backed or bent forward, looked like brooding Rodin figures, black-robed and black of mood, almost resentful that this insoluble problem had been put before them."

DeBlanc and Wright's hopes lay with Hugo Black. If Black's question regarding "sufficient punishment" reflected his belief that Willie's second execution would indeed violate the Constitution, then Black would surely argue to his fellow justices that Willie Francis—not the State of Louisiana—should be given a second chance.

weeping no tears

Where life is to be taken, there must be no avoidable error of law or uncertainty of fact.

—JUSTICE HAROLD H. BURTON

On November 23, the Saturday following oral arguments, the justices convened to discuss the cases they had heard that week, Willie Francis's among them. Chief Justice Vinson announced the case by its docket number: 142.

Customarily, the initial vote of each justice at the conference table is registered along with any commentary on the case he or she may wish to offer. The justices then further discuss the case as they see fit, and after they have debated the various issues that have affected its initial outcome, one justice in the majority is assigned to write a draft opinion. (If the chief justice is in the majority, he selects the justice who will write the opinion; if not, the senior justice in the majority assigns the opinion to one of his colleagues.)

The first vote registered that Saturday was that of the chief justice. Neither a brilliant jurist nor the sharpest legal mind in history's estimation of him, Vinson was first and foremost a conservative, and he usually voted that way. When casting his vote, he commented only upon Wright's double-jeopardy argument—arguably, the weakest claim raised in Willie's defense—and voted to affirm the judgment of the Louisiana courts: Willie should not be spared a second electrocution.

The next to vote, per seniority on the court, was Hugo Black. Willie's case afforded Black the perfect opportunity to forward his conviction that the Bill of Rights should be applied unequivocally to the states. After all, didn't Louisiana have the responsibility to ensure that, if it was to electrocute an individual, the machinery used to effect that end would at the very least be in full working order so as to guarantee the subject an instant and painless death, as the Supreme Court had previously held regarding cruel and unusual punishment in *Kemmler*? Black could easily have made the case that, because of Louisiana's own inattention and neglect, the chair had malfunctioned and thus denied Willie Francis the humane execution to which he was by law entitled. The state by its own irresponsibility had forfeited its chance to effectively execute Willie Francis. For the Court to so hold would have marked a threshold in the evolvement both of American jurisprudence and of Black's judicial career.

Black's advocacy of the extension of rights granted in the Constitution would eventually help usher in an altogether new era of Supreme Court jurisprudence to the states, allowing Americans to enjoy their protection in every court in the land. He would indeed make history in the Court over the extension of the tenets in the Bill of Rights, but not until one year later, with *Adamson v. California*, when he wrote, "I cannot consider the Bill of Rights to be an outworn eighteenth-century straight-jacket." Skelly Wright would later say of Black, "If I had had to pick one sure vote [for Willie], I would have picked him." But Hugo Black voted to send Willie Francis back to the electric chair. Without discussion or explanation, he indicated that he would affirm the Louisiana court's decision. "Why Black did not take that position in the *Francis* case," Miller and Bowman note, "is an unresolved mystery."

Stanley Reed, like Justice Jackson, a former U.S. solicitor general, often cast the swing vote on the Court, and he, like Black, voted to affirm. Willie's chances for a reversal of Louisiana's ruling were slipping away.

Surprisingly, it was Frankfurter, not Black, who expressed reservations about the determination of the Louisiana courts. "This is not an easy case," he said, and then proceeded to discuss and dispense with double jeopardy as grounds on which to reverse the Louisiana courts. He wrestled more particularly with the issue of cruel and unusual punishment. Frankfurter felt, overall, that judicial restraint compelled the Court simply to defer to Louisiana's own interpretation of the death penalty statute. Still, he took time to consider whether Willie Francis had been accorded due process under the Fourteenth Amendment, which would, in turn, determine whether or not the Eighth Amendment regarding cruel and unusual punishment would apply. Strangely, that consideration led the coldly logical, assiduously unemotional Frankfurter to a test articulated by his old friend Oliver Wendell Holmes, whose mantel as court scholar Frankfurter liked to think he had inherited. Holmes would not rule a state's law unconstitutional unless it made him "puke." Frankfurter noted that, while Louisiana's second attempt at electrocution was "hardly defensible," the thought of it did not make him puke. He voted to affirm.

And down the line it went.

Justice William O. Douglas, a known liberal and former Yale Law School faculty member who, like many on the Court, had served in government shortly before his appointment—he was chairman of the Securities and Exchange Commission when Roosevelt nominated him to the Supreme Court in 1939—usually voted with Justice Black. That Saturday was no exception: affirm.

Justice Frank Murphy—a former mayor of Detroit and governor of Michigan whom Roosevelt had named U.S. attorney general and

later nominated to the Court—frequently championed the underdog and individual rights. Murphy usually voted with the liberal
bloc of the court led by Black. Splitting with Black, he followed his
liberal sympathies and voted to reverse.

Justice Jackson, former counsel to the IRS, solicitor general, and
attorney general, as well as Nuremburg prosecutor, unsurprisingly
voted to affirm.

Justice Wiley Rutledge, another known liberal and formerly a law
professor on the faculties of numerous schools before becoming a
judge on the court of appeals for the District of Columbia, voted to
reverse.

So, too, did Justice Burton, the one-time mayor of Cleveland who
in 1941 became a U.S. senator and had been recently nominated to
the Court by Truman. Burton, in fact, had been opposed to having
the Court take Willie's case in the first place and had earlier remarked
to Frankfurter, "Felix, as you know most of the time I agree with you
and certainly I can understand why you take the position that you
take. But for the life of me I can't see why a man of your intelligence
should think that simply because something went wrong with an electric wire, for which nobody was responsible, the State of Louisiana
cannot carry out a death sentence imposed after a fair trial."

Thus, the Court's initial vote stood at 6 to 3 against Willie Francis. Chief Justice Vinson assigned to Justice Reed the writing of the
opinion.

Willie's fate had not yet been decided, however. The highly contentious Court, true to its form, would continue to impose ego upon
the deliberations and allow abstract philosophies of judicial restraint
to overshadow the more consequential reason they had gathered on
this Saturday, that is, to determine the fate of a young Negro named
Willie Francis.

In the Supreme Court, the first vote initiates a round of debate
among the justices, who engage in a back-and-forth over the drafted
majority opinion and any other final opinions drafted by dissenting

justices. The various drafts provide justices with the means to influence their colleagues to alter their position or to incorporate particular legal points from a draft into the final Court opinion. Justices do have changes of heart and of mind, and politics—as ugly as it might be in the context of some cases, and as it was in Willie Francis's—does indeed rear its head.

Reed's first draft of the majority opinion was written, printed, and circulated among the justices within two weeks. By then, too, each of the three dissenters—Murphy, Rutledge, and Burton—had drafted three dissenting opinions by which they hoped to do some coalition-building and turn Reed's majority opinion into a dissent.

What became evident as all four drafts circulated among the justices was that a crucial element—the circumstances of Willie's execution, from the setting up of the electric chair to the actual nature of the suffering Willie had endured during the electrocution—was not a matter of firm record before the Court. That element became an issue central to the conflict among the justices.

Reed viewed the failure of Willie's execution essentially as an act of God. "Accidents happen for which no man is to blame," wrote Reed of the botched execution attempt. The malfunction of Louisiana's electric chair being such an accident and therefore utterly unforeseeable, it could thus not be considered "cruel," Reed argued. Indeed, Reed's opinion suggested that, had the malfunctioning of the chair been the result of "malevolence" on the part of Louisiana state administrators, the state court's ruling on Willie might be reversed. The opinion, however, asserted nothing in regard to the State's possible negligence. By contrast, two of the three dissents maintained that Louisiana's negligence in failing to ensure that the electric chair was in good operating order was such that the State may as well have intentionally injured Willie.

With regard to the notion that Willie suffered mental stress leading up to the electrocution and that it was thus cruel and unusual punishment to submit Willie to undergo the anticipation of execution a second time, Reed hewed to previous Court decisions (like *in re Kemmler*) that had found the use of the electric chair to be humane. Reed's opinion did not address the notion that Willie had experienced severe pain when he underwent the electrocution, hence apparently Reed deemed Willie's actual pain to be negligible or nonexistent. In fact, Reed wrote that Willie Francis's re-electrocution would not violate "national standards of decency."

As to the issue that Willie had not received a fair trial, Reed wrote that "there is nothing in any of these papers to show any violation of petitioner's constitutional rights." In addition, Reed applied the rules of appellate review: the Supreme Court could not review the question because Wright and DeBlanc had not raised the claim in the Louisiana courts.

Burton's dissent was everything that Wright and DeBlanc could have wished for. Although Burton, like Frankfurter, subscribed to the philosophy of judicial restraint—Burton often voted against criminal defendants and with state governments—he found Louisiana's treatment of Willie Francis wholly repugnant. In Burton's mind, there was no question that repeated attempts at execution constituted torture. Nor could any point raised in Reed's opinion in any way have affected his position; he had begun writing his dissent on the same day as Reed, and on the same day as Reed, too, he'd had printed copies of it awaiting the attention of his fellow justices.

Burton declared the treatment of Willie to be not only cruel and unusual in the extreme but also absolutely inhumane. In his opinion, he revisited an issue with which the Court had wrestled earlier: whether electrocution was a humane form of execution. The Supreme Court in *Kemmler* had reasoned that it was essentially humane on the basis of its reckoning that death would be virtually instantaneous and relatively painless.

Burton, like justices before and after him, implicitly accepted the finding of *in re Kemmler* that electrocution was instantaneous and painless, despite the fact that the Supreme Court had considered Kemmler's case before Kemmler was sent to the chair and later accounts of his horrific death had not been part of the record. Burton felt strongly, however, that reapplication of electric current after one failed attempt at electrocution ceased to be humane. He stated his position forcefully:

> If the state officials deliberately and intentionally had placed the relator in the electric chair five times and, each time, had applied electric current to his body in a manner not sufficient, until the final time, to kill him, such a form of torture would rival that of burning at the stake. Although the failure of the first attempt, in the present case, was unintended, the reapplication of the electric current will be intentional. How many deliberate and intentional reapplications of electric current does it take to produce a cruel, unusual and unconstitutional punishment? While five applications would be more cruel and unusual than one, the uniqueness of the present case demonstrates that, today, two separated applications are sufficiently "cruel and unusual" to be prohibited.

Burton accepted Wright and DeBlanc's argument that to inflict upon a condemned person a repetition of the significant mental stress and anguish already suffered in the face of execution indeed constitutes a form of torture. As Miller and Bowman write, the Supreme Court would later recognize the "fate of ever-increasing fear and distress" that must be endured by condemned prisoners—an anxiety so forceful that "the onset of insanity while awaiting execution of a death sentence is not a rare phenomenon." But Burton was years ahead of the Court in this regard. He argued further that the re-execution of Willie, so to speak, might in fact violate Louisiana's death-penalty statute, which allowed only that a continuous stream of electric current, as opposed to an indeterminate number of successive shocks, be applied to the condemned person's body until death resulted.

Murphy, the Court's humanist, agreed, and Burton managed to persuade both Murphy and Rutledge to join him in his dissent. By standing together, the three dissenters could make their position stronger and more readily draw judges away from the majority opinion. They needed just two more votes to gain a solid Court majority.

After the initial opinions had been circulated, dissenters and the majority alike waited to see if any justice would waver in his position. Justice Douglas was the first to express reservations. He may have decided that the case hinged, after all, on what Willie Francis actually experienced during the first electrocution, because, on December 20, 1946, he abandoned his original position and joined Burton's dissent, which ordered that the case be sent back to Louisiana for hearings to determine "the extent to which electric current was applied to [Willie Francis] during his attempted electrocution"—in other words, to see just how much Willie had suffered. As Burton had written, "Where life is to be taken, there must be no avoidable error of law or uncertainty of fact."

Burton's opinion did not call for outright reversal; rather, it ordered that the execution be stayed pending further investigation. It nonetheless marked a significant victory for Willie. Wright's tactic had worked: Burton referred explicitly to the affidavits appended to Wright's brief as evidence of the need for a hearing in the Louisiana courts. Despite the strength and passion with which Burton's dissent was written, it in fact called for Louisiana to determine first whether Willie Francis had suffered significantly in the course of the attempted execution and then, if he had, whether it would be a violation of due process or cruel and unusual punishment to force him to undergo it again. Indeed, under Burton's decision, Louisiana could attempt to execute Willie again if it determined that Willie had not actually received a painful shock from the electric current or if it found that he had just been "tickled."

The crux of the matter, then, became whether or not a simple question of fact—what had Willie really suffered as he endured current in the chair—had any relevance to the case. The majority based its opinion solely on the facts presently before them. Five of the justices were still willing to accept that the chair's malfunction was an unavoidable accident for which no one—specifically, the State of Louisiana—bore any blame.

To convert his dissent into the majority opinion, Burton had to convince one more justice to move to his side. Would Black, who so often voted with the intellectually compatible Douglas, reconsider?

Apparently not. No record of communications between Black and Burton exists to indicate that they shared any ideas about the matter with each other. Black's writings do show, however, that he felt the record in no way demonstrated that Willie Francis's conviction had been improperly reached.

But another of the justices appeared at least to be thinking about changing his vote. On December 13—seven days before Douglas joined the dissent—Frankfurter sent a note to Burton in which he expressed some difficulty in staying with the majority. "I have to hold on to myself not to reach your result," he wrote in his typically grandiose fashion, and added that "only the disciplined thinking of a lifetime" prevented him from joining the dissent. He also reiterated his feeling that the case did not meet the Holmes "puke" test.

Frankfurter wavered, and thus began the battle for his vote. Desperately trying to hold in the majority, Reed, in an exchange of memos with him, made a multitude of subtle changes in his opinion to satisfy Frankfurter, and then made a multitude more in accordance with suggestions from Frankfurter. Over Frankfurter's other shoulder, Burton was urging the justice to forgo his commitment to judicial restraint and follow his heart instead.

Reed watched anxiously as the majority grappled with his opinion. His "national standards of decency" test did not enjoy popular-
ity with the justices. The general tenor of its reception among the
majority was conveyed in a concurrence circulated by Justice Jackson. As something of an intellectual rebuke to Reed, Jackson expressed his doubt that the framers of the Constitution "ever
intended to nationalize decency." Suddenly, Reed was staring at the
disorder and turmoil the public had come to expect from the U.S.
Supreme Court of late. Four justices were now in favor of reversing
the Louisiana court's decision to return Willie Francis to the electric
chair. Now only two of the nine justices, Reed and Vinson, had
agreed to affirm, with Jackson, Frankfurter and Black all claiming
they could not agree with the majority opinion, although Jackson
had indicated he would not vote to reverse. Reed had to move
quickly, and he set off on a mission to appease the wavering justices.

In all probability, Reed adopted the standards of decency test in
part to bolster the majority opinion with reasoning that both Frankfurter and Black, on opposite sides of the fence with regard to "incorporation" cases, would find acceptable. Black was in favor of
"incorporating" the Bill of Rights to the states through the due process clause in the Fourteenth Amendment. Frankfurter opposed
constitutional challenges as long as they did not "shock the conscience." "Whose conscience?" Black would wonder, and back and
forth it went. Reed was trying to sidestep the incorporation debate
entirely by premising the decision on a standards-of-decency test,
which he'd drawn from a previous Court case, *Palko*, and which he
hoped would prove to be acceptable to both Frankfurter and Black.

Reed hoped in vain. Frankfurter's frequently expressed notion
that the states should be left to conduct their own affairs—that the
Bill of Rights did not in fact apply to them—was, in Black's mind,
absurd. Surely, in Black's view, the Bill of Rights had not been enacted so that, in the majority of cases throughout the United States,

it would not apply. Nor did Black, any more than Justice Jackson, find the adoption of a "national standards of decency" test a reasonable measure, for it gave judges no guidance on how to apply such a test: It was purely subjective.

At the very least, incorporation of the Bill of Rights into the states, by which particular standards could be applied to determine what constituted due process, was less subjective than the standards of decency test. Still, the phrase "cruel and unusual," for instance, provided no specific guidance, Black believed, as to how it might be practically applied to particular cases. That Reed chose to ground his decision in "national standards of decency" prompted Black to circulate a concurrence savaging Reed's test. The concurrence also offered some explanation as to why Black had voted to affirm. "I cannot agree with them that any provision of the federal Constitution authorizes us to rule that any accidental failure to carry out a valid sentence of death on the first attempt bars execution of that sentence," Black wrote. On the record before the Court, Black found no cause to impute responsibility to the State of Louisiana for the mishap that befell Willie Francis; he assumed that the chair had been prepared properly and that the State had done all that it could to ensure that it functioned correctly, for the record did not indicate otherwise.

To persuade Black to withdraw his concurrence, Reed offered to include a sentence in the majority opinion suggesting that the Bill of Rights applied to the states. That was apparently good enough for Black. Black did not join the dissent.

Meanwhile, Frankfurter wrote to Reed on December 14, 1946—the day after he had sent the note to Burton—asking that Reed insert a paragraph into his opinion further emphasizing that, because the official record was silent on the actual circumstance of Willie's failed execution, the Court had to assume that the malfunctioning of the chair was accidental:

I assume that you will add something like this to your opinion, even if it is already implied: "We have not before us a situation where officers of the State acted with malevolence or callousness or carelessness toward human life. Nothing in the record remotely warrants such imputation. On the contrary, the case presupposes the appropriate precautions were taken and the abortiveness of the attempted execution is one of those contingencies which is not the fault of man. Any other consideration is unfair to the State and disregards the very narrow scope of our authority to limit the powers of a State."

Reed quickly obliged by inserting into the body of his opinion a paragraph in word and substance very much like Frankfurter's own. Frankfurter had thus managed to lobby successfully for a majority statement that, not incidentally, entirely furthered his view of judicial restraint, that is, that the federal government's powers over the states were severely and narrowly restricted.

Burton himself was a proponent of judicial restraint, but in this case he felt that action, not restraint, was necessary. Burton, for his part, tried to convince Frankfurter that the dissent was not proposing the use of federal power to regulate the state but, rather, that the opinion argued only for Louisiana to correct the misinterpretation of its own statute: "Consider that in enforcing the 14th Amendment against these state officials we are enforcing not only the *federal* amendment *but also* the *express* language of the *state* legislature," Burton wrote on December 26.

Even if Frankfurter did not wholly agree with Burton's dissent, he might easily embrace Burton's plea that Willie's second execution be stayed pending the result of an inquiry into the circumstances of the first by the state. On December 31, Frankfurter responded to Burton's entreaties with a memorandum. "I think I can say without the slightest exaggeration," it began, "that, knowing the care that you give to the writing of your opinions, I try to bring the same kind of care to their consideration." As happy as Burton may have been to receive the praise, he was surely more eager to discover whether he had convinced Frankfurter to join the dissent. "And, in a case like that of Willie Francis, my high regard for the quality of your work is reinforced by my feelings regarding the duty of States not to fall short of the standards which it is within the competence of the Court to enforce," continued Frankfurter, teasing Burton with the possibility that he might side with the dissent for reasons not unlike Burton's own.

But it was no more than a possibility, for Frankfurter concluded that the Louisiana court's ruling on the basis of what the state's own laws meant had to be respected. "All this is purely a State question beyond our purview," wrote Frankfurter.

In his memorandum, Frankfurter expressed his concern that, should he alter his majority stance, he would be ruling according to his own private view "rather than the allowable consensus of opinion in the community which, for purposes of due process, expresses the Constitution." Apparently, Frankfurter assumed that the ruling of the Louisiana court somehow expressed the wishes of the community, which in fact had showered newspapers and the governor's office with letters urging, almost pleading, that Willie Francis's life be spared. Felix Frankfurter evidently failed to consider that his personal inclination—he was, after all, against capital punishment—might not be the same as that of the community. Ironically, in adhering to his dictum not to follow his own personal preferences in arriving at his decisions, he may have been allowing a Louisiana state court judge to follow his.

"I am sorry that I cannot go with you," Frankfurter wrote to Burton, "but I am weeping no tears that you are expressing a dissent." The apology would likely mean little to Willie Francis.

just like a movie star

If anybody's gonna sit, I'm gonna.

—WILLIE FRANCIS

By January of 1947 Willie Francis had been locked up in the New Iberia Parish jail for seventeen long months. DeBlanc would visit him regularly and bring candy, magazines, and comic books, which Willie was grateful for. In the back pages of one magazine, Willie happened upon an ad that promised a cure for stuttering. He was allowed to order it, and when the booklet arrived, Willie studied it and practiced his enunciation. Sheriff Ozenne believed Willie's speech improved.

Since being detained, Willie had been outside the jail only a handful of times, like when he'd helped Sheriff Resweber and his deputies locate evidence—later used against him in court—at the Selon Canal behind Andrew Thomas's house and at Rivere's jewelry store in New Iberia, where he'd identified Thomas's watch. Willie had also made a few trips back and forth to the St. Martinville courthouse on the occasions of his indictment, trial, and sentencing, not to mention that long, slow drive on the morning of May 3, 1946, to receive 2,500 volts of electricity in Gruesome Gertie.

Against all odds, though, Willie had lived through that last experience, and contrary to any reasonable expectations, he'd also made the drive back to New Iberia that afternoon. Since then, he'd waited optimistically while Bertrand DeBlanc petitioned the supreme court of Louisiana. He'd kept his hopes up, too, when DeBlanc argued before the Louisiana Pardons Board. Both times his spirits had been dashed. Three times since the failed execution on that hot morning in May, he had attempted to prepare himself mentally for a second electrocution; three times he'd been granted a stay. In addition, a clerk's error in Washington had led Willie and his lawyers to believe that the nation's highest court had refused to hear his case, thus obliterating his final chance for a reprieve. Only when he'd awakened the next morning did he learn that the U.S. Supreme Court had decided just the opposite. The emotional stress had to have been unbearable for Willie at times.

The winter of 1946, however, five months after Willie Francis was first sentenced to death by Judge Simon and five months into his confinement in his cell in New Iberia, was, quite possibly, the most anguished time of any that Willie would spend in jail. At that point, Governor Jimmie Davis had not issued a death warrant stating exactly when the death sentence would be carried out. And the mail was bringing no letters from supporters to bolster him. Except for family, visitors were few. His public defenders had essentially deserted him. Willie knew that he was going to the electric chair sure enough, but he had no idea when. The uncertainty no doubt took a toll on him.

A letter written by Willie to Sheriff Resweber on February 15, 1946, sheds some light both on the state of Willie's mind and perhaps on the quality of his representation by public defenders Mestayer and Parkerson. The letter was buried in a file at the St. Martinville courthouse among dozens of others sent to Sheriff Resweber months later, after Willie survived the execution in May. It is signed, and the handwriting unmistakably matches Willie's. Willie wrote:

Feb. 15, 1946
Mr. E. L. Resweber

Dear Sir

*I heard about my second trial. I don't want to be trial again Do
I have to get a lawyer to close my case. And just get my sentence
by the judge. It suppose to be the state of law. Of course I plead
guilty the grand jury and the judge won't mind.*

*I don't mind getting A death penalty or life. My grand jury
knows about my case. They find me in first degree murder.
When a person don't want to heard his second trial again he
don't have too. Mr. Resweber will you please have a talk with
judge and grand jury for me.*

I'm a negro, I killed A white man.

I know that your are trying to give me a death penalty.

I don't mind at all.

*I'm willing to pay for my crime any sort of ways. When you
come over in New Iberia come and have a talk with me.*

(Willie Francis)

No official documentation regarding the possibility of a second
trial seems to exist. As the court-appointed attorneys Mestayer and
Parkerson had made not even a half-hearted effort in Willie's defense, it is unlikely they would have pursued the possibility of a retrial. Besides, by February of 1946, all deadlines for appeals had
expired. At that point, too, Bertrand DeBlanc, who had only re-

cently returned from his postings in France and Germany during World War II, was not yet involved with the Willie Francis case (and would not be until the morning after the failed execution four months later). Neither did the NAACP enter into the case until after the botched execution, so it may simply have been that Willie's family was talking to him about a retrial in an attempt to bolster what little hope remained in the boy.

As Willie's letter indicates, in February of 1946 he was willing and apparently prepared to die. Around that time, too, Sheriff Resweber revealed to a reporter that, according to Sheriff Ozenne, Willie had threatened to kill himself with a safety razor. Someone had evidently smuggled the razor into his cell in New Iberia, and Willie, Ozenne claimed, had hidden it in his Bible. While there is no other evidence that Willie was considering suicide during those winter months when he was being guarded by Sheriff Gilbert Ozenne and his deputy Gus "Killer" Walker, his letter to Resweber rather clearly states that, as far as his death sentence was concerned, Willie didn't "mind at all."

Just because Willie had accepted the possibility that his fate was sealed that winter did not mean that those who would spend ensuing months defending him would be ready to do the same. For three weeks, Skelly Wright had been calling the court every Monday to learn if the Supreme Court had reached a decision. Finally, on January 13, he spoke with a Court clerk who told him that the Court had, indeed, reached a decision, and he spoke the word both Wright and DeBlanc had been praying for.

Reversed.

Willie had won! Wright was elated. He rushed by taxi to the Supreme Court building, his heart pounding with excitement. He'd call DeBlanc with the good news from there.

He looked out the window of his taxi as the grand monuments and impressive federal architecture flashed by on his way to the court that promised Equal Justice Under Law. Upon his arrival,

Skelly Wright bounded up the stairs of the Supreme Court building and rushed through the bronze doors. He was eager to see the decision in writing, eager to read it to DeBlanc over the phone. It was a spectacular win. Most likely, Willie would have his sentence commuted to life imprisonment and spend a long time at Angola. Maybe he'd even be granted a new trial. But at least Willie wouldn't be going back to the chair that had haunted his dreams and those of his counsel.

With a new spring in his step, Wright walked across the marble floors of the Great Hall. But his elation was short-lived.

Once again, a Supreme Court clerk had erred.

The clerk on the phone had read the wrong result to Wright. The Louisiana decision had been *upheld*. Not reversed. Willie Francis was going back to the chair. The Court announced the opinion and decision on January 13, 1947, one day after Willie's eighteenth birthday.

"When I got to the courthouse after a much excited ride in a taxi," Wright would relate afterward, "I called to a friend that I saw in the hallway, 'I won my case!' I said it twice, and he kind of looked at me like I was crazy because he knew the truth. He had been there, and when I got to the clerk's office I got the bad news myself. I had actually lost."

"Skelly was crushed," Helen Wright recalls. "Just devastated. He didn't think justice had been done."

The U.S. Supreme Court had been Willie's last hope. He had not stepped outside the small, filthy jail on the top floor of the New Iberia courthouse since Captain Ephie Foster's chair had failed to kill him. And he can't have found comfort in knowing that the next time he left the jail might well be while traveling to the end of his life.

Willie had passed the long, uncertain months visiting with family, reading his Bible, and writing letters. After his story had gained the

national headlines, an abundance of mail offering prayers and sup-
port had been pouring into the jail. Money came, too, and Bertrand
DeBlanc had established a defense fund to cover the costs of what
had become a time-consuming and expensive struggle to save
Willie's life. He'd kept a log of these funds, most of them very small
donations under $10, which arrived daily. Every little bit helped.
Not only did DeBlanc have to pay for trips to New Orleans and
Washington, DC, but in the year or so that he'd been working on
Willie's appeal, he'd had to pass up other cases that would have paid
him a fee.

The volume of mail and number of donations increased significantly after the Supreme Court agreed to hear Willie's case. The
generosity could be quite unusual. A letter from Mrs. John Kenney
of Washington, DC, for instance, came with the offer that her husband—a "totally and permanently disabled World War II veteran"—sit in the executioner's chair in place of Willie. DeBlanc
politely declined the offer, as did his client. "If anybody's gonna sit,
I'm gonna," Willie said.

Another letter, this one from Mrs. Wilmer Cox of Dallas, Texas,
in May 1946, brought an odd request. It embarrassed her to ask,
Mrs. Cox wrote, but if Willie's appeals turned out to be unsuccessful
and he was sentenced to die, would he consider willing his eyes to
her brother Rufus, who had been without sight since childhood.
Willie was moved. As a child growing up in St. Martinville, he had
befriended an old blind neighbor with whom he kept company.
Willie wrote a letter to Mrs. Cox: "We cannot judge ourselves right
now. I do wish every thing was quiet and peaceful. When I was a
small child there was a blind neighbor who used to romp with me.
He was much older as he is 72 years of age now. He always kissed
me on the forehead. Right then and there I wanted to help someone
who was blind. I always had a deal of sympathy for any one that was
blind."

His fond memory of the man prompted Willie to have DeBlanc draw up a will, which read:

> *This is my last will and testament knowing life is not sure and God may call me to life everlasting. I want to atone for my life. I leave and bequeath to Rufus Allen of Dallas, Texas, my eyes and that being all that I will dying, have left, I have no other things to will.*

> *Yours truly, Willie Francis*

Willie then wrote to Mrs. Cox informing her that he would comply with her request "if it is God's will I should be electrocuted again." In the letter, he also included a "mimeographic plea" prepared by DeBlanc asking that petitions for a change in sentence to life imprisonment be circulated.

According to a story in the *World's Messenger* in July 1946, Willie's mother, ill and confined to bed, learned of the will and demanded that her son break it. Willie's eyes would not be taken from him, even in death. In a June 2, 1946, letter to Jessyl Taylor, the reporter friend of Mrs. Cox in Dallas, Willie explained the change of plans, which, clearly, he regretted.

> *Dear Mrs. Taylor,*

> *I received your letter and really was glad to hear from you. About my past, I didn't mean no harm. I received a Rosary. I didn't know who sent it. Since you mentioned about it that you sent it I really do thank you. I didn't receive the magazines yet. I think I will get them Monday. I have written to Mrs. Cox and explained to her about the will I made for my eyes. I had to make my mind up for me to break the will. I hope Mrs. Cox*

will understand. I had made a promise to her. My mother had wrote to me and told me to break the will up. It took four days for me to write to her and explain everything. I was sorry to break my promise.

Things are not going so good in my case—I am not afraid to die. Only one thing I am worrying about is my soul. Now that I am going to die Friday, I am prepared to meet the Lord. This may be my last letter to you. I won't say "goodbye," because we will meet in Heaven.

Your friend in Christ,
Willie Francis

He later told Mrs. Cox, in another letter written before the Supreme Court agreed to hear his case, that "last night I had a long dream. I dreamed I was blind and I didn't rest well all night."

It was evident even to Sheriff Gilbert Ozenne that, after the Supreme Court agreed to hear Willie's case, his mood picked up considerably. Ozenne observed that Willie started talking and kidding around with another condemned inmate, whose cell was just down the corridor; he noted, too, that Willie was eating better and that his lanky body was filling out. Otherwise, Willie attended to his mail, occasionally sang spirituals he'd learned as a boy, and read the magazines posted to him by strangers who wished him well. Willie was also visited regularly by his family, DeBlanc, and Father Hannigan.

With all the attention he was receiving, Willie "felt just like a movie star." Certainly he had achieved some celebrity. A song about Willie's dance with death had even been published: "Da Lord Fool'd around Wid Dat Chair," written by Eugene Cortinas and Lester Lalande under the pen names Gene Carter and Joseph Lester. Bertrand DeBlanc negotiated the contract with the two songwriters, by which Willie retained one-third of all moneys and revenues generated by the song.

Regardless of the hopes Willie may have clasped that the Supreme Court might commute his death sentence to life in prison, he still feared the "bad chair." He had met with Father Hannigan nearly every day throughout the months since the failed execution, and the priest had done his best to sustain Willie's optimism and at the same time prepare him for the possibility of death by electrocution. No longer, though, did Father Hannigan need to help Willie face the unknown. Willie knew exactly what it was like to be strapped into Gruesome Gertie.

better with an ax

I reckon my time has plumb done come.

— WILLIE FRANCIS

By the early and mid-1800s, abolitionists, who had been clamoring for an end to slavery, began speaking out on the brutality of hanging, which "had no place in a civilized society." Much of the debate over capital punishment centered on biblical passages, with proponents arguing that God demanded "an eye for an eye and a tooth for a tooth," while opponents pointed to the Commandment, "Thou shalt not kill."

While most northern states were soon, at least, entertaining legislation to repeal the death penalty on the grounds that the punishment was cruel, it was in fact U.S. Senator Edward Livingston of Louisiana who led the most significant charge for the abolition of capital punishment. A former congressman from New York as well as mayor of New York City, Livingston moved in 1804 to New Orleans, where he had acquired a large law practice. Appointed to the Louisiana state legislature in 1821, he wrote the "Livingston Code" (published in both French and English), which provided for significant changes in criminal laws and procedures as well as for the abolition of capital punishment on the grounds that it was not an effective deterrent and that juries often freed guilty criminals rather than impose death sentences. Livingston's legal genius was praised throughout Europe—the United Provinces of Central America adopted his reform code—and his good friend President Andrew Jackson appointed him U.S. secretary of state in 1831. The state of Louisiana, however, never enacted the Livingston Code.

Until William Kemmler became the first beneficiary of a more "humane" execution, the method preferred by most sheriffs in those states that still permitted death sentences was death by hanging. Mostly conducted in public parks or the center of town and usually attracting large crowds, these morality lessons designed by the State to deter serious crimes generally proved to be abhorrent to those who witnessed them. In most cases, the condemned person's neck was not broken, and victims often "slowly strangled to death." Dangling from the gallows, frequently urinating and defecating themselves, they convulsed for long minutes in what newspaper reporters described as the "dance of death." Increasingly, public hangings were less a solemn, "civic ritual of retribution and reconciliation" and more a festive bout of "drunkenness, gambling, profanity and almost all kinds of debauchery" around the gallows.

Toward the end of the nineteenth century, proponents of capital punishment challenged anti-death penalty advocates by proposing the use of a means of execution more humane than hanging, and in 1886, the New York state legislature passed a bill to create a commission to "investigate the most humane and approved method" of execution. Behind the bill was Alfred P. Southwick, a dentist from Buffalo who had been collecting hundreds of stray dogs and killing them in a metal box with electric shocks. Southwick had secured the endorsement of the Society for Prevention of Cruelty to Animals (SPCA), which had been trying to find a method less cruel than gunshot and asphyxiation to destroy unwanted animals; the SPCA noted that dogs died "instantly and seemingly without pain" in the dentist's contraption. Southwick would soon after become known as "the father of the electric chair," but not without some help from the Wizard of Menlo Park.

Thomas Alva Edison made it known that he was opposed to capital punishment and refused to offer any advice when Southwick contacted him on behalf of the death penalty commission. Undaunted, Southwick pleaded that science and civilization demanded a "more humane method than the rope" in death sentences and begged Edison to give the commission the "benefit of your knowledge." Edison reconsidered. He and George Westinghouse had been engaged in "a great political, legal and marketing game" over the development of electricity for consumer use, with Westinghouse's alternating current emerging as a serious rival to Edison's direct current. In Southwick's plea, Edison saw an opportunity to bury Westinghouse: He recommended to Southwick and the commission that the "the most effective" machine to inflict "the least amount of suffering upon its victim" was, in fact, one utilizing alternating current, like the type being manufactured by Westinghouse.

Thomas Edison thus began the "war of currents" as he set out to convince consumers that it would be dangerous to use Westinghouse's alternating current electricity in their homes because it was lethal. In 1888 Edison began holding public executions of animals—dogs, calves, horses—outside his laboratory in West Orange, New Jersey, and of course he advertised the use, in doing so, of Westinghouse's alternating current, which he had gone to great lengths to obtain since Westinghouse had refused to sell him a generator. Killing criminals with electricity, or "Westinghousing" them, was "a good idea," Edison said, coining a new verb for the American lexicon. "It will be so lightning quick that the criminal can't suffer much." To further demonstrate the power of alternating current electricity, Edison fitted a Coney Island circus elephant named Topsy with copper-lined sandals on her feet, wired to a dynamo. A crowd of 1,500 people and Edison's cameras then witnessed Topsy take 6,000 volts of electricity, stiffen, and crash "over on her right side, dead."

Westinghouse was understandably livid. Facing a loss of millions of dollars in contracts as a result of Edison's public relations campaign, he tried to convince consumers that his electric system was safer than his competitor's. But Edison had more credibility, and Westinghouse was forced to resort to the courts if he wanted to stop the bad publicity resulting from these electrocutions. He contributed $100,000 in legal fees toward the appeal of William Kemmler before the U.S. Supreme Court in the hope that it would rule the electric chair cruel and unusual punishment, thereby ensuring that New York State would continue hanging its condemned prisoners. (Kemmler was on trial for the murder of his common-law wife.) During the Supreme Court's deliberations on whether electrocution fell into the category of cruel and unusual punishment in May of 1890, however, no condemned man had yet faced this method of execution and, hence, there were no accounts or studies of death penalty electrocutions on record to lend support to a finding either way.

After the death penalty commission had considered using lethal injections of morphine to execute condemned prisoners—an alternative rejected because it might "make death somewhat agreeable" and "rid it of its terrors"—and after George Westinghouse had lost his battle to convince the U.S. Supreme Court that death by electrocution was cruel and unusual punishment, William Kemmler was taken from his cell and led to the death chamber at Auburn Prison. When they reached the chair, a deputy sheriff fumbled with the straps, prompting Kemmler to say, "Don't get excited, Joe. I want you to make a good job of this."

Once Kemmler was secured to the chair, the warden spoke: "Good-bye, William," he said.

When the current hit him, Kemmler convulsed. His mouth "twisted into a ghastly grin," and his fist clenched with such force that a fingernail cut his palm and "blood trickled out onto the arm of the chair." After seventeen seconds the current stopped. Doctors pressed the flesh on Kemmler's face, then pronounced him dead.

The "father of the electric chair" faced the witnesses in attendance and announced, "This is the culmination of ten years work and study. We live in a higher civilization today." But behind him, Kemmler was suddenly gasping for breath.

"Great God!" someone cried. "He's alive!" A "purplish foam" dribbled from Kemmler's mouth, and he began shaking and moaning in the chair. Southwick wheeled around as someone shouted, "Turn on the current! Turn on the current instantly! This man is not dead!"

But with the voltmeter back to zero, Kemmler was forced to endure the current as it rebuilt. Kemmler began wheezing and struggling to breathe; his head began to smoke, and the back of his coat caught fire. Some witnesses were fainting and vomiting; others thought Kemmler was on the verge of regaining consciousness. All of them were horror-stricken. Finally, Kemmler went rigid. The current was shut down, and Kemmler, slumped in the chair, was pronounced dead by Dr. Edward C. Spitzka, who soon after predicted, "There will never be another electrocution."

Thomas Edison was less dour. "When the next man is placed in the chair to suffer the death penalty," Edison predicted, "that death will be accomplished instantly and without the scene at Auburn today." George Westinghouse, however, was horrified. "It has been a brutal affair," he said from his home in Pittsburgh. "They could have done better with an ax."

In spite of the grisly reality of this new form of capital punishment, the wheels of so-called progress moved inexorably forward. After the first electrocution of William Kemmler in 1890, use of the electric chair climbed steadily around the country and reached an all-time high by the 1930s when nearly two hundred condemned souls were being killed by a fatal surge of current each year. By then, too, the electric chair had worked its way into popular culture, and movie gangsters were routinely being sent to Sing Sing to "fry," or get "juiced," or sit in the "hot seat."

On February 9, 1934, four months before the Louisiana state legislature's House Appropriations Committee voted to spend $10,000 on the purchase of an electric chair, five Negroes were successively strapped into the same chair at Kilby Prison in Montgomery, Alabama, and electrocuted "swiftly and with little talk" in less than forty-five minutes. Actually, nine black men were scheduled to die that day in the brightly painted chair known as "Yellow Mama," but one had died in prison, one had received a thirty-day reprieve, and the other two had had their sentences commuted.

Following the lead of neighboring Alabama, the Mississippi state legislature passed Act 14 in May of 1940, replacing hanging with electrocution. The following month, Mississippi purchased, for the sale price of $3,980.45, an electric chair, generator, and truck built by International Harvester in Memphis, Tennessee. Louisiana received a similar deal from the farm equipment manufacturer, and shortly afterward, the state had its own portable electric chair. After June 1, 1941, all prisoners sentenced to death would be strapped into the state's new portable electric chair, which would be driven to the parish jail at which they were incarcerated.

But before the electric chair was available, there were still prisoners to be executed, and on March 7, 1941, Louisiana performed its last execution by hanging. Four escaped convicts were marched to the gallows at the Caldwell Parish courthouse in Columbia, Louisiana. Radio station KMLB of Monroe, in cooperation with the sheriff's department, had arranged to broadcast, live from their jail cells, the condemned men's final statements, which included the message that "crime doesn't pay" and one prisoner's opinion that "I think you have a mighty fine sheriff." But Louisiana Attorney General Eugene Stanley cancelled the plan for a live broadcast on the morning of the executions. The mass hanging lasted just under two hours.

After that point, "prisoners sentenced to death in Louisiana," one newspaper noted, would "have the 'satisfaction' of knowing they will die in one of the finest electric chairs in the country." On September 11, 1941, Eugene Johnson, convicted of robbing and murdering a white man in Livingston Parish, was electrocuted. He was the first of the twenty-one men and one woman to fry in the lap of Gruesome Gertie before Willie Francis, number twenty-three, got "lucky."

●   ♦   ●

By January 12, 1947, the day that Willie turned eighteen, two months had passed since his lawyers had argued his case before the Supreme Court. On January 13, Willie was standing by the small, barred window of his cell when Sheriff Ozenne brought him the news of the Supreme Court's decision. A cruel irony colored the moment, for on a radio in the guards' bullpen blared the voice of Louisiana's singing governor himself, Jimmie Davis, belting out his hit song, "You Are My Sunshine." The last legal barrier that might have prevented Willie's second trip to the electric chair had been toppled, and the State of Louisiana would move quickly. Davis's executive counsel, George Wallace, said that the governor would issue a new death warrant "once he receives the Supreme Court's mandate."

The news was a blow to Willie, who, according to Ozenne's account to reporters, "sat down hard on his cot and then got up and started walking around the room."

"It's the same thing all over again," Willie told the sheriff. "I got to start worrying again, and Boss, I thought I'd get out of it. But I guess a man's got to die sometime," he said. "And I reckon my time has plumb done come.

Ozenne lingered for a moment. "This time it'll be different," Willie told him. "That electric chair is going to work." Ozenne offered to inform Willie's family, then asked if there was anything he could do.

Willie smiled politely. "No, thanks," he told the sheriff. "If I need you, I'll let you know. I got four bucks and some funny books and the good Lord's Bible, and I still got the breath in my chest. No, thanks."

An editorial in the *Pittsburgh Courier* noted Willie's poise when he received the bad news. "Here speak the poet and the philosopher out of the mouth of an unlettered boy, a voice from the mudsill of a color caste-ridden society, calmly uttering sentiments that somehow come out as a cleansing fresh breeze to dispel the miasma of stuffy and distorted legalism, or a hymn to drown out the moans of violated justice."

Bertrand DeBlanc arrived at the jail and visited Willie soon after he himself had heard the news. Staggered and despondent, he was at a loss for words, and it was Willie who ended up assuring DeBlanc that everything would be okay. Once he'd composed himself, De-Blanc told reporters that Willie "is a lot calmer than he was last May when he walked away from the chair. He's amazing. And he's still got a chance, since the Supreme Court ruling against him was only 5 to 4. We're filing for another hearing as soon as possible."

Reporters visited Willie in his cell, where one described him as "singularly cool" upon learning of the decision. "Death and me is old neighbors," Willie said. "But remember this, I'm a closer neighbor of the Lord."

Did he have nightmares, a writer wanted to know? "Everybody has, I guess," Willie said. "No, the ghost of Mr. Thomas doesn't come back to sit beside me in my cell at night. I haven't seen him, anyway." Willie told another reporter that he was "right interested to find out if I can die like the man I thought I was." He added, "I always sort of wondered if I was a brave man. Now I guess maybe I'm going to find out. And I'm gonna find out the hard way, Boss, so there won't be no doubt in my mind when I leave." Echoing the thoughts of Father Hannigan, Willie told the reporter, "A lot of men never find out. A lot of men die still wondering if they was the man they thought they was."

Later, Willie was nonchalant about the Court's decision. "Five of the Justices voted against me and four for me. That's pretty close to happiness, I guess. I am not complaining or anything like that, because I know down in my heart everybody has tried to do the right thing for me and for everybody else. It is just that there has never been another case like mine before and I see how hard it is to say what is the right thing in my case. If I ever get to heaven I guess I'll get to know."

One reporter wondered if Willie could overhear "the various conversations" outside his cell, like those from the bullpen of the fourth-floor jail where Deputy Gus Walker, Sheriff Gilbert Ozenne, and the jailer, Clemarie Norris, sometimes gathered, for their conversations bluntly summarized Willie's prospects and the task before Bertrand DeBlanc. "His lawyer can take his case wherever he wishes," the reporter himself overheard, "and the NAACP or any other of the agitating organizations may protest, but that's one nigger who is going to die."

strong and easy boy

May God forgive you. Man will not.

—ADRIAN CONAN DOYLE

When news of the Supreme Court's decision reached the press, newspapers across the country reported it, and many editorial writers lambasted it. One writer in Louisiana suggested that, when Willie goes to the chair, he ought to "sit on the Bible and the Constitution so that all three be destroyed at once."

"Where five men weigh the legal arguments in one fashion and four in another," columnist Max Lerner wrote, "the margin of legal doubt should surely have been great enough to allow a sense of humanity to operate."

Especially critical of Justice Frankfurter was the *Pittsburgh Press*, which commented on the "crowning irony" in Frankfurter's admission that he "was 'strongly drawn' by the views of the minority, but voted the other way because the Supreme Court has no legal right to interfere with a 'state's insistence on its pound of flesh.'" The newspaper observed that, "if the chair works the next time, Willie Francis will be just as dead as if the high judges had agreed 9 to 0 on what the law requires and permits. Then he won't have to worry about ironies."

James Marlow of the Associated Press wrote an open letter to Willie Francis:

Dear Willie:

I thought you'd like to know how it was when nine men you never saw, sitting in a marble palace, talked about your future.

You stutter badly and don't read very well but still this will tell you a little of what it was like here yesterday.

You may not understand it, but you were very important for a little while in a very important place, the U.S. Supreme Court.

It's all marble, not like any court you ever saw down there in bayou country. It has great, red velvet curtains, a real palace.

And the nine men—everyone of them famous—sat in a row in black gowns behind a long walnut desk.

They're the nine justices of the Supreme Court. And for 45 minutes they talked of nothing but Willie Francis.

They already had talked a lot about you among themselves, behind closed doors. But yesterday they talked for the whole world to hear.

It all started when Justice Reed suddenly mentioned "Willie Francis, colored citizen of Louisiana."

The other justices listened very carefully. They were all deeply interested for a couple of reasons.

This was their decision they were announcing about a human life, yours. It was important to them.

And, besides, you were making history. Your case is what lawyers call historic. Nothing like it had happened before. It was all on the record.

Marlow went on to fill in the background of Willie's arrest, trial, and execution; then he continued:

Four of the nine justices said it would be cruel and you shouldn't have to sit in the electric chair again.

But five of the nine said it wasn't cruel. They said it was an accident with no one to blame for it, that the chair didn't work.

So back you go to the chair again. But you almost made it: Five to four. Pretty close. But five was one too many.

Justice Frankfurter spoke up. He was one of the five. He used to teach law in college. He has a wide forehead and white hair.

He spoke for a long time, explaining why he thought you ought to die. He used some very big words you wouldn't understand.

He said the accident to the chair in May was an "innocent misadventure." (I thought you'd like to know that.)

And he said the whole situation was very "disturbing." I thought you'd like to know that, too.

I bet you never dreamed in all your life that some day you'd be very "disturbing" to a Supreme Court justice.

But in the end he agreed with the other four justices, that send-
ing you back to the chair isn't cruel.

The *Norfolk State News* stated that the Court's decision "does not find widespread public acceptance," contrary to Frankfurter's belief that Willie's fate of a second execution was the "consensus of society."

"It would be unfortunate, indeed," the *New York Law Journal* stated, "if this young colored boy should now be put to death over the protests of four Justices of the Supreme Court of the United States. Any chance for the further infliction of injuries upon society could be eliminated by his permanent incarceration."

Noted radio and newspaper commentator Walter Winchell made a public plea to Governor Jimmie Davis. "You can commute the sentence to life," Winchell stated. "If Justices Frank Murphy and Frankfurter were in doubt in placing their vote with the majority in sending Francis to the chair for a second time, certainly you, Mr. Governor, should be in doubt."

Other publications praised the majority opinion. Conceding that "mercy has a useful and rightful place in any democratic system of law enforcement," the *Washington Post* then added that "mercy ought to be applied on some other basis than mere mishap in carrying out a sentence." The *Times-Picayune* editorialized, "It would be anything but comforting in the way of criminal justice were such superficial interpretations of the Constitutional safeguards for accused and convicted persons to prevail," in commenting on Wright and DeBlanc's argument before the Supreme Court.

And in Birmingham, Alabama, an *Age Herald* editorial proffered this send-off for "poor, ignorant Willie Francis."

So long, Willie. You're going to die again. But the people of America have given a lot of their time thinking about your case. It's cost the country a good bit of money, more than you could ever earn if you lived to be a hundred. . . .

When you go this time, Willie, walk in straight and sit down and smile and say "good-bye" in a strong voice. Maybe you'd have been better off if you died all the way that first time. Take it strong and easy boy.

But no one responded to the Court's decision with more passion—or more distaste—than NAACP secretary Walter White. White was familiar with southern justice, but he had clung to his belief that the Supreme Court of the United States would deal fairly with Willie Francis. His association with A. P. Tureaud enabled White to stay abreast of the case, which he had been following closely. His editorial ran in newspapers around the country; it no doubt echoed the private sentiments of both Bertrand DeBlanc and Skelly Wright. White wrote:

William Shakespeare should have been in the United States Supreme Court on Jan. 13. Had he been there he most surely would have ruefully remembered his famous line, "The quality of mercy is not strained." For on that day five Justices of the Court—Mr. Chief Justice Fred M. Vinson, and Mssrs. Justices Hugo Black, Robert H. Jackson, Stanley F. Reed and Felix Frankfurter—hewed bitterly close to the line of "justice" and the "law" while humanity and equity hung their heads in shame.

After describing the mental torment of Willie's "dying but not quite achieving death," White lashed at the justices in the majority.

And now five men wrapped snugly in the silken robes of the high court and seated in the marble aloofness of the building in Washington dedicated to equity and human kindness as well as the strict letter of the law have said that Willie Francis must sit again in the Louisiana electric chair—and again, and again, and again until the sentence of the court that electric currents be made to pass through his body until he is dead has been fulfilled.

Gentlemen, you have done your duty. Cold justice has been upheld. Only if there be pity in the heart of the governor of Louisiana can Willie Francis' second—or maybe third or fourth—long walk of the last mile be stayed.

We hope, gentlemen of the majority of the United States Supreme Court, that you will not jump also in pain in your warm comfortable beds in Washington the night Willie Francis again jams his feet against the floor when the switch is thrown.

Messrs. Burton, Douglas, Murphy and Rutledge need fear no such bad dreams the night Willie Francis crosses Jordan because they tempered justice with mercy in their dissenting opinion.

Swing low, sweet chariot.

White said the column was "the most praised—and damned—of any piece I have written in a long time," and it "brought down on my head an avalanche of letters."

White was not the only one at the NAACP angry with the Supreme Court. An indignant Thurgood Marshall had been speaking to similarly outraged "Hollywood people" who had been following the case. Knowing well that Governor Jimmie Davis was enamored with show business and spent a great deal of time in Los Angeles, Marshall thought some "interested friends" might be able to apply some political pressure on Davis. Among others, the actors Burgess Meredith and John Garfield approached the governor about the possibility of his intervening on Willie Francis's behalf. Davis told them he had "no control whatsoever."

Marshall wrote Daniel Byrd, president of the NAACP's New Orleans branch and former member of the Harlem Globetrotters basketball team, that "we should corral our forces, especially in Louisiana, and make every effort to get this commutation." Byrd set his sights high. Noting that all three members of the Louisiana Pardons Board were Roman Catholic, as was Willie Francis, and that the Catholic Church did not believe in capital punishment, Byrd sought to appeal to Pope Pius XII. "If the Pope would ask for mercy," Byrd wrote to Marshall, "it would certainly give the Board a reasonable out for recommending commutation and not create any political revenge on the part of the White Citizens of St. Martin Parish, which is practically wholly Catholic." Byrd felt that "one person on the Board would appreciate a good reason to commute the sentence" and that such a plea from the pope "would eliminate any political apprehension he would have."

The NAACP's attempt to reach the Holy See did not get very far, however. Bishop Jules B. Jeanmard of the diocese of Lafayette, who had proposed Father Maurice Rousseve for the parish of Notre Dame Church in St. Martinville, replied to Byrd, "Whilst I cannot but commend you for your zeal in trying to save Willie Francis from the electric-chair, I do not think it would be fair or proper on my part to do so for the reason that the Holy Father cannot be expected to intervene in individual cases of this nature." Bishop Jeanmard closed by saying he was "sincerely hoping and praying that our efforts in behalf of this poor boy will be successful."

It is doubtful that Felix Frankfurter was unaware of the widespread controversy surrounding the decision, or of Walter White's eloquent and well-circulated criticism. Coming off the term he viewed as "the worst" in the Court's history, he was fully cognizant that the 5–4 decision allowing Louisiana to return Willie Francis to the electric chair had only battered the Court's image even more in the eyes of the public. Frankfurter's detractors often accused him of being cold and impervious to criticism; in the matter of Willie Francis, however, he soon proved to be anything but. In truth, the criticism regarding Willie's case stung him, and it came to him in letters from around the world that expressed everything from disappointment to horror over his and the Court's ruling against Willie.

Reflecting the emotional tone of a country still reeling from World War II, one letter writer concluded, "It is almost impossible to believe that a human being, who does not happen to be a Jap or a Nazi, should condemn Willie Francis to death a second time!" Adrian Conan Doyle, son of Sir Arthur Conan Doyle who famously authored the Sherlock Holmes detective mysteries, wrote simply in his letter to Frankfurter, "May God forgive you. Man will not."

In his concurrence on the Willie Francis case, Frankfurter stated that Supreme Court justices should not impose their private views upon their judgments, but rather they should determine "the consensus of society's opinion, which, for purposes of due process, is the standard enjoined by the Constitution." The method and measure by which Frankfurter was able to ascertain the "consensus of society's opinion" remain a mystery, however. Surely, whatever societal consensus in St. Martinville he might have discerned from court documents differed from that of the country at large. National polls on the Francis case were not taken, but even if they had been, it is still not likely that Justice Frankfurter would have deferred to public opinion in rendering his decision. In fact, thousands of letters and telegrams urging clemency for Willie Francis had been and still were pouring into the offices of the governor of Louisiana, while editorials around the country were condemning a second execution; yet, in face of these facts, Frankfurter managed somehow to believe that he had correctly measured the pulse of society when he'd rendered Willie his destiny.

More puzzling is the fact that Frankfurter admitted to being "deeply disturbed" by his vote in the Francis case, no doubt because he disapproved of capital punishment. In a later case (*Haley v. Ohio*), in which a fifteen-year-old black youth was convicted of murder and sentenced to life imprisonment on the basis of a confession that may have been coerced, Frankfurter ruled that the "deeply rooted feelings of the community" dictated a reversal of the youth's conviction and punishment. Despite Frankfurter's often stated conviction that a Supreme Court justice should eschew "personal feelings" when arriving at a decision, by applying vague, subjective measures like the "consensus of society's opinion" and "deeply rooted feelings of the community" to his rulings, he himself was doing exactly that. Of course, so were the dissenters in the Willie Francis case; they had clearly determined by virtue of their private views to save Willie and "advance humanitarianism," according to Miller and Bowman in *Death by Installments*, whereas Frankfurter "relied on his private view to advance an abstract judicial philosophy. That philosophy was more important to Frankfurter than an impoverished youth's life."

Not long after the Supreme Court announced its decision in the Francis case, Frankfurter received a letter from Mrs. Harold Evans of New York. She wrote:

> That boy committed the crime at 15 and since has gone through the valley of the shadow of death and God gave him another chance and you took it away from him. As a white mother please help this boy. Had he been white he could have been sent to a reformatory in the first place, or perhaps gotten a suspended sentence. Perhaps you could instruct their governor to help him. Thanks for what you will do to help this child.

Frankfurter received countless letters during his years as a justice of the Supreme Court. Normally, he chose not to acknowledge those regarding opinions of the Court. Frankfurter usually let the decisions speak for themselves. But Mrs. Evans's letter struck a nerve and moved Frankfurter to respond just days later: "You will permit me to say that I quite appreciate your compassionate feeling on the Willie Francis case. I share it. But a judge of this Court isn't God—he is not even the Governor of the State, in whom is vested the power of executive clemency. You may care to see the opinion of the Court in this case."

However much Frankfurter stood by his contention that he had accurately measured the "consensus of society," and despite having barred his own "compassionate feeling" in the Willie Francis case, he still found Louisiana's conduct in the case "shocking" and "a barbaric thing to do." He'd later admit that the Francis case "told on my conscience a great deal. I was very much bothered by the problem, it offended my personal sense of decency to do this. Something inside of me was very unhappy, but I did not see that it [the second execution] violated due process of law."

Perhaps guided by his conscience, or maybe prodded by Mrs. Evans's letter urging him to "help this child"—and despite the fact that the Supreme Court had already rendered its decision, which he believed, as a Frankfurter biographer notes, "provided a classic proof of the judicial process at its very best"—Felix Frankfurter set out on an extraordinary and virtually unprecedented course: behind the backs of the other justices, Felix Frankfurter sought to effectively overturn the Willie Francis decision.

In his concurring opinion, and in not particularly subtle language, Frankfurter had expressed a "personal revulsion" at the state's "insistence on its pound of flesh," but evidently Frankfurter was beginning to realize that his broad hint had been lost on the "singing governor" of Louisiana. So Frankfurter turned to Monte E. Lemann.

A highly respected member of the Louisiana bar, Monte E. Lemann had remained friendly with his former Harvard Law School roommate since their graduation in 1905. In 1938, Frankfurter, in recommending Lemann to President Roosevelt for an appointment on the U.S. Court of Appeals for the Fifth Circuit—an offer that Lemann declined—Frankfurter described Lemann as "about the best lawyer south of the Mason and Dixon line." Noting further that Lemann "really cared about the social reforms of the New Deal," Frankfurter characterized him as being mindful of "the basic function of the law as the body of arrangements for realizing social needs," a man whose "progressive outlook" reflected Roosevelt's own political philosophy.

On February 3, 1947, in a letter to Lemann, Frankfurter exhorted the "progressive" Louisiana attorney to use his influence on Davis to have the death sentence of Willie Francis commuted to life imprisonment. In the letter, Frankfurter spoke of the bar's responsibility in general to intervene and "clean up" any legal or judicial "mess" created by the courts of a state, for to do so "would be true to the best traditions of our profession and save the State much future misery." Then, more particularly, Frankfurter warned Lemann, "I have little doubt that if Louisiana allows Francis to go to his death, it will needlessly cast a cloud upon Louisiana for many years to come, and, what is more important, probably leave many of its citizens with disquietude."

The justice who had cast the deciding vote that would ultimately return Willie Francis to the electric chair was recruiting Lemann to save Willie's life. Frankfurter acknowledged to Lemann the division within the Supreme Court on the Francis case, then asked, "Is there any possible reason for saying that, if Francis is allowed to go to his death instead of imprisonment for life, the restraints against crimes of violence will be relieved?"

Concluding, Frankfurter openly expressed the emotional toll his decision on the case was taking on him. "This cause has been so heavily on my conscience that I finally could not overcome the impulse to write you," wondering if—or hoping that—the State of Louisiana could show "humaneness" and "compassion" by granting clemency to Willie Francis. "It is difficult for me to believe that clemency would not be forthcoming, whatsoever may be the machinery of your state for its exercise, if leading members of the bar pressed upon the authorities that even to err on the side of humaneness in the Francis situation can do no possible harm and might strengthen the forces of goodwill, compassion, and wisdom in society."

When Frankfurter mailed his letter to Monte Lemann, he also sent a copy of it to Justice Burton. It was marked "Strictly Confidential" and had the following note attached: "H. H. B., For your information, F. F."

Shortly after receiving Frankfurter's letter, Monte Lemann wrote to Judge James D. Simon, who had formerly been his student at Tulane University Law School. Certainly, for a fourth-generation trial judge with a family history in the Louisiana State Supreme Court to grant clemency to a black youth convicted of murder in his own jurisdiction could present serious political problems down the road, and Lemann addressed this potential political albatross by noting that, in their jurisprudence, the English, who are not "soft people," often took "considerations of humanity" into account. He further noted that "it does not seem to me to be a determining factor whether electric current passed through Willie Francis' body or not. The controlling circumstance would be the fact that he was exposed to the ordeal of an abortive execution."

Then, without specifically mentioning Frankfurter by name (though it was hardly necessary as Lemann's friendship with Frankfurter was well known, especially to Simon), Lemann underscored the importance of the Willie Francis case before the Louisiana Pardons Board: "I realize that the eyes of the world are in a sense upon us in this case, because I have myself had communications from lawyers of high standing, for whose opinions I have great respect, one of whom wrote me recently that he felt it would be a serious blot upon our State if Francis was permitted to be executed. These considerations," Lemann wrote, "do not, of course, relieve the Pardons Board of its responsibility of reaching its own decision, but I imagine that you and the other members of the Board will feel as much influenced as I have been by opinions so entitled to respect."

Lemann concluded by pleading that, "where at the very least there is so much room for doubt as to what is the proper course to adopt, the further punishment of Francis is not as important as adherence to the highest standards of decency and humaneness which a large and informed body of public opinion feels would be betrayed by Francis's execution." As Miller and Bowman note, "It is ironic that Lemann's plea to Judge Simon" should assert that a "large and informed body of public opinion" would be betrayed by the execution of Willie Francis, when Frankfurter stated in his concurrence that a second execution attempt would *not* be "repugnant to the conscience of mankind" or the "consensus of society."

On April 23, 1947, Frankfurter sent to each of his fellow Supreme Court justices a copy of Monte Lemann's letter to Judge Simon. With it, he included the following note: "Dear Brethren: Monte Lemann is, I suppose, unexcelled at the Louisiana bar. He happens to be an old and close friend so it is natural for him to send the enclosure. I thought it might interest the Brethren. F. F." Notably, Frankfurter did not mention to the other justices the fact that he himself had reached out to Lemann and asked his old college roommate to act on Willie's behalf. Justice Burton, apparently, did not raise the point either. Also on April 23, Frankfurter wrote again to Lemann and praised his old friend's efforts. "You could not have made a better plea for saving Francis from death than by your letter to Judge Simon. Your letter may perhaps be more effective than a formal association as counsel for Francis."

Throughout his career, according to Miller and Bowman, Frankfurter consistently advocated judicial self-restraint, which ultimately left litigants with no option other than to attempt to "influence the political process." In the *Gobitis* case seven years earlier, Frankfurter had voted to reverse the holdings of the Philadelphia courts and urged the powerless litigants to seek recourse in a political process that had already failed them. In fact, though, Frankfurter had shorn the litigants of their last hope: a ruling in their favor by the U.S. Supreme Court. Or perhaps Frankfurter had known then, as he may have fully realized in the Willie Francis case as well, that the political process had indeed failed the litigants once and was sure to fail them again. As Miller and Bowman write, "Frankfurter was deeply troubled by the consequence of his decisive vote and enmeshed in an intellectual swamp, his secret attempt to gain clemency for Willie Francis can only be recognized for what it was: a pitiful attempt by a jurist to assuage his conscience for allowing a youth to be put to death in the name of abstract principles of judicial self-restraint."

By the spring of 1947, both Lieutenant Governor Emile Verret and Attorney General Fred LeBlanc had been mentioned as possible gubernatorial candidates for the 1948 election, and Judge Simon, a former state senator, likely had his eye on election to the supreme court of Louisiana. Despite whatever political influence might be brought to bear on them by "lawyers of high standing" or "opinions so entitled to respect," not one of these three members of the Louisiana Pardons Board had anything to gain by recommending that the life of Willie Francis be spared.

a disgraceful and inhuman
exhibition

I've gotta die.

— WILLIE FRANCIS

Sitting at his desk on a late afternoon in February 1947, Bertrand DeBlanc was mulling over his options. Despite the Supreme Court decision, he was unwilling to give up on Willie's case, and with Skelly Wright, he had filed a desperate petition for rehearing with the Court—a petition based on an amendment that Louisiana had added to the electrocution statute two weeks after the botched execution in St. Martinville in May of 1946. The amendment stated that the operator of the electric chair "shall be a competent electrician who shall not have been previously convicted of a felony." Under this statute, both Ephie Foster and Vincent Venezia would have been prohibited from operating the electric chair, for Foster was not a competent electrician, and Venezia was a convicted felon.

The Supreme Court rules state that a petition for rehearing will not be granted "except at the instance of a Justice who concurred in the judgment or decision and with the concurrence of a majority of the Court." Once again, Felix Frankfurter was afforded the opportunity to thwart the execution of Willie Francis that he so opposed.

Instead, he voted not to grant the petition, which the Court then denied.

Having failed twice before the nation's highest court, DeBlanc figured that he had exhausted all legal options. It seemed that he could do nothing more to prevent the State of Louisiana from sending Willie back to the chair; nevertheless, he sent a telegram to the New York office of the NAACP asking for $5,000 so that he and Wright could further pursue a rehearing. Walter White thought the telegram "impudent" and bristled at the fact that DeBlanc had not provided the NAACP with any legal documents from Willie's case or allowed them to intervene in any fashion, except by now paying the lawyer a fee. But Thurgood Marshall pointed out to White that DeBlanc was not "demanding" a fee, rather he was requesting one, and that from a public relations perspective, it was important that the NAACP not distance itself from either DeBlanc or Willie Francis. Still, DeBlanc never received the fee he requested.

DeBlanc was preparing yet another plea for the Louisiana Pardons Board when Louie M. Cyr, an old law school friend and former city judge in New Iberia, stopped by for a visit. Amused as Cyr often was at some of his friend's unorthodox positions, he admired the fact that DeBlanc, whom he considered an unusual and "determined fellow," cared not a damn what other people thought. Cyr knew DeBlanc to be very conscientious, but he was surprised on that late February afternoon to learn that DeBlanc was still working on the Willie Francis case. Cyr had been under the impression that there was nothing more to be done. It was a shame, Cyr sighed, that a young boy had to suffer so much anguish because of two drunken executioners.

Cyr's remark left DeBlanc dumbfounded. It was the first he'd ever heard anything about two drunken executioners.

Cyr assured him it was true. A day after the botched execution, George "Squirrel" Etie, the one-armed owner of the Green Lantern, had visited him in his New Iberia office and had given him an eye-witness account of the entire spectacle. While Etie had witnessed other executions, Willie's, he'd said, was the most horrible, "most disgraceful and inhumane" exhibition he had ever seen, in no small part because the men responsible for executing Willie "were so drunk that it was impossible for them to have known what they were doing."

Etie had described how Willie's nose had flattened so that it no longer even looked like a nose and how his lips had swelled beneath the leather hood until they were protruding from the slit. Willie was awake, Etie had said, but he was in intense pain; he was jumping and kicking so much that he'd ultimately lifted the 300-pound chair six inches off the ground—it had made a full quarter turn before coming to rest.

It was Etie's opinion, according to Cyr, that the reason the execution had failed rested with the two drunken executioners, Foster and Venezia. Etie had told Cyr how the muzzy Foster had cursed Willie the moment the execution was aborted. Not many hours before, in the early morning of May 3, Etie had evidently accompanied Foster and Venezia and others to various saloons in New Iberia, where he had witnessed the two men from Angola inviting people to attend Willie's execution.

DeBlanc was horrified. It was bad enough that the State of Louisiana had placed the execution in the hands of two men like Foster and Venezia; worse, though, was the fact that, if DeBlanc had had this information earlier, he could have used it in his appeal to the Louisiana Pardons Board or in his attempt to sway just one of the Supreme Court majority who had referred to Willie's ordeal as "an innocent misadventure." DeBlanc and Wright had argued before the Court that the botched execution demanded a full investigation, but if DeBlanc himself had done an investigation, he might have uncovered the information about his client's drunken executioners, which might have been enough to save Willie.

Over the next several weeks, DeBlanc focused on the facts of the failed execution. He managed to find another witness to the execution attempt on May 3, 1946—Ignace Doucet of St. Martin Parish—who swore in an affidavit that he saw the two men with the electric chair "drinking during the whole last part of the morning." He also confirmed that "the man who pulled the switch to electrocute the prisoner Willie Francis was the same tall large man whom I saw drinking."

DeBlanc attempted to get an affidavit from George Etie, but the owner of the Green Lantern was reluctant. It's unclear if Etie's reticence came from fear of reprisal or from the belief that it would simply be bad for business for him to be testifying for Bertrand De-Blanc in his effort to save Willie Francis's life. Or perhaps Etie had attended the execution in the St. Martinville jail at the express invitation of Ephie Foster, and he wanted to be involved no further. Whatever the case, Etie refused to sign, so DeBlanc was forced, instead, to use the secondhand account of the events in Cyr's conversation with Etie, which was recorded in a sworn affidavit.

Newly energized and in possession of Doucet's and Cyr's two sworn affidavits to demonstrate that the State of Louisiana had in fact failed in its responsibilities, DeBlanc drove to New Orleans, where he appeared before the Pardons Board and pled again for Willie's life. Secretary Lawrence Sauer of the Pardons Board admitted that his office had received more than seven thousand letters, "some from as far away as Europe," pleading a pardon for Willie Francis. Surely, under the newfound circumstances of negligence on the part of the State of Louisiana, DeBlanc argued, his client's death sentence should be commuted to life imprisonment.

The board took the new evidence under consideration. On April 22, 1947, it announced its ruling. Willie Francis would receive no mercy.

Willie was eating boiled meat and potatoes in his cell that April afternoon when a journalist delivered to him the news that, once again, the Louisiana Pardons Board had rejected DeBlanc's appeal.

Willie glanced at the Bible on his cot. "I'm gonna die," he said softly. "There ain't nothin' I can do. I've gotta die."

"It's pretty tough," the journalist replied.

"It ain't tough," Willie answered. "I've gotta die."

Five days later, on April 28, 1947, the State of Louisiana concurred. With the singing governor Jimmie Davis again out of state, Acting Governor Emile Verret signed Willie's death warrant. Willie Francis was to be executed on May 9, 1947, between the hours of noon and 3:00 p.m. Reporters in the New Iberia jail asked Willie if he wouldn't mind posing for a picture. They handed Willie a calendar opened to the month of May 1947. Sitting on his cot with his hair grown out again, Willie drew a big circle around the ninth of May, a Friday. He tilted the calendar toward a photographer and raised his eyebrows for the picture. There is a good-natured smile on his face. But there is also a glint of unease, as if the photographer had him hold the pose a little too long and, in that moment, the smile faded a bit as the significance of the date settled on him. Willie Francis was the only person on earth who knew exactly what it was like to go to the electric chair, and in less than two weeks, he'd be going back.

Bertrand DeBlanc grew desperate. With next to no legal avenues left to pursue, DeBlanc radically shifted his strategy. In a marked departure from his earlier argument that the State of Louisiana had violated Willie's constitutional rights in its ruling to return him to the electric chair, DeBlanc decided to request a new trial on the grounds that evidence germane to the case had not been presented in the first trial. He filed papers with Judge James D. Simon in which he stated that Mrs. Van Brocklin should have been called as a witness, since her testimony in the coroner's inquest "would have been material, valuable and of a nature to serve the ends of justice." "Justice," DeBlanc added, "would be served by granting a new trial."

Since the day that Frederick Francis, seeking a lawyer for his son, had appeared on DeBlanc's doorstep, the Cajun attorney had implemented a legal strategy based on the premise that sending Willie

Francis back to the electric chair amounted to cruel and unusual punishment. From the outset, DeBlanc had been adamant in his assertion that the innocence or guilt of his client was immaterial, for he was not trying to free Willie Francis—he was attempting merely to have his sentence commuted to life imprisonment. This strategy had enabled DeBlanc to maintain his reputation in St. Martinville as an "unusual" but determined man of principle.

Now taking a stance more in line with the strategies that the NAACP employed when it came to the legal aid of condemned blacks in the South, DeBlanc had decided to argue that the all-white jury had erred in convicting a young Negro for the murder of a white man. This change of heart must have finally pleased Tureaud, as *Louisiana Weekly* described the "valiant attempts of Bertrand De-Blanc, brilliant young Lafayette, La lawyer" to save Willie's life. De-Blanc was surely aware that attacking the jury and the prosecution would have negative consequences for him and his career. For one thing, he would now be viewed as an agitator—as if he were some New York lawyer sympathetic to the cause of the NAACP who'd come into town to impose northern values on the South. For another, DeBlanc's new strategy was likely to turn white public opinion against Willie in Louisiana. But DeBlanc also knew that he had no other options left and very little time.

Any short-term affection Tureaud may have had for DeBlanc quickly evaporated. In the event that NAACP attorneys might attempt to usurp the case from him, DeBlanc wrote a letter on May 1, 1947, to M. A. Barras, the chief deputy clerk of court in St. Martinville, stating that, in the case of Willie Francis, DeBlanc was "the only attorney authorized to initiate any proceedings in your Court." Furthermore, and no doubt with A. P. Tureaud in mind, DeBlanc warned that, if "some unscrupulous attorney" attempts to initiate any proceedings, "I will not hesitate to bring disbarment proceedings against any such attorney and I would appreciate your calling this to their attention."

On May 5, in what must have felt like an exercise in futility, De-Blanc argued his motion for a new trial before Judge Simon and District Attorney Pecot, the two men least likely to find fault with the criminal case against Willie Francis. Pecot simply countered that such a motion as DeBlanc was proposing would have to have been filed as a Bill of Exception at the time of Willie Francis's trial or before sentencing. Willie's public defenders had filed no such bill, and the deadline to appeal had long passed; DeBlanc's motion came too late. Not surprisingly, Judge Simon agreed with Pecot. He denied DeBlanc's motion for a new trial. DeBlanc then asked Simon to suspend Willie's sentence pending an appeal to the supreme court of Louisiana—a request that Simon denied immediately from the bench.

The next morning, standing before Judge Simon, DeBlanc argued that the State of Louisiana had, as a result of the Willie Francis case, amended Article 570 of the Louisiana Code of Criminal Procedure to the effect that the operator of the electric chair *"shall be a competent electrician who shall not have been previously convicted of a felony"*—an amendment, DeBlanc asserted, that amounted to an admission on the part of the state of Louisiana legislature "that the failure of the execution of Willie Francis resulted from the incompetence of the execution officials." Once again, Simon quickly dismissed DeBlanc's motion.

That day in the St. Martinville courthouse left Bertrand DeBlanc convinced that every opportunity for Willie in Louisiana had now truly been exhausted. "Well, I guess it's all over now," he told a reporter. "I shall not try to get the matter before the United States Supreme Court again." Yet, if the execution of Willie Francis were to be stayed, the reprieve would have to come from outside the state. So the next morning, DeBlanc called Skelly Wright, who had been expecting the denials DeBlanc received in Louisiana and for two weeks had been preparing a petition for habeas corpus to be filed with the U.S. Supreme Court. With the date of execution looming, both lawyers knew that in all probability this was going to be their last chance to save Willie Francis.

On that same morning of May 6, 1947, the dull gray 1941 International Harvester cornbinder pulled up behind the St. James Parish jail in Convent, Louisiana, where Gruesome Gertie was unloaded and conveyed into a small execution chamber. At 12:11 p.m., twenty-eight-year-old Alonzo Ellis "Blackie" Jones was ushered into the chamber and strapped into the chair. The sheriff asked Blackie if he had anything to say. "I want you to know that in my heart," Jones said, "there is no malice towards those who have given false witness against me. They have my complete forgiveness. In a few minutes I shall go to my God, the beginning, and only the beginning of a better life than we can ever know on earth."

At 12:21 p.m. the switch was thrown. Seven minutes later, Blackie Jones was pronounced dead. Gruesome Gertie was then driven back to Angola, but she wouldn't stay there long. In just two days, again loaded into the back of the cornbinder, she'd be heading south, then west, into Evangeline country—back to the town of St. Martinville.

Bertrand DeBlanc flew to Washington, DC, on the morning of May 8, 1947, the last full day of oral argument in the Supreme Court for the October 1946 term. After studying the opinions of the Court on Willie's case, he and Wright had decided that their best bet to save Willie lay in an attempt at changing the mind of Felix Frankfurter. Wright believed that Burton's dissent was worded in a way that made it seem as though it had at one point been the majority opinion, and he felt there might have been a last-minute change of vote, rendering it the minority opinion. In his concurrence, Frankfurter had clung to the reasoning that, if the execution had failed because of recklessness on the part of the State, then due process would have been denied. Wright felt that his petition satisfactorily proved that the actions on the part of the two drunken executioners were tantamount to wanton recklessness, and he hoped that he might therefore be able to convince one of the justices in the majority, most likely Frankfurter, that the electrocution of Willie Francis on May 3, 1946, was clearly not, as Frankfurter had described it, "an innocent misadventure."

Neither Wright nor DeBlanc likely knew it at the time, but Felix Frankfurter had, in 1940, demonstrated a flair for the dramatic when, as an associate justice, he intervened on behalf of a death row inmate just moments before his execution. Joe Vernon had been sentenced to death after his conviction for killing a young college student in Alabama, but the Supreme Court had twice refused to hear his case. On the night Vernon was to die, his desperate attorney called the Supreme Court and asked specifically for Justice Frankfurter. The Court managed to reach Frankfurter at his home, and after speaking with the attorney, Frankfurter, new to the bench and still uncertain as to the extent of his power and authority, called a deputy clerk at the Court and shouted, "Stop the execution!"

When it was determined that Frankfurter did indeed have such authority, the clerk telephoned the warden at Vernon's prison, who sternly informed the clerk that he took orders only from the governor of Alabama—"not from some stranger on the phone." The clerk finally managed to contact the attorney general of Alabama, who was able to halt Vernon's execution "with only minutes to spare." The U.S. Supreme Court subsequently heard and reversed *Vernon v. Alabama* in 1941.

Wright and DeBlanc felt that they had stumbled across the kind of information that would stun the justices and put a halt to Willie's execution. According to Wright's petition, "the executioner and other persons connected with carrying out the execution were so drunk that it was impossible for them to know what they were doing." It was "negligence on the part of the State," since there was no competent electrician on site, "only a convict." He added, "The scene was a disgraceful and inhuman exhibition, that as soon as the switch controlling the current was taken off, the drunken executioner cursed Francis and told him he would be back to finish electrocuting him, and if the electricity did not kill him he would kill him with a rock." Wright concluded by accusing Foster and Venezia of being motivated by "sadistic impulses and either willfully, deliberately or intentionally applied less than a minimal lethal current, for the purpose of torturing the petitioner. As a consequence, the petitioner was cruelly, inhumanely tortured."

As DeBlanc had done in Louisiana, Wright asked the Court to stay the execution of Willie Francis. He suggested furthermore that the Court itself appoint a special commissioner to investigate the facts behind the failed execution, or else order the Louisiana courts to do the same.

The Supreme Court justices received Wright's habeas corpus petition just twenty-four hours before Willie's scheduled execution, but just ten minutes before oral arguments were to begin on the last day of the October 1946 term. The justices gathered hastily in the conference room; before each of them lay a file with a label marked "capital case" in red on the cover. Wright's petition, they decided, required discussion for which they hadn't the time. The Court convened at its usual 12:00 noon starting time, but what Chief Justice Vinson did next was not usual in the least at the U.S. Supreme Court. Vinson called an immediate recess in the Court, and the justices filed back to the conference room to once again determine the fate of Willie Francis.

An hour later they returned. Vinson held a typewritten statement in his hands. As he read the Court's decision, Wright heard the words he had dreaded. "Petition for writ of *habeas corpus* is denied."

Vinson referred to the1944 *ex parte Hawke* case as reason for the denial. That decision held that a petitioner who seeks habeas in federal court must beforehand exhaust all state remedies. With less than twenty-four hours remaining until Willie again faced electro-cution, DeBlanc and Wright hardly had the time to file yet another petition back in Louisiana and then, should it fail, return to Washington in the hope of securing a stay of execution.

Wright "slumped forward." His worst fears had been realized. "Abstract principles of federalism outweighed the facts of the bungled execution." With Willie's life on the line, the Court was apparently more concerned with political theory and procedures.

Then Wright heard something that surprised him, for the Supreme Court usually denied petitions of habeas corpus in a single sentence. This time, however, Chief Justice Vinson seemed merely to pause. He'd caught Wright's attention.

Vinson continued, "In view of the grave nature of the new allegations, set forth in this petition," he read, "the denial is expressly without prejudice to application to proper tribunals." Vinson then added that the present request for habeas corpus should be revised as a petition for a rehearing by the Court of its earlier decision in regard to the fate of Willie Francis. Justice Rutledge, he said, wanted that decision thrown out and returned to the supreme court of Louisiana "to determine the issues of fact."

Although Wright and DeBlanc had been unable to persuade Frankfurter to change his vote, the language in which the Court had couched its denial afforded the two attorneys a glimmer of hope. Something had happened in that conference room. Both Wright and DeBlanc believed that the Court, shocked by the allegations of the executioners' drunkenness, was giving them a hint as to how next to proceed, as well as conveying to them the message that the Court might be more inclined to favor their plea after the petition had gone through federal district court in Louisiana. Chief Justice Vinson seemed to be providing the two young lawyers with legal advice—a road map they could follow to spare the life of their client.

Wright and DeBlanc felt they owed it to Willie to take this one final shot at saving his life. At the same time, they knew it was altogether possible that Willie might be executed before the Louisiana court would even have a chance to review the petition.

That evening Bertrand DeBlanc shook hands with Skelly Wright and then boarded a plane from Washington to New Orleans. De-Blanc spent the flight time drafting the petition he was planning to file with the Louisiana court on Friday morning, May 9, 1947—the day Willie was scheduled to die.

my hell on earth

That child could cook and make a bed as good as womenfolks.

—LOUISE TAYLOR FRANCIS

"I used to walk by that jail and it just looked like a little old red building," Louise Taylor Francis said. "The brick was kind of pretty on a sunny day. Never thought my baby'd be going there to die."

The mother of Willie Francis sank into the cushioned back of her soft easy chair the evening before the youngest of her thirteen children would return to the hardest chair of all. Her eyes drifted outside to the dusty street where young children played in the last moments of daylight.

"My Willie was always kind. He used to play with little children, even when he was a big boy he used to play with 'em," she said. "There wasn't no bad in him. I just don't understand."

The "gentle, gray-haired Negro woman" had been ill lately, and bedridden, but she was still hoping to leave town before Willie came back to St. Martinville to die.

"You know, Willie was a funny boy," she said. "Times he'd sit here on the floor and play with clothespins, rubbin' 'em in his hands and countin' 'em, and stackin' 'em on top of one t'other. He'd make little fences and pig styes with 'em, and he smiled a lot when he was doin' it. Sometimes I'd get wonderin' how Willie could have himself such a time with those old clothespins. I believe his mind would run off places. Not bad places, but places."

Willie was not like any of Louise Francis's other boys. He was an unusual child. "He didn't like no baseball or football," she said. "Didn't even shoot marbles. Most times he was around the house when he wasn't in school, and he was the Lord's own blessing when it come to helping his mama. That child could cook and make a bed as good as womenfolks."

Willie was the "family pet" until he got in trouble with the law. Although the family would visit Willie in his cell in New Iberia, "it's not the same," Willie's mother said. "He gets scared, we are scared, and he don't say much to us."

At that same moment, a big, gray 1941 International Harvester truck with a muffler on the roof of its van and a "spring-loaded chrome handle" on the door was driving toward the red brick jail that stood just blocks from the Francis house. Louise Francis did not see it.

"Never thought my baby would be goin' to die there," she said to the reporter. "He told me he's ready, but I just don't understand it. And, mister, I ain't ready at all."

The reporter was thirty-year-old Elliott Chaze, born and raised in southern Louisiana. He'd attended Tulane University, and after graduation and a string of jobs, which included selling refrigerators, oil-field work, and scraping paint off old Greyhound buses, Chaze had found steady employment as a reporter for the Associated Press in New Orleans. World War II had interrupted the job, but following service in Japan as a paratrooper in the U.S. Army's 11th Airborne, Chaze had returned to New Orleans and the Associated Press, which in the spring of 1947 dispatched him to St. Martinville to cover the Willie Francis story.

Two years earlier, Chaze had covered the last days of Toni Jo Henry, managing to land a jail cell interview with the comely prostitute who was going to the chair in Louisiana for murder. The night before her scheduled execution, a photographer persuaded Toni Jo to pose for a picture. Seated in a chair, she arranged her dress to show off her shapely legs. Chaze reported that the photographer, who was slow in setting up the shot, asked his subject to smile, to which Toni Jo replied, "I've smiled twice, Mister. You haven't shot yet. Have you any idea how much talent is being wasted here today?" Later that evening, Toni Jo Henry, who until then had faced her execution with style and wit, broke down and cried, Chaze wrote, because prison officers were going to shave her head.

Chaze would in time gain some fame as a prolific southern writer and author of eight novels, but in May 1947, he was a young, unknown Associated Press reporter whose stories about a Negro teenager at death's door would soon be syndicated across the country. In St. Martinville, Chaze took the time to interview Willie's family, and in the days leading up to the May 9 execution date, he began visiting Willie regularly in the New Iberia jail.

After speaking with Louise Francis on the evening of May 8, Chaze visited Willie in his cell in New Iberia. Willie was sitting calmly on his cot, and he showed "no alarm over a second trip to the chair." Neither he nor Chaze was aware that Willie's date with the executioner might again be averted, that a last-minute legal maneuver conceived by his attorneys that afternoon in the U.S. Supreme Court might yet again "halt" what Chaze called "the fatal throw of the switch."

"But tomorrow noon has already arrived in some parts of the world," Chaze wrote, "and it's coming quickly in St. Martinville."

●   ●   ●

HORRIBLE!
MURDER, ROBBERY

THE BLACKEST CRIME EVER
COMMITTED IN THIS PARISH
MOTHER AND DAUGHTER SLAUGHTERED IN BED
IN THE HEART OF ST. MARTINVILLE.

Those were the headlines of the *Weekly Messenger* after Mrs. J. S. Robertson and her daughter, Isabella, were found dead in their home on Main Street near the railroad depot. Mrs. Robertson's throat had been cut while she was sleeping and "her mosquito bar torn to pieces." "Miss Belle," the paper speculated, must have heard a cry or a groan and come to her mother's aid, but "her strength failed," and she, too, fell "victim of the villain." Marks on her neck appeared to indicate she'd been strangled to death.

Justice Ralph DeBlanc, son of Alcibiades DeBlanc, had begun an inquest in the absence of the coroner, and the sheriff's investigation had determined that an intruder or intruders had apparently scaled a ladder outside the Robertson house, then entered and exited through a window, where they'd left bloody handprints on the sill. Bookcases and other furniture had been "raked of their contents," which led law enforcement to suspect robbery as the motive.

As word of the vicious double homicide spread, dozens of townspeople in St. Martinville rushed to the scene of the crime. The next day, "several squads of armed men" came to town to "help law have its course," but, the paper noted, "this case should have been in the hands of a shrewd detective rather than be in the hands of an armed crowd, however good may have been their intention." The paper added that Lewis Chambers, a Negro, had been arrested and jailed: "He is believed to be the right man."

Doubts lingered, however, and in the following week, "three more negroes were arrested and jailed," though none of them was ever charged. A professional detective from New Orleans, who had been hired to solve the Robertson murders, concluded in his final report that one man alone committed the crime: Lewis "Boy" Chambers. "Most of our people disagree with the detective," reported the *Weekly Messenger*, which held with the "popular opinion" that two or more men were implicated. Still, the paper did concede that there was "little evidence to sustain this belief," while also pointing out that the evidence against Chambers was nonetheless questionable: "Someone lied in their evidence, which tends to increase the doubt against the prisoner." Indeed, the paper doubted that any evidence in the report was sufficient to "bring a verdict of guilty, even a qualified one."

Months dragged on, with Lewis "Boy" Chambers locked in jail and with the law still unsure that they had the right man. Then Louis Michel, aka Louis Broussard, aka Grand Louis, was apprehended in Plaquemine, Louisiana, and conducted to St. Martinville to be charged alongside Boy Chambers for the Robertson murders. Brought before the bar of the court, Louis Michel, whom the paper described as "a negro with a very unsavory reputation" from St. Martinville, pleaded not guilty. During the "Republican reign in the 1870s," Louis Michel, according to the *Messenger*, had been a "prominent politician, exercising a great influence upon the voters of his race. He figured prominently in several intrigues during that time that made him an obnoxious character. He was considered a brave, bold and dangerous character."

In February 1892, Louis Michel and Boy Chambers both stood trial for the murder of Belle Robertson. Seven Cajun jurors were assembled. They heard testimony from the witnesses for the prosecution as well as eight witnesses for the defense. They deliberated, and after two days, they returned with a verdict. Both men were found "Guilty Without Capital Punishment" and sentenced to "imprisonment at hard labor in the State Penitentiary at Baton Rouge for the term of your natural life." Michel took the verdict "coolly." But Chambers was deeply affected; "his hands and lips trembled and tears rolled down his cheeks."

In September of 1892, a second trial—for the murder of Mrs. J.
S. Robertson—was held in the crowded courthouse where "there
was not a standing place that was not occupied," for, according to
the paper, this was "the first case in which the ladies have taken such
an interest as to attend the trial." The testimony was inconsistent
and contradictory, and all the evidence was circumstantial (the *Messenger* reported that "there was not a single direct evidence brought
against either of the accused"). Edward Simon, grandfather of Judge
James D. Simon, had been the judge in the first trial, but he had
consented to represent both Michel and Chambers in their second
trial. Because of the conflicting testimony from the first trial, Simon
requested that Judge Felix Voorhees separate the witnesses, and at
the end of a five-day trial, the jury was sequestered. They deliberated for "a considerable time" with "no prospect of them agreeing
on a verdict," but by September 26, they had managed at last to
reach a verdict. Again Michel and Chambers were found guilty, only
this time they were sentenced by Judge Voorhees to "death by hanging by the neck until you are dead and may God have mercy on your
souls." It was the first time since the war that a jury rendered a verdict of death in St. Martin Parish, and it would be "the first legal
hanging in this parish for over forty years."

In March of 1893 a reporter for the *Messenger* accompanied the
sheriff when he informed Louis Michel and Boy Chambers that all
appeals had been denied and that Governor Murphy J. Foster had
signed their death warrants. The condemned men, who were being kept in steel cages in an apartment near the courthouse, agreed
to talk to the reporter. "We were expecting that [the death war-
rants] ever since we were put in this cage. We never expected to
have any justice from men; but God knows we are innocent," both
proclaimed.

Michel was described by the *Messenger* as "a fine specimen of the
African race . . . tall, a little stoop, but . . . a good looking negro with a
smooth face, which, outside of his flat nose, was devoid of any negro

features." He was calm and cool, and "when prevailed upon to save Chambers if he would throw some light on the murder," Michel said that, "to his regret," he could not because, being innocent, he knew nothing of either of the killings. He said further that he "wished the day of his death was nearer," for he was ready to "enter the glories and delights of the beautiful kingdom above." Michel professed he was going to "die like a man," and he noted that, for nineteen years, the people of St. Martinville had been trying to kill him and that they had succeeded at last. Town lore had it that Michel had angered anti-Republicans not just with his political aspirations and influence among members of his race but that he had also pointed out to federal troops and Metropolitan police searching for Alcibiades DeBlanc a location where many of the town's guns were hidden.

Both Louis Michel and Boy Chambers requested gin on the reporter's next visit, the paper noted. It also mentioned that one of Chambers's sisters was circulating a petition to have her brother's sentence commuted. And not to no avail. Just a few days before Chambers was to hang, the governor had him sent to Baton Rouge for life imprisonment at hard labor. Many people in St. Martinville believed that, even if Chambers, who was "no doubt a bad man," had not been involved in the Robertson crime, "he had committed others for which he should hang." Other townspeople felt that he should be given the benefit of the doubt since there was "too much doubt" for a death penalty. Officers kept the news of Chambers's commutation a secret, fearing "violence on the part of our people if they knew." Perhaps, the *Messenger* noted, more clear evidence of Chambers's guilt would be found, and he could be returned to St. Martinville to "be hanged."

Edward Simon told the *Weekly Messenger* that the evidence against Chambers was "so doubtful and indirect" that both the judge and the district attorney had consented to a new trial for him.

"The public seem to think," the paper noted, "that the evidence against Chambers was not sufficient for a verdict of death." The supreme court of Louisiana agreed and "reversed the judgment of the lower court."

Louis Michel was not so fortunate. On Friday, March 24, he awoke and requested from the sheriff a "cake of the finest perfumed toilet soap" for his bath, as he "wished to wash his body as clean as his conscience and his soul was, for he was innocent of the diabolical crime of which he had been convicted." He had a hearty breakfast, which he proclaimed to enjoy, then received communion from a Catholic priest who remained with him the whole morning. At 11:30 a.m., Louis Michel was taken from a cell in the St. Martinville jail and marched to the scaffold, his hands tied behind his back and a "cigar in his mouth." After Sheriff David Rees read the death warrant, he asked Michel if he had anything to say. Michel asked the sheriff to remove the cigar from his mouth and then spoke "at some length," according to the *Messenger*. In a "cool and calm way," Michel laughed and joked, and the nearly 1,000 spectators who stood outside the jail yard were greatly amused. Louis Michel looked at the rope: "This is quite a big rope," he noted, then remarked that the gallows was "quite high for a man to fall through." He asked for, and was given, more wine. But he was not through talking.

What happened in the last few minutes of forty-two-year-old Louis Michel's life will never be fully known. Newspaper accounts of hangings at the time often included highly provocative and lurid details to boldly demonstrate the morality of the occasion—the guilty receiving their horrible but just desserts at last. A newspaper story about an execution often made that issue the best-selling one of the year. Most papers, though, withheld the "too delicate" but quite common features of hangings, like a hanged man urinating or defecating himself or speaking ghastly last words from the gallows (and if he did, superstition demanded that he be "buried at the crossroads" so that his ghost would not return to haunt the town). Details of hangings that would go unprinted would, nonetheless, survive through their retelling from generation to generation—no doubt with colorful embellishments. This oral tradition is likely how Grand Louis Michel came to be known as "Too Tall Man" around St. Martinville.

After Michel had drunk more wine, he resumed his speech for some time and "protested his innocence to the last," according to the *Messenger*. He avouched that he "was not hanged for the Robertson murders, but for an old grudge the people had against him which dates back 22 years." Louis Michel's mood darkened. He accused some of the townspeople in the crowd of having knowledge that he was innocent of the Robertson murders and refusing to speak out. Then he silenced the crowd that had gathered around the jail, and with his priest holding a crucifix beside him on the scaffold, he cursed the town of St. Martinville—cursed it so that it would never grow or prosper.

After a prayer at 12:17 p.m., Michel's legs were bound, and the noose was fitted around his neck. A "black cap" was placed over his head. At 12:20, the trap was cut. Michel dropped through, but because of his height and the length of the rope, his "feet reached solid earth." The astonished crowd watched as Too Tall Man "stood there on his tip toes with the noose slack around his neck—like a dancer in a macabre ballet." The executioner, thinking quickly, placed a board under Too Tall Man's feet to support him, then proceeded to dig a hole beneath it. The way it is told, he whistled while he dug.

When the hole was deemed deep enough, the executioner "calmly kicked the board away," and Louis Michel danced frantically for a few moments as he slowly strangled to death before the gaping crowd. "Louis was bold and plucky while on the gallows," the *Messenger* reported, "and died brave." The following week, the paper noted that

its issue on the hanging of Louis Michel "was the largest edition of
the *Messenger* ever printed, and it met with a splendid success."

On April 8, 1893, it was reported in the *Lafayette Advertiser* that a
newsboy who'd noticed a "strange negro loitering about" a train depot in Houston, Texas, had identified him as a man from St. Martinville who had disappeared shortly after the Robertson murders.
The boy had alerted the police, and the negro, Paul Cormier, had
been detained in Houston until St. Martinville Sheriff David Rees
arrived to retrieve him. "It is hoped," the paper reported, "that Paul
Cormier will suffer the full extent of the law in a short time, as evidence is at hand to show that he was the man who choked Mrs.
Robertson to death."

Corrompre. It's a dirty town, some have said.

●   ●   ●

By late Thursday night, May 8, Willie was ready. Sheriff Gilbert
Ozenne allowed Willie, in Ozenne's words, to practice "walking the
last mile, like a debutante practices," for Willie wanted to make sure
he would go "like a man"; he had promised Father Hannigan that he
was going to "walk it steady. I'll be darned if I'm going to act like a
cry-baby." Then Sheriff Ozenne brought Willie a "specially prepared meal," after which Willie again went through the condemned
person's head-shaving ritual so that he'd be ready for "the lethal cap."

Bertrand DeBlanc's plane had not yet landed in New Orleans
when the reporters left Willie alone in his cell for the night. During
the flight, DeBlanc had prepared the papers he would file in court
the next morning, after he'd seen Willie. The closer he got to Louisiana, the more confident DeBlanc became that he could now finally stop Willie from going to the chair. His plane began its
approach to New Orleans, and he still had a long drive ahead of
him. He'd be cutting things close. But he was looking forward to
telling Willie the news.

Unlike DeBlanc, who had been rushing from courtroom to courtroom in the year since Willie had walked away from the chair, Father Hannigan had been visiting him in jail nearly every day, and his effect on the teen was patent. Willie told a reporter that "Heaven is a place where you have a white suit. I don't mean a seersucker suit but a white suit and tie . . . a linen suit and a fine, spreading tie. For going to heaven, I want the white suit to show off my shoulders." Willie believed that he had survived the chair because, as Father Hannigan had reasoned it, the Lord "wanted me to get my hell on earth." Only now the Lord had seen him suffer enough. "I have been in this jail sweating it for a year," Willie said. "Now I'm ready to go. I want the machine to work this time. I want to die because as soon as I do I am going to the Lord."

Willie was having his big meal when he was visited by Father Hannigan, who talked to him about what was transpiring in Washington. "Who would think," Willie sighed, "that one Negro boy could get all those big men to talk about him?" Reporters had come by again while he'd been practicing walking his last mile, but Willie by then was growing weary of them. "The whole thing is in God's hands now," he told them. "Now let me be." He hadn't heard from his lawyer yet, but from what he could tell, he'd be going back to St. Martinville in the morning, back up the stairs to the second floor of the red brick jail, back to the small L-shaped room where the chair would again be waiting.

For the past year and a half he'd been waiting here in the New Iberia jail. For a year and a half he'd been finding some comfort in everyday sounds that had become familiar: the dogs barking in the lots across Iberia Street, the slow, steady rumble of the passing freight trains, the bells of St. Peter's Church, and country music from a radio in the bullpen where Sheriff Ozenne and Gus Walker and the other deputies gathered just outside the elevator.

The filthy pink walls of his cell, though, were cheerless. Willie didn't mind the color, he said, "but I wish the walls weren't behind the paint." Between the bars on his small window he'd stuffed dozens of letters he'd received, as well as some photographs and a roll of toilet paper. On the radiator beside his bed lay some loose change, a few more letters, and the Bible his father had placed in his hands on a visit that had to seem a lifetime ago. The narrow cot with the striped pillow and mattress was barely long enough to accommodate his lanky body. The lights were out, but he could still read the words he'd written on the wall.

OF COURSE I AM NOT A KILLER

In the morning, Willie would pay the price for murder. He no doubt turned his thoughts to heaven and the Lord, as Father Hannigan had advised. Still, he'd have that entire night to reflect, too, on his life—and on the night when he'd so drastically altered its course. On the night of November 7, 1944, according to the State of Louisiana, Willie Francis had tried to rob Andrew Thomas and ended up killing him. That night had led Willie to where he was now, and to where he'd be in the morning.

Why'd you do it, Willie? He'd been asked the question countless times, and each time he'd answered, the words faded like a distant whisper from his lips: "I don't know," he'd said. "I just don't know."

That was his answer later. But the first time he was asked, Willie did have an answer to the question. In custody in Port Arthur, Willie tried to explain his motive with eight mysterious words scrawled on a piece of paper for the police.

It was a secret about me and him.

ruining my life

Is it a foolish dream, an idle vague superstition?
Or has an angel passed, and revealed the truth to my spirit?

—HENRY WADSWORTH LONGFELLOW,
Evangeline: A Tale of Acadie

Before and after the murder of Andrew Thomas, gossip that the druggist had been carrying on affairs with married women was rampant in both white and black St. Martinville. At the coroner's inquest shortly following Thomas's murder, Dr. Sidney Yongue pointedly questioned Alvin Van Brocklin about the rumors making their way around town that "somebody across the bayou might have had something to do with this," and Van Brocklin stated that he had seen Thomas's car "at a lady's house out there several times." In fact, at the time of the murder two ladies were rumored to be having affairs with Andrew Thomas. Both lived in houses across the bayou, and both were married.

Sue Martin remembers the rumors. Still a resident of St. Martinville, she has lived her whole life in a house behind the courthouse along the Bayou Teche. She was working as a clerk in the courthouse when Thomas was killed and when Willie Francis was sent to the chair. An opponent to capital punishment, Martin had been so horrified by the prospect of Willie's execution—what with both her

home and her place of employment being in such close proximity
to the St. Martinville jail—that she and her sister had gone by bus
to Lafayette for the day to escape the State of Louisiana's grim
business on May 3, 1946; she had been shocked to learn from the
driver on the bus ride home that "that boy didn't die." Months
earlier, in the period immediately following the Thomas murder,
before Willie had been apprehended, Martin had heard rumors in
the courthouse itself that tied the killing to a jealous lover. It was
there that Alida Thomas (Mrs. Zie), the wife of Andrew's brother
Zie and the secretary-treasurer of the St. Martin Parish Police
Jury, frequently aired reckless theories and pernicious rumors linking various women to her brother-in-law's death. "Mrs. Zie was
trying to solve the case and get to the bottom of it," said Sue Martin, who worked in the courthouse with Mrs. Zie.

The two women who figured most prominently in the rumors
were Henrietta Duplantis and Bea Nassans. In his testimony at
the coroner's inquest, Alvin Van Brocklin stated that he saw
Thomas's car "several times" both at the home of Mrs. Nassans
and at the home of Mrs. Duplantis. Both women lived in houses
across the bayou, near Pine Grove. Police Chief Claude Thomas,
another of Andrew's brothers, and Sheriff E. L. Resweber followed up on these leads and were satisfied that the victim's alleged relationships with the two women in no way connected
them to his murder.

But the rumors, indeed, infuriated the ladies. James Akers, another lifelong resident of St. Martinville, was friendly with both of
them. Akers says that the happily married Henrietta Duplantis was
so upset by the rumors in St. Martinville that she wrote a letter—or
so she claimed—to the editor of the Weekly Messenger before
Willie's arrest. In it, Akers said, she chided the town and sarcasti-
cally thanked its citizens "for ruining my life." Akers recalls Mrs.
Duplantis telling him that such rumors were preposterous. She was

nearly twenty years younger than Andrew Thomas, and her husband was always present whenever Thomas visited.

Genevieve Duplantis Lasseigne, the daughter of Homer and Henrietta Duplantis, was one of several young ladies in St. Martinville who worked in Andrew Thomas's drugstore after school and on weekends. Genevieve was sixteen years old at the time of Thomas's murder in 1944. In addition to the shock of learning that her boss had been murdered, she recalls the pain and humiliation her father felt when he was treated as a possible suspect in Thomas's murder and was questioned by police. "It was bad," Genevieve recalls. "Andrew was a family friend. My father was so gentle. He was very upset by the rumors." Genevieve remembers that Andrew Thomas loved baseball and would often take the Duplantis family to minor league games in New Iberia. "We'd watch the games together, my father, my mother and Mr. Thomas. He was a very nice man."

According to Genevieve, her mother, Henrietta, and Bea Nassans would commonly walk down Cemetery Street across the bridge to Main Street and to Thomas's drugstore, where they were virtually fixtures. They'd spend hours at a table, drinking Cokes and talking. Homer Duplantis was a welder who worked long hours in the oil fields, and Louis Nassans, also an oil worker, would sometimes take assignments out of the country. The ladies had time on their hands, and both of them enjoyed the company and friendship of Andrew Thomas.

James Akers recalls a similar conversation with Bea Nassans back in the 1970s, when she, too, scoffed at any suggestion that she might have been carrying on some kind of affair with the bachelor pharmacist. "Besides," she told Akers, "Andrew Thomas was gay."

Could it be, then, that Thomas had purposefully chosen to lead a life that might at times occasion rumors, possibly even eliciting the threats of jealous men, to hide a sexual preference he felt compelled

to keep secret in a small southern town in the 1940s? Were his relationships with married women in actuality strictly platonic, as Henrietta Duplantis and Bea Nassans asserted?

Nolan "Cabbie" Charles, who grew up in St. Martinville, remembers rumors of Thomas as a "lover boy" who was "popular with the
ladies" because of the fancy facial creams he sold in the drugstore.
The ladies in St. Martinville loved these beauty products, Charles
said, and they loved having Thomas come around to show them
how to apply the creams for facial treatments. Were the prevailing
perceptions of Andrew Thomas as a ladies' man simply the naïve but
most obvious conclusions drawn by Cabbie Charles and others in
town about a very private single man who chose to keep company
with married women?

•   •   •

In 1943, twenty-two-year-old Stella Vincent—like her sister Lillian
Vincent DeBlanc and like Genevieve Duplantis—began working at
the pharmacy on Main Street in St. Martinville, her boss being Andrew Thomas. She helped out at the busy soda fountain where the
kids of St. Martinville liked to spend time. People would gather at
tables in the front of the store after church, and boys would socialize
there after school. While Stella was working at the pharmacy,
Thomas hired a young Negro to do odd jobs like sweeping the floor
and helping with deliveries. Though segregation was in "full swing,"
the Thomas family, according to Claude's son Otis Thomas, prided
themselves in their relations with blacks in St. Martinville. "My father, as chief of police, was always on good terms," he said. "And I
know the Francis family was well thought of."

Sue Martin also remembers seeing the Negro boy around town;
she recalls that he walked kind of funny and didn't seem very bright
by the way he talked. The boy was fifteen-year-old Willie Francis,
whom Genevieve Duplantis remembers as a "nice boy" who was

mostly cleaning the drugstore whenever she saw him around. "I didn't work for him steady," Willie later said. "I would run around the corners with a package or sweep the floors when he asked me to."

Stella had been clerking and waiting tables at the pharmacy for more than a year when she came home from work one night and told her sisters that she didn't want to work for Mr. Thomas anymore. She offered no explanation as to why. Increasingly, though, she talked about wanting to leave St. Martinville. The options for a young, single woman being limited, Stella ultimately decided that, without a job or a husband, the only way she could leave St. Martinville was to enlist in the services. By this time, Andrew Thomas was dead, and Willie Francis had been arrested, convicted, and sentenced to death. Just two weeks before Willie was sent to the chair, Stella Vincent left St. Martinville for good. She enlisted in the Women's Army Corp in New Orleans on April 15, 1946.

While she was stationed in San Antonio, Texas, Stella met air corpsman Robert Baker, and the two were married. The couple eventually settled in Pinellas County, Florida, where they raised a family.

Unlike her older sisters who have enjoyed good health and longevity, Stella Vincent Baker was long dogged by illness as a result of a battle with anorexia nervosa. In 1972, at age fifty, Stella was confined to her bed. Sensing the end was near, her sister Edith, still a resident of St. Martinville at the time, flew down to Florida to spend some time with Stella in her final days. It was then, according to various family members, that Stella, wracked with guilt for thirty years, confessed to Edith why she had quit her job at the pharmacy and had left St. Martinville forever.

Stella had witnessed something at the drugstore that had so disturbed her she could not bear to return. In a back room, she had seen "an incident" involving Andrew Thomas and Willie Francis, an incident followed by the druggist yelling and lashing out at the boy.

Young, scared, and confused, Stella had told no one—not the police, not the sheriff's department, not anyone in her family. She'd
been horrified when she'd heard of Thomas's murder, and sickened
when she'd learned the young boy in the store had been found
guilty of the crime and was sentenced to die in the electric chair.
Still, she had told no one, not even her brother-in-law Bertrand De-
Blanc when he was trying to save Willie from going to the chair a
second time.

Stella's daughter, Diane Baker Godwin, long suspected that her
mother was haunted by a memory of St. Martinville that was so
shocking she could not even talk about it. Godwin believed that her
mother had witnessed an incident in St. Martinville that was sexual in
nature, and that it was related to Stella's subsequent health problems.

Lillian DeBlanc, too, believed that her sister's guilt over not
speaking up about the incident at the time either of Willie's arrest or
of his indictment negatively affected her health. She also believed
that Bertrand knew nothing about an encounter of whatever sort
Stella may have witnessed between Thomas and Willie. Daniel De-
Blanc, Bertrand's oldest son, however, did recall speaking with his
father about the incident after he learned of Stella's admission.
"Aunt Stella was very religious," Daniel says. "She would not lie."
Was sexual abuse of some sort the "secret" Willie was referring to in
his confession to police upon his arrest in Port Arthur, Texas? Was
this the secret that lay behind the true motive for the killing of Andrew Thomas?

Jessyl Taylor, the writer for the black newspaper the *World's Messenger*, spent time with the Francis family following Willie's failed
execution. Though she does not get specific, in her story, Taylor
refers to an "altercation" that the Francis family apparently shared
with her. This incident may have inspired murderous revenge but,
most likely, will remain forever unknown. Taylor wrote, "The allegation further has it that after the altercation, and murder seemed

eminent [*sic*], that this white person offered the services of his gun. Further rumor has it, that there was a hidden motive behind the move that probably will never be told."

Taylor seems to imply that Willie did not steal August Fuselier's gun; rather, she suggests, the deputy sheriff, who had, according to Father Rousseve, once threatened to kill Andrew Thomas, was aware of the "altercation" and had put the gun in the boy's hands.

Had an altercation or interaction of some kind transpired between Andrew Thomas and Willie Francis, an interaction so shocking that Willie himself would not reveal it, even if it meant the secret—*a secret about me and him*—might take Willie to his grave?

"That was it," said Daniel DeBlanc. That was the question he had asked his father, but instead of an answer, his father had discussed how a "manslaughter with mitigating circumstances" defense might have played out in St. Martinville had it been known what Stella had presumably seen in the storage room of Andrew Thomas's drugstore on Main Street, just across from St.-Martin-de-Tours Catholic Church.

On January 16, 1981, when Gus Weill contacted Bertrand De-Blanc to discuss a play he was hoping to write, the two held a telephone conversation about the Willie Francis case—a conversation DeBlanc kept notes on. Weill asked DeBlanc if he was aware that Andrew Thomas was "queer." ("DeBlanc's word, not mine," Weill later noted.) DeBlanc responded that he "didn't know then but I heard so later." Weill then referred to Willie's Port Arthur, Texas, confession, when Willie "said why he killed Thomas was a secret between me and him." Weill knew DeBlanc had surely asked Willie about the secret, so he asked DeBlanc directly.

"What did he mean by that?" Weill pressed. "What was the secret?"

Nearly forty years later, the lawyer struggled to answer. Finally, he relented. "It would be interactions," DeBlanc said.

Weill later added that DeBlanc would not elaborate further.

see you on the other side

I can still stop this thing. I'm almost sure I can stop it for you.

—Bertrand DeBlanc

Willie Francis awoke before dawn on the morning of May 9, 1947, for an early transfer from the New Iberia jail to St. Martinville. Unlike his first trip to the chair just over a year ago, for which he had worn drab prison grays, Willie looked quite dapper in dark, pinstripe slacks, black dress shoes, and a clean white shirt with thin, dark stripes. "I'm wearing my Sunday pants and my Sunday heart to the chair," Willie said. "Ain't going to wear no beat-up pants to see the Lord. Been busy talking my way into heaven for this past year. Them folks expecting me to come in style."

This time he was also coming without chains, as Sheriff Gilbert Ozenne was doing Willie the courtesy of not shackling his legs. Willie was determined that he'd walk like a man to the chair, so determined that he'd been practicing. As Ozenne had had no reason to expect any trouble from him, the sheriff had let Willie out of his cell in the mornings and allowed him to rehearse his final steps by walking up and down the east wing of the jail.

Elliott Chaze met Willie at the New Iberia jail that morning. Chaze wrote that Willie, upon leaving the jail, "walked lightly and with shoulders squared." The young AP reporter also noted that Willie wore a "wide uncertain grin on his face."

The early morning sky was still dark when they ducked through a back exit of the jail to a waiting sedan. A year ago they had taken Willie out the front door, where the statue of Lady Justice had stood before him. This time the only view he got was that of a graveyard, Bruce's Place, and the still-quiet shotgun shacks surrounding it. One of the deputies puffed on a cigarette. The wind whipped smoke into Willie's face. Willie turned his head away and frowned, then "grinned apologetically at the deputy." He had quit smoking just over a year ago—on May 3, 1946, the day he had walked away from the electric chair.

The deputy opened the rear door of the sedan, and Willie got in; the officers escorting him followed. Chaze noted that the car tires had "kicked up a couple of dark plumes of gravel" when Willie turned and waved at him with his manacled hands. Chaze was making the trip in a car behind.

In the darkness just before dawn, Willie traveled the same nine-mile stretch of gravel road from New Iberia to St. Martinville that he'd traveled one year earlier. Traveling toward West Main Street, the sedan passed under the same sign that hung over the street the last time Willie had made this ride: "Come Again," the sign read. The headlights illuminated the moss hanging from the live oak canopies; in flashes, they lit the cane fields that ran alongside the road. The sedan crossed the Bayou Teche, then approached St. Martinville. Willie had again come home.

The *Weekly Messenger* on May 9 ran a small headline, "Francis To Be Electrocuted Today," above a two-paragraph story stating that Willie's execution would bring "to an end one of the longest delays of justice in the Parish's history." An article just above the Willie

Francis story reminded the town of St. Martinville that Sunday was Mother's Day, "and we should all make an effort to do something very special for our mothers."

The sedan stole down Claiborne Street, past Bertrand DeBlanc's old place across from the courthouse. Willie might have wondered if he'd see DeBlanc again that morning. He knew nothing of his lawyer's last-minute efforts in Washington, but experience had taught him that even DeBlanc's good news had a way of turning bad.

The sedan parked behind the St. Martinville jail, where Paul Guilbeaux, the jailer, and E. L. "Brother" Resweber, the sheriff's son and a deputy, met Willie. The two men led Willie toward the jail. Trailing behind was Elliott Chaze, whose car had pulled in just behind the sedan. A few spectators had already gathered, as had a photographer, who snapped a picture of Willie being escorted into the jail. Wearing his Sunday pants and an uncertain grin, he's walking with his hands cuffed in front.

The men walked him past the camphor trees and then into the jail, to a cell on the second floor of the small, redbrick building behind the courthouse. Willie was superstitious about the number thirteen. He was the last of thirteen children, he was convicted on the thirteenth day of September, 1945, and on January 13, 1947, the U.S. Supreme Court had "turned me down." He had counted, and he remembered the number of steps from the cell to the chair from the last time he had come here to die. "It's a long 13 paces," Chaze wrote. "But it's still 13." There, Willie waited.

Farther than thirteen steps, but not much farther, back at the Francis family house on Washington Street, Frederick and several of Willie's brothers and sisters sat in a "pleasant living room" and talked "nervously of trivial things." Occasionally, someone would mention Willie, and the room would grow silent.

Frederick Francis would stay at home this time rather than stand outside the jail the way he had a year ago, when he had suffered the horrific roar of the gasoline engine and the blazing noonday sun and, pacing frantically, had waited with the coffin to bury his youngest son. "I'm goin' to stay here and wait for the body," Francis said. "I got to make arrangements for my boy."

Even though Francis chose to remain at home, six members of Willie's family—a brother, two brothers-in-law, and three sisters—arrived at the jail at 9:30 a.m. for a final visit. They stood "in a stunned semicircle" around the chair that would take Willie's life. None of them spoke, and although they all remained "dry-eyed," they refused to look each other in the eyes. Finally a deputy let them into Willie's cell.

"How are you feeling?" a sister asked Willie.

"I feel good," Willie answered.

Then Willie "must have said something humorous, because several of them laughed. They didn't laugh hysterically, but rather as if Willie had said something genuinely funny."

One by one, they left. At the cell door one of Willie's sisters turned to him. "I hope we have the faith to take it the way you're taking it," she said. "We'll see you on the other side."

"You folks got to be brave," Willie said. "You just got to be brave."

As Willie's six visitors staggered out to the jailhouse yard, where a sizable crowd had already begun to gather, a man in the crowd pushed himself against them and hurled at them an indignity to compound their pain that morning: "They ought to do away with all the niggers," he said.

At 10:15 a.m., less than two hours before Willie was scheduled to die, Bertrand DeBlanc finally arrived at the St. Martinville jail. Looking "haggard and sleepy-eyed after a flying trip to Washington," DeBlanc filled Willie in on what had happened the day before: how he had failed to get a stay before the Supreme Court and how, with hope and confidence, he now planned to petition the Louisiana courts on Willie's behalf one more time. He explained to Willie that the Court seemed primed for a reversal now. Chief Justice Vinson had said as much.

Willie simply shook his head. He had had enough. His hopes had been dashed again and again, and each time he'd had to prepare again for his impending death. He was tired of it all. His parents were both getting on in age; his mother was also very ill. He just couldn't put them, or himself, through it again.

DeBlanc was stunned. This couldn't be. "I can still stop this thing," DeBlanc strove to assure Willie. Searching for Willie's eyes, he pressed, "I'm almost sure I can stop it for you. The Supreme Court said I can go back and stop this execution."

No matter how desperately DeBlanc pleaded, though, Willie insisted. "No, Mr. B-B-Bertrand. No, don't go back. I'm ready to die. I'm ready to go. I don't want you to do nothing."

DeBlanc heard in Willie's voice the calm strength that comes with determination. Exhausted, DeBlanc looked Willie steadily in the eye and asked, "O.K. Are you sure?"

Willie nodded. Staring out the window of the cell, he said, "Leave it alone, Mr. Bert. Thank you, but just leave it alone. I'm ready to die. And the sooner the better."

Bertrand DeBlanc cared not even a little about what people said or thought about him. The handkerchief he always carried with him was not just for allergies. An emotional man, he was prone to well up with tears in moments of intensity. He might be overwhelmed by exquisite beauty or moved deeply by sadness and loss, but either way, DeBlanc felt no shame over crying in public. "I like the guy," DeBlanc had said a year earlier. "And I got to liking him more." As he stood in the cell with his client for the last time, DeBlanc's eyes filled with tears. And once again, it was Willie who tried to console DeBlanc.

"I'm ready to die," Willie whispered.

Then, he and Willie, born to two widely different worlds that lay just blocks apart, closed the distance. They embraced and said good-bye.

With Willie ready for the execution, the State of Louisiana was taking no chances this time. One front-page headline on that morning read:

EXPERT SET TO THROW SWITCH ON WILLIE
No More Amateur Executioners in Louisiana

Gone were Ephie Foster and Vincent Venezia, the two men from Angola who had drunkenly botched Willie's execution the year before. The State made sure that Grady Jarratt, Louisiana's official executioner, was there to do the job on May 9, 1947. Jarratt, in fact, had been in charge of the chair since 1941 when Louisiana first switched from hanging to electrocution for death-penalty sentences, but he had been unable to attend to Willie Francis's first execution. A big, tall Texan in a white hat and cowboy boots, Jarratt made a habit of greeting witnesses and shaking their hands while they all stood by and waited uncomfortably for the moment when he'd finally throw the switch. His meticulous yet sociable manner must have been a relief to Sheriff Resweber, who'd not have to deal alone with the people milling about the jail all morning.

Unlike Mississippi's official traveling executioner Jimmy Thompson, whose body was "tattooed from clavicle to toe with black cats, snakes and strawberries" and who brought a P. T. Barnum-like showmanship to his executions ("I just seem to have a talent for this sort of thing," Thompson admitted), Grady Jarratt was all business. And unlike Jimmy Thompson, Jarratt didn't blow part of his execution fee posting bail for drunk-and-disorderly charges, which Thompson usually faced in the mornings following his executions.

Hilton Butler, former Angola warden, remembered that Jarratt would arrive at an execution very early and "go through the chair with a fine-tooth comb. Everything had to be right up to snuff. Even the leather. He would take it in his hands and ply it. If it had a crack in it, then we'd have to make a new one. He was very, very particular." Right before he pulled the switch, Jarratt would say good-bye and then state the condemned person's first name. "That's the way he did them all," Butler said. "The last thing he said to them was, 'Good-bye, whatever-their-name-was.' Then he pulled the lever." Ephie Foster had tried to emulate Jarratt a year before with his good-bye to Willie, but he had managed only to sound churlish because he'd failed to capture any of the dignity to which Jarratt rose. Captain Ephie Foster would continue to make death runs with the portable chair into the 1950s as a security man. He remained employed at the Louisiana State Penitentiary until he ended his life by suicide in January of 1956.

As Jarratt went about his preparations, Father Charles Hannigan, who had visited Willie nearly every day for a year, arrived at the jail in New Iberia. On May 9, he, too, drove to St. Martinville so that he could offer counsel and prepare the eighteen-year-old Willie for death while together they awaited noon in the cell. He would later tell reporters that Willie was in great shape, "physically and spiritually."

DeBlanc was present in the cell during Hannigan's visit and, in a later interview, recalled the priest saying, "Willie, at 12 o'clock sharp they're going to pull that switch and you're going to die just like this" (this being a snap of his fingers). "The minute you die, Willie, you're going to be walking to the Lord. And when you meet him now, Willie, he'll be there to welcome you."

Hannigan continued: "Now listen, Willie. There are several things you've got to do. When you go to the Lord, you've got to talk to him about your family. The next thing is to put in a good word for your lawyer. Finally, and do listen," Father Hannigan said, smiling, "don't forget to put in a few good words for me, too."

Always striving to be a good Catholic, Willie decided that, since it was Friday, he'd have to pass on his favorite: fried chicken. "I'm hungry, mostly," he told Guilbeaux. "But I don't want nothing but fish." The wife of jailer Paul Guilbeaux brought Willie's last meal to his cell. Mrs. Guilbeaux had prepared catfish, fried potatoes, and pickles for him.

"I brought him a soft drink, too" Paul Guilbeaux said, with a modest shrug. "He didn't ask for it, but I brought it to him. You know how it is."

Years later, Paul Guilbeaux was badly beaten by a prisoner inside the St. Martinville jail. He died not long afterward.

Soon after his meal, Father Maurice Rousseve arrived at the jail, and with another Negro priest, he administered the last rites of the Catholic Church, just as he had the year before. Outside the jail, the generator had been fired up and was beginning to roar. At noon the bells of Notre Dame sounded the hour, and at 12:02 p.m., Willie rose from his cot and began the thirteen paces to the execution room. There the chair was waiting.

By now, a crowd of nearly five hundred people had gathered outside the St. Martinville jail. Some had climbed onto the branches of the large oaks surrounding the jail in the hope of catching sight of the execution over the eight-foot wooden fence, just as they had done a year before. Among the crowd stood about two hundred "colored spectators," many of whom had come from out of the state to protest in silence. The crowd spilled out of the jailhouse and over to the courthouse, then up both Claiborne and Saint Martin streets. Armed guards stood around the executioner's truck to discourage any attempt to disrupt the progress of the electrocution. Though the mood was "openly hostile to Francis," there was no disorder.

Elliott Chaze was waiting inside the death chamber for Willie to arrive. He could hear the crowd outside, "the steady murmur of . . . curious citizens in the jail yard. They talked steadily, lolling beneath a giant, bearded oak, sometimes laughing, sometimes swearing. Across the street in the jailer's sun-browned yard sat more than a score of Negroes, many of them with their hats in their laps despite the brilliant sun. They said nothing." But Paul Guilbeaux's "mud-crusted black pig" in its wire cage behind the jail was grunting steadily and "resentfully" throughout the proceedings. "Only the pig," Chaze wrote, "of all living beings present, seemed unimpressed."

In his walk to the chair, Willie refused the assistance of Father Hannigan and motioned for the priest to precede him. He'd been practicing this walk; he didn't need any support. When Willie entered the chamber, he would have noticed that one of the witnesses in the small anteroom was Claude Thomas, Andrew's brother and the town's chief of police. Chaze reported a small smile on Willie's face as he calmly walked the last six paces to the chair "without a flicker of fear."

Twice he wiped the palms of his hands on his Sunday pants before sitting down. No sooner was he seated than the officials began strapping Willie into the same chair he'd walked away from a year earlier. They were fastening broad straps across his arms and chest when Willie caught a glimpse of Chaze. He snapped the reporter a "one-finger salute" and silently mouthed him a "hello" by "moving his lips exaggeratedly to shape the word."

Willie was looking down at his lap while the leg straps were being adjusted. Deputies would cut a small slit in the left pant leg to attach the electrode. When he looked up, he spotted another familiar face. It was Sidney Dupois, the barber on Main Street to whom Willie had spoken briefly in this same room one year ago. Then, Willie had wanted to ask Dupois about his nine-year-old son, but Willie had been so gripped by fear that his mouth was too dry to speak. Dupois, much to his wife's dismay, had once again agreed to Sheriff Resweber's request that he serve as an official witness to the execution, and this time Willie managed a few words. "How's little Sid?" he asked.

"Fine, Willie. Just fine," Dupois replied.

"Well, you tell him to be a good boy now, 'ya hear." There was no time for any further words.

For a second, Willie Francis closed his eyes. When he opened them, it was the last time anyone would ever see his dark, wide eyes, for Grady Jarratt stepped forward, the black leather mask in his hands. "Are the straps too tight?" Jarratt asked.

"Everything is all right," Willie replied, a smile still on his face.

Jarratt then asked him if there was anything he wanted to say.

"Nothing at all," Willie said.

Jarratt placed the mask over the face of Willie Francis and plunged him into a world of darkness. Stepping aside, Jarratt took hold of the switch.

All eyes were on the boy in the chair, and the room was still. Still, until the words came.

"Good-bye, Willie," Jarratt said, then pulled the lever. It was 12:08 p.m.

When the 2,500 volts of current hit him, Willie held himself still as he sat small in the big chair. His chest didn't heave; his body did not convulse. He took the electricity without a tremor. The jolt picked him up stiffly as his fingers lay "motionless against the scarred wooden arms of the chair." His body sagged when the current was shut off. A second charge was applied, just to make sure. Thirty seconds later, the current stopped, but the tension and uncertainty remained—an unspoken expectation, perhaps, that the hand of God might once again save him, that the indestructible Willie Francis might still have breath in his chest.

"Are you sure he's dead?" Resweber asked.

Jarratt picked his cigar off the floor and walked over to the chair. He opened Willie's shirt.

"He's dead," Jarratt said. The time was 12:12 p.m.

●   ◆   ●

Louisiana Taylor Francis had gotten herself out of bed that morning with the intent of taking a train to Port Arthur, Texas, to visit her daughter Lucille for Mother's Day. She wanted to get away from St. Martinville on the day her youngest son was to die in that terrible chair. But Louise Francis didn't make the trip. Instead, the ailing sixty-two-year-old mother of Willie Francis staggered five blocks to the St. Martinville courthouse, and there, by herself, she waited, like Longfellow's Evangeline, in "dull, deep pain, and constant anguish of patience." She waited much the way her husband Frederick had waited by himself with a coffin twelve months earlier, while the State of Louisiana prepared for a son's execution.

Just after noon, she saw a man signal from the jail to tell the crowd that Louisiana justice had been done. There were no miracles this time. Her Willie was no more.

It was hot in St. Martinville that afternoon of May 9, 1947, and as soon as they got the word, the bystanders began to slowly disperse, the blacks going one way and the whites another, back toward the heart of the town, past the little Catholic churchyard where the two Acadian lovers rest in their nameless graves. Alone on the courthouse steps in the accursed town, Louisiana Taylor Francis, her heart broken, wept for her dead son.

the nerve to kill a man

All was ended now, the hope, and the fear, and the sorrow,
All the aching of heart, the restless, unsatisfied longing,
All the dull, deep pain, and constant anguish of patience!

— Henry Wadsworth Longfellow,
Evangeline: A Tale of Acadie

Willie Francis was buried at the Union Baptist Cemetery, just a short walk from the house he grew up in. Unlike St. Michael's Cemetery across the Bayou Teche, Willie's graveyard has none of the ornate tombs and crypts that distinguish the plots where the Thomases, the Simons, the Fuseliers, the DeBlancs, and most of the white Catholics of St. Martinville eventually came to rest. Nor was there a headstone to mark Willie's grave. Frederick Francis had smashed it a year earlier, after his youngest son had walked away from Gruesome Gertie, and had not purchased another stone to take its place. Andrew Thomas had left behind, in succession to his brothers and sisters, a house, the drugstore, a car, furniture, some stocks and bonds, and $2,473 in cash. Willie Francis left all of his belongings with Sheriff Gilbert Ozenne at the New Iberia jail.

The Good Will Mutual Aid Association, with which blacks in southern Louisiana, with small monthly premiums, ensured proper burials for their dead, paid for Willie's funeral. "Everyone came out," Nolan Charles said. The women wore black skirts, white blouses, and black hats; the men dressed up in their best suits and wore black armbands as well as Good Will member badges, which were black with white and gold fringe. Solemnly, quietly, they followed the coffin of Willie Francis through the parish streets to the Union Baptist Cemetery.

James Akers, then a young, blond boy living in St. Martinville, thought that he was watching a parade when he saw the funeral procession. He tagged along behind the mourners all the way to the graveyard. He recalls that, when he returned home and reported to his mother what he had witnessed that afternoon, he got punished. That was not a parade, she told him. And that's how it happened that Akers "was the only white person at Willie Francis's funeral," as he tells it.

Bertrand DeBlanc, perhaps the only white person one would have expected at the funeral, was missing. He was in St. Martinville a few days later when Frederick Francis once again appeared before him. Francis was wearing the same expression he'd worn a year earlier, when the aging subsistence farmer had desperately sought out the young Cajun lawyer to help him save his son from a second trip to the chair. In the year since, DeBlanc had lost the long legal battle, and Frederick Francis had lost his youngest son. Standing before the Cajun lawyer, Francis handed DeBlanc a sack of onions—the only payment DeBlanc would ever receive from Willie's family. His handkerchief at the ready, DeBlanc shook hands with Frederick Francis, and the two men said good-bye. Francis would outlive his youngest son by nearly a quarter century. He died in St. Martinville in February 1971 at the age of ninety-one.

Although a small story in the *Weekly Messenger* on May 9, 1947, stated that Willie Francis was scheduled to "die today," Willie's name would not again appear in the St. Martinville newspaper until two years later when one Clarence Joseph Jr. was scheduled to be executed, like Willie, at the jail in the same infamous chair. The *Messenger* quoted officials as saying that they wanted "no repeat of the Willie Francis incident." Since then, the name of Willie Francis has been relegated to the footnotes of capital punishment texts and Supreme Court citations, where it remains today. The boy who was named Willie Francis has been long forgotten.

Willie Francis did not take the stand during his trial. He never gave sworn testimony before the court as to what happened that night in November 1944 outside Andrew Thomas's garage. But in the words of Willie Francis that have survived on record lie clues to critical factors in the unfortunate turn of events. Upon examination, in fact, the words of this stuttering, undereducated black youth in the rural South of the postwar forties speak volumes.

August Fuselier may have been, as Father Rousseve said, a "bad man," but Willie Francis did confess to stealing Fuselier's gun, a .38 caliber Smith & Wesson. It disappeared along with its holster from a car parked on a street just off Main Street in St. Martinville. A prosperous farmer and deputy sheriff, Fuselier claims to have told both Sheriff Resweber and District Attorney L. O. Pecot about the theft of his gun in September 1944. According to the prosecution, Andrew Thomas was shot and killed two months later, on the evening of November 7, 1944, in a "stickup" behind his garage, where Willie had waited for as little as a half hour to as much as three hours allegedly to rob him.

In the two months between the theft of Fuselier's pistol and Andrew Thomas's death, not a single incident of a robbery at gunpoint in St. Martinville was reported. If Willie Francis stole the gun of August Fuselier for the purpose of robbing Andrew Thomas, then he patiently waited two months before attempting the robbery. And of all the people in St. Martinville to rob, why would Willie choose a man who knew him, a man who employed him and could easily identify and report him to police? Why, too, would Willie wait behind Thomas's garage, perhaps for as long as three hours, until his victim returned to his rural home, more than a mile from town, on this particular night two months after stealing the gun? If Willie's motive was financial gain, why not break into Thomas's remote home when he knew Thomas was not there and assure himself of takings better than the subsequent four dollars and a watch?

The murder of Andrew Thomas bore all the markings of a planned confrontation, not a random robbery. If Willie did wait as many as three hours behind that garage, it was probably not to rob Thomas but to take a stand against him, perhaps just to threaten him although, if so, something must have gone very bad. According to the prosecution, "The motive for this crime was robbery (in underworld parlance, 'a stick-up'), and to perpetuate this robbery, this murder was committed." But the theory of a robbery gone bad was simply the prosecution's easiest, most believable means to convince a jury to convict Willie Francis. And the prosecution was not required to prove a motive. Later, in the hearing before the Louisiana Pardons Board, Resweber did allude to the possibility of a relationship between Thomas and Willie prior to the robbery. He stated that Thomas may have chastised Willie at the drugstore. The sheriff claimed that Willie Francis told him that he'd "had a little trouble with Thomas," but then, according to Resweber, Willie changed his mind and said that he'd had no problem with Thomas, who was a "fine fellow." According to Willie, Thomas had even invited the youth to his house where he would pay Willie "a dollar or fifty cents for cleaning or raking his yard." In his confession in Port Arthur, Texas, Willie more enigmatically said, "it was a secret about me and him."

According to the coroner's report, five bullets struck Andrew Thomas. It would appear, then, that the alleged armed robber had waited behind the garage until Thomas parked his car and shut the garage door before confronting him. The *Weekly Messenger* reported that Thomas died after a "terrific struggle," yet the coroner's report did not cite any evidence of a struggle. It simply stated that Andrew Thomas had been shot five times in the head and body with a .38 caliber gun. Presumably, one of the shots, perhaps the first, from the stolen .38 caliber gun knocked Andrew Thomas to the ground; the coroner's report stated that "anyone [sic] of these wounds would have produced death." If so, the shooter then continued to fire the gun at close range into Thomas's head and body, possibly even after he was down. Two bullets, however, may have penetrated both Thomas and the side of the garage while he was still standing. The ballistic details of the crime that ended Thomas's life will never be known, for the evidence was lost in transit to Washington, DC. Still, the fact remains that someone was waiting for Andrew Thomas with a gun. Most probably what started out as a premeditated confrontation quickly escalated into rage and gunfire that left St. Martinville's congenial bachelor pharmacist lying dead.

While Willie himself did admit repeatedly to killing Andrew Thomas, he denied that the motive was robbery. Nor did he ever divulge his actual motive; when asked why he did it, he'd say only, "I don't know. I just don't know." He did say why he didn't do it, though. On the night of May 3, 1946, just after he had walked away from the chair, Willie told a reporter, "I wasn't after money."

Sheriff Gilbert Ozenne and his men may have had a history of terrorizing blacks in New Iberia, but Ozenne did not force Willie to scrawl "I killed Andrew by accident" on his pink jail cell wall. And twice in writing—once quite freely—Willie confessed his guilt to Sheriff Resweber. Unquestionably, though, the trial of Willie Francis was a travesty of justice, and quite possibly it was efficiently manipulated to hide the truth behind the death of Andrew Thomas.

Indeed, if Willie's confession is to be believed, clearly something had to have happened that was serious enough to bring the two of them to that confrontation behind Andrew Thomas's garage, across from Evangeline Park on the evening on November 7, 1944. On his jail cell wall, Willie wrote that he had killed Thomas practically "by accident" and that it will "happen once in a lifetime." In his letter to Mrs. Taylor, he said, "About my past, I didn't mean no harm." Willie may have been armed with a stolen gun, but he may not have intended to fire it.

Willie's most telling comment on the matter came in January 1947 after he learned that the U.S. Supreme Court had rejected De-Blanc's appeal by a vote of 5–4. Willie told a reporter that he was confident the chair would work the second time, and the reporter asked, "Do you think you can take it?" Willie replied, "I'm sure I can. I had the nerve to kill a man so I guess I can take it."

Father Hannigan, most likely, never learned the motive behind the killing of Andrew Thomas, yet he was nonetheless convinced that Willie was no threat to society. It would seem the priest's comments to reporters in early 1947 that Willie "has changed" were indicative of Hannigan's perception of Willie as a young man whose motive had never been robbery; rather, he may have seen the murder as an act of catharsis. Willie's alleged possession of the wallet, which could read-ily place him at the scene of the murder, showed that the killing of Andrew Thomas meant more to him as a personal deliverance than as the commission of a crime. "He would be all right if they let him out," Hannigan said, seeming to support Willie's own claim that the incident behind Andrew Thomas's garage was a "once in a lifetime" occurrence.

Although he certainly welcomed Bertrand DeBlanc's efforts to spare his life, Willie always demonstrated willingness to pay for his crime, although he did not talk specifically about his motive. Even if his initial confessions were coerced by racist law enforcement officers, Willie never denied his guilt. "I was convinced he did it," DeBlanc would say years later. In the spring of 1947 Willie was collaborating with a local writer, Sam Montgomery, on his pamphlet, *My Trip to the Chair*, which DeBlanc was going to use to raise money for a last-minute appeal to the U.S. Supreme Court. Surely, had Willie claimed in his pamphlet to be innocent of the murder of Andrew Thomas, DeBlanc might have been able to raise more money. But Willie wrote, "I don't want to talk about the killing of Mr. Thomas. When they asked me to write this story I said I would only [write it] if I didn't have to say anything about that part. I was tried and convicted of the killing, and as far as I think, that's all over." Devoutly religious and preparing to meet God, Willie Francis would not lie. Not even to save himself.

In 1981, Gus Weill, a Louisiana author, television host, and political consultant, spoke at length with DeBlanc about the murder. He believes that any "interactions" between Willie and Andrew Thomas that may have led to the latter's death were not matters DeBlanc would have pursued as a young lawyer with political aspirations in southern Louisiana. As a result, the issue for DeBlanc was never a matter of Willie's innocence or guilt. A "strict constitutionalist" and not opposed to the death penalty, DeBlanc simply and profoundly believed that a second trip to the chair constituted cruel and unusual punishment. DeBlanc acted in accordance with the truth as he perceived it—that Willie Francis had killed Andrew Thomas—and he defended Willie tirelessly in a manner he considered to be fair and just.

Those like DeBlanc who believed that Willie had likely pulled the trigger of Fuselier's gun and killed Thomas never took much interest in discovering why, even after Willie's cryptic references to a deeper story. The town of St. Martinville buries its secrets, and so did Willie Francis.

When he told Bertrand DeBlanc to "let it go" because he was "ready to die," it may have been the only time in the short life of Willie Francis that he felt he had any power, any say, in a system of laws and mores that could only crush him. In the end, the deeply religious Catholic boy condemned himself—for sins he would not discuss, sins, to him, perhaps worse than murder. Willie Francis took his secret, "a secret about me and him," to a small patch of dirt in the Union Baptist Cemetery, beneath a pecan tree and the shattered remains of his own gravestone.

no matter how small

I want to do what's right.

—J. Skelly Wright

The year 1947 was a particularly deadly one in Louisiana. Willie Francis was one of eight men who were put to death in the lap of Gruesome Gertie that year—the most until 1987 when another eight were killed in the chair. Between 1941 and 1991, when the state of Louisiana adopted lethal injection to execute capital punishment, Gruesome Gertie ended the lives of eighty-six men and one woman. Today a replica of the chair sits in the Louisiana State Penitentiary Museum at Angola, although it has on occasion been moved from the museum to the prison for appearances in films like *Monster's Ball* (2001).

There are people in St. Martinville today who believe the town is cursed. Just as many believe that Willie Francis was innocent, as did—"with deep conviction"—Father Maurice Rousseve. A few years before his death in 1985, Father Rousseve spoke to a writer, Nicholas Lemann, about the Willie Francis case, and in that conversation, he named August Fuselier as the man behind the murder of Andrew Thomas. While many men in town might have wished Thomas dead, Rousseve reasoned, none of them could match the

288

marksmanship of the deputy sheriff, whose gun was in fact used to kill the druggist. Rousseve suggested, too, that Willie might have been set up, for he was "simple-minded" enough to have accepted Andrew Thomas's wallet as a token or gift from someone he barely knew and then to consider it his own. And with the dead man's wallet in his pocket, Willie would almost surely be charged with the murder. Nor would it have taken much, in Rousseve's view, for the authorities to wrest a confession out of Willie Francis once he was in custody. And while it is conceivable that Willie might have wanted to take some vengeance on Thomas—he had caught Willie trying to steal from the safe in the drugstore, according to Rousseve—it is unlikely that a Willie wanting vengeance would have translated into a Willie planning murder. Rousseve was convinced that, indeed, the person with the most compelling motive and real means to kill Andrew Thomas was not Willie Francis but August Fusilier.

"Anyway," Rousseve said, "if Willie Francis had done it, why would he carry around the wallet for almost a year? Why had the murder weapon disappeared?" Rousseve's theory reverberates, some sixty years later, in St. Martinville still.

Father Rousseve noted also that in 1946 it was unheard of for a white man in southern Louisiana to spend a year defending a poor black youth. Bertrand DeBlanc had demonstrated "great courage," said Rousseve, and had been "completely honest and sincere throughout." But the Cajun lawyer had one failing, according to Rousseve: "The sad part is this. He didn't believe the boy was innocent. He would not believe the boy was innocent." Rousseve pointed to entreaties, late in the case, from NAACP attorney A. P. Tureaud that DeBlanc more aggressively attack the fairness of Willie's trial—entreaties that DeBlanc rejected.

"My approach to the case was," a terse DeBlanc said in retrospect, "I wasn't trying to stir up controversy. I just didn't want him going back to the chair. Some groups were interested in that. But you see, when a person is convicted of a crime, you appeal on a question of law, not fact."

After Willie's death, DeBlanc served as district attorney in Lafayette, Vermillion, and Acadia parishes for eighteen years. But his heart, according to family members, was never in prosecuting the endless stream of Louisiana's poor. Upon leaving office, he did not turn to a more lucrative career in private practice. Instead, De-Blanc became the first former district attorney in Louisiana to become head of the indigent defender's office in Lafayette. It was a job that better suited his passion and idealism, friends and family noted, and when it came to his clients, every man was king. "He would get so many Christmas cards and letters every year, thanking him for caring," his daughter Veronica says, adding that they came even from prisons.

Before his death in 1992, and nearly forty years after the Supreme Court decision that broke his heart, Bertrand DeBlanc returned to the Union Baptist Cemetery with a group of journalists. He solemnly gazed at the small family crypt and the unmarked grave where Willie lay buried. Brushing away a tear, DeBlanc said, "If Willie's appeal was today we'd win."

When Bertrand DeBlanc spoke those words in 1981, Thurgood Marshall had been serving on the U.S. Supreme Court for fourteen years, during which time the criminal justice system—from its police investigations to criminal trials to death-penalty appeals—had changed so profoundly that what had happened to Willie Francis in 1946 would at that point have been close to unthinkable. And in March 2005, the U.S. Supreme Court voted to abolish capital punishment for offenders who committed crimes when under the age of eighteen. The decision was 5–4, with the majority concluding that the death penalty for minors is cruel and unusual punishment, while citing a "national consensus" against the practice and promoting the "evolving standards of decency that mark the progress of a maturing society." In his dissent, Justice Antonin Scalia chided the majority opinion, stating, "The court thus proclaims itself the sole arbiter of our Nation's moral standards." The language calls to mind the self-imposed dilemma of Felix Frankfurter during the winter of 1946, when he embraced the maintenance of national standards of decency at the same time that he vainly wanted, given his personal standards in regard to the questionable humanity of his own decision, to save the life of Willie Francis.

● ● ●

Alexander Pierre Tureaud, who viewed civil rights as a legal issue, never wavered in his dedication to the achievement of "scattered little victories" in the courts—victories that, he hoped, would someday reverse the ruling in *Plessy v. Ferguson* and bring an end to legalized racism in America. After gaining equal pay for black public school teachers in Louisiana, Tureaud took on the far more ambitious and contentious issue of public school desegregation in the state of Louisiana. The battles he waged throughout the 1950s and 1960s were long; large though the victory would ultimately be, it might also have cost him his life. That was never more apparent than in 1951 when he filed suit in *Bush v. Orleans Parish School Board*, calling for the desegregation of public schools in New Orleans. The lawsuit dragged on for nearly ten years, and it launched a decade of constant death threats targeting not only Tureaud himself but his family as well. It was the "second battle of New Orleans."

Late in his life, when the civil rights movement had become more confrontational, Tureaud reiterated his preference for the rule of law over protest:

I'm more in favor of that than all this damn stuff they are carrying on in the streets. I never had to participate in one single demonstration and I've gotten all these things.

All the schools that are desegregated now came as the result of litigation, not . . . demonstrations. Demonstrations
haven't desegregated anything but lunch counters and we
had to make it possible for them to carry those on. . . . We
had to defend them in the courts.

Before Thurgood Marshall became a Supreme Court justice, at a
time when the hotels in New Orleans were closed to blacks, he and
his associates on visits to the city would often stay at Tureaud's
home. Marshall delivered the eulogy for his frequent host at
Tureaud's funeral in 1972, and suitably so. Tureaud was, as historian
Adam Fairclough avows, "the most important strand of the complex
fabric that made up the civil rights movement in Louisiana."

At best, Tureaud's relationship with Bertrand DeBlanc throughout the Willie Francis ordeal was strained, although Tureaud, deep
down, must have had a begrudging respect for the Cajun lawyer. In
the early 1960s, when Tureaud's own son, A. P. Jr., was attending interracial student council meetings in college, the elder Tureaud
asked him, "Do you know who the heroes are?" The NAACP
lawyer's answer to his own question possibly surprised his son, for
he declared that the white students were the real heroes. Whereas
blacks had to take action to change the system because the struggle
was theirs, said Tureaud, the white students didn't. And because
they did, heroically, they faced ostracism.

J. Skelly Wright would learn a thing or two about such ostracism
in Louisiana. Three years after arguing the Willie Francis case before the U.S. Supreme Court, Wright was back in New Orleans
working for the U.S. attorney's office. There, as throughout the
South during the 1948 presidential election, many Louisiana De-
mocrats abandoned their party for Strom Thurmond, who promised
to protect the "Southern way of life" from an oppressive federal
government and made "Segregation forever!" the rallying cry for his

new "Dixiecrats." Skelly Wright, however, was not one of them. By a narrow margin that year, President Harry S Truman won reelection, and among his judicial appointments was the loyal Wright. Almost immediately after the Senate confirmed him, Wright was thrown into battle at the U.S. District Court, Eastern District of Louisiana, where he was assigned "many race cases he would decide as spokesman for the federal Constitution in his corner of the world."

Six years after the 1954 U.S. Supreme Court ruling in *Brown v. Board of Education of Topeka*, which outlawed racial segregation in public schools, A. P. Tureaud became increasingly frustrated but no less determined in his attempts to effect the desegregation of New Orleans schools. By then hundreds of schools in bordering states had desegregated, but not one had done so in Louisiana. School boards simply refused to appear in court; unsympathetic judges dragged their feet or dug in their heels. Jimmie Davis meanwhile won a second term as governor in 1960 by promising the citizens of Louisiana that he would uphold segregation in public schools four more years. (Davis took 82 percent of the vote.) For Tureaud to succeed in his lawsuit to desegregate schools in New Orleans, he needed a judge who would be willing to stand up to the governor, the state legislature, and a city populace that was certain to ostracize him, or worse. Tureaud found that judge on a spring day in 1960 when he stood in the courtroom of the Honorable J. Skelly Wright.

Having run out of patience with the city's stalling techniques over the past four years, Wright presented the Orleans Parish school board with an ultimatum: come up with a plan to desegregate by May 15, or "I will come up with one myself." When the board returned to court on the 15th, their "briefcases empty," Wright devised what he termed his "desperation plan" and ordered that it be implemented when the schools opened in September. The desegregation would begin with the first grade, because, Wright said, children at that age are "not color conscious; they haven't been taught to hate." Another grade would be desegregated each year thereafter, until the schools in their entirety were racially mixed. However much Wright's reputation had preceded him, Tureaud had to have been stunned by the judicial activism he witnessed in the courtroom that day.

Governor Davis was livid. He issued a statement to the press in which he declared that "the people of Orleans parish and the state of Louisiana can be assured that every necessary legal step will be taken to preserve and maintain segregation in this state." On May 17, Roy V. Harris, the National Citizens' Council president and one of the "roving ambassadors of segregation," told an enthusiastic crowd: "Get ready for war!"

Orleans Parish board attorneys quickly took the case to the U.S. Supreme Court (adjourned for the summer) in an attempt to stay Wright's order, but acting on behalf of the Court, Justice Hugo Black (who would later become one of Wright's closest friends in Washington) refused, and Wright's order stood. Tureaud, meanwhile, knew the clock was ticking; he told Thurgood Marshall that "it looks like New Orleans may be the next battleground for massive resistance or closing of the schools in the state." Governor Jimmie Davis, who had vowed to "fight to eternity" for Louisiana's right to disobey a federal court order, suspended the Orleans Parish school board and took control of the city's schools himself. But Davis was nowhere to be found when federal marshals, at Wright's behest, attempted to serve him with a summons. The court thus instructed the parish board to move forward with the ordered desegregation.

The hatred and threats that Wright (as well as wife Helen and son Jimmy) endured in the ensuing months became so intense that New Orleans police squads were camping in Wright's basement around the clock. Federal marshals protected Wright during the day. Around the city, coffins appeared displaying Wright's name. Everywhere placards proclaimed, "Wright is Wrong!" and he'd hear himself described as a "nigger-loving traitor to his race." Wright estimated that he was "hated by 80 to 90 percent of the people in New Orleans," and he and his family became increasingly isolated. Still, Wright maintained perspective. On the back of a Mardi Gras program, he wrote the words that would eloquently formulate his opinion on *Bush v. Orleans Parish School Board*—words his wife, Helen, would encase in a plastic plaque, which Wright took to Washington when President Kennedy appointed him to the DC circuit court—words that read:

> The problem of changing a people's mores, particularly those with an emotional overlay, is not to be taken lightly. It is a problem which will require the utmost patience, understanding, generosity and forbearance and from all of us, of whatever race.
>
> But the magnitude of the problem may not nullify the principle. And that principle is that we are, all of us, free-born Americans with a right to make our way unfettered by sanctions imposed by man because of the work of God.

Meanwhile, Tureaud and the NAACP were searching the Ninth Ward for children who, along with their families, might be able and willing to commit themselves to the upcoming battle on D-Day (Desegregation Day) in New Orleans. A mass desegregation, they knew, would be too difficult and chaotic to implement, so they screened prospective first-graders and their parents through "rigorous testing required by the pupil placement plan" until they found four strong candidates. All the students chosen were girls, three of whom would attend McDonough 19, while the other six-year-old would enter first grade at the William Frantz Elementary School in the Ninth Ward.

Skelly Wright summoned a corps of federal marshals to his chambers early on Monday morning, November 14, 1960 (he had been forced to reschedule Desegregation Day, which had originally been set for September), and provided each of them with copies of his court order. A gold stamp and seal of the court as well as the blue ribbon wrapped around the rolled document were intended "to make it look more legal than usual" when the marshals flashed the order at any state troopers who might try to block their entrance. Wright instructed the marshals to proceed assertively but, if guns were drawn, to back off; the safety of the girls was at all times to be their top priority.

At approximately 9:30 a.m., two sedans pulled up in front of the William Frantz Elementary School, and a little girl in a white dress and with white ribbons in her hair hopped out. Her name was Ruby Bridges. As marshals led her to the front steps of the school building, they also shielded her from rotten eggs, spit, and vicious racial slurs slung at her by a rabid crowd. That moment—immortalized by Norman Rockwell in his painting *The Problem We All Live With*, in which four faceless marshals wearing yellow armbands are escorting the little girl in the white dress past a schoolhouse wall splattered by the juice of a tomato and fouled in a crude scrawl with "KKK" and the word "Nigger"—would make Ruby Bridges the symbol of desegregation in the South. Skelly Wright hung a framed print of the Rockwell painting on the wall of his office.

Ruby Bridges spent her first year of grade school in a classroom for one at William Frantz Elementary, and each day there she was greeted by "cheerleaders" who blocked, shoved, shouted, spat, and snarled at her in angry demonstration against Wright's plan. The writer John Steinbeck observed the protestors and noted, "No newspaper had printed the words these women shouted. It was indicated that they were indelicate, some even said obscene. On television the sound track was made to blur or had noises cut in to cover. But now I heard the words, bestial and filthy and degenerate." Ruby held up well, although her sudden loss of appetite puzzled her parents. School staff had found a stash of uneaten sandwiches in Ruby's locker; only later was it learned that one of the "cheerleaders" accosted Ruby each morning with the threat that "we're going to poison you until you choke to death."

In the end, despite counterefforts by Louisiana's legislative majority, the state superintendent of schools, Governor Jimmie Davis, and the state police force, Skelly Wright and A. P. Tureaud did segregate the schools of New Orleans. Unlike Felix Frankfurter, Wright did not hesitate to use judicial activism to advance the cause of justice for all. He and Tureaud both "stared down the entire state of Louisiana in one of the most dramatic confrontations between law and mob rule the nation has ever witnessed."

Over the next several years, Wright would be responsible for desegregating the professional schools of Louisiana State University, the public buses, and the city parks. He would restore the names of countless blacks to voting lists and uphold interracial sporting events. He would stand firm always, and frequently he'd be vilified by friends and foes alike in New Orleans. Former political associates would refer to him as Judas Scalawag Wrong and publicly call for his impeachment, not to mention his arrest and imprisonment. Yet Skelly Wright would remain calm, even in the face of daily death threats and at the sight of burning crosses on the front lawn of his house on Newcomb Boulevard. "Lots of people don't like what I have done," he said. "But more and more are coming to understand that it is something we must do."

In 1962, President Kennedy appointed Wright to the court of appeals for the District of Columbia, known as the "home court for the federal government." Kennedy ranked the Louisiana native as "one of the great judges of America," but reputation could not erase the pain Wright had experienced during the Willie Francis Supreme Court appeals. Nearly forty years after the execution, Wright admitted to a biographer that Willie Francis "still weighed heavily on his mind," and he told a journalist in 1983 that had he and DeBlanc been able to send the case back to Louisiana, as Justice Burton had suggested, "the Court today would find some way to alleviate the situation."

In words that stand in stark contrast to Felix Frankfurter's deeds in the Willie Francis case, Wright once said, "I want to do what's right. When I get a case, I look at it and the first thing I think of automatically is what's right, what should be done—and then you look at the law to see whether or not you can do it. That might invert the process of how you should arrive at a decision . . . but in my case it developed through making decisions, which involves solving problems."

Earlier in their careers, Wright and Tureaud—these two accomplished, earnest, Catholic Louisiana attorneys—had been unable to solve the problems of the Francis case. They had been unable to save the life of a poor, stuttering, barely educated, devoutly Catholic boy from St. Martinville, but their memory of Willie Francis lingered long and hardened them for future battles. For Skelly Wright and A. P. Tureaud, Ruby Bridges represented all the young lives that could be saved. As Wright observed, "These children have a right to accept the constitutional promise of equality before the law, an equality we profess to all the world."

To state his credo more plainly, Skelly Wright, who served more than a quarter century on the U.S. court of appeals for the District of Columbia circuit until his death in 1988, borrowed the words of Theodor Geisel, better known as Dr. Seuss, from his book *Horton Hears a Who:* "A person's a person, no matter how small."

Unlike Wright, Bertrand DeBlanc received no prestigious political appointments and tried no further high-profile cases to make a national name for the attorney from southwestern Louisiana. He was essentially a country lawyer, but not a narrowly provincial one. He came back to Louisiana from a world war and, like millions of returning servicemen white and black, he now saw America a little differently. The caste system in St. Martinville as well as his own family's tradition-bound biases represented the old order, which was beginning to collide with new national standards—standards of perceived fairness and justice, with laws to protect, as Hugo Black wrote, the helpless, the weak, and the outnumbered.

Bertrand DeBlanc was more than a witness to the collision. He was also a party to it, because he chose to take a stand. DeBlanc, though, made his choice, just as he would make his case for Willie Francis, on the grounds not of race but of American values. The color of Willie's skin was inconsequential to DeBlanc; what was at stake in the case was the right of all Americans as equals to fairness and justice. Arguing Willie's claim to that right, DeBlanc was able to rally a nation, white and black. In Willie Francis, DeBlanc humanized poignantly the cruelty being inflicted by the government on a black youth, and he struck a chord nationwide with white Americans who responded with outrage at southern justice, as they would again in 1955 after the murder of fourteen-year-old Emmitt Till, and in 1963 when four little girls died in the bombing of the 16th Street Baptist Church in Birmingham, Alabama.

Outrage, in the two decades following Willie's sad case, would more and more motivate whites in the long struggle of American blacks for their civil rights. Social change in America would come slowly. It would be achieved, as A. P. Tureaud said, in "scattered little victories," not only in the courts but in the actions of ordinary men and women, like Bertrand DeBlanc, making what they perceived to be simple decisions or unexceptional choices and, little by little, altering a nation's collective consciousness.

•   •   •

In 1986, the writer Ernest Gaines was teaching at the University of Louisiana at Lafayette. He was also researching a book that would become the best-selling novel *A Lesson Before Dying*. The story is of a young, nearly illiterate black youth in southern Louisiana who is accused of killing a white man and condemned to die in the state's portable electric chair. A student in one of Gaines's classes asked him if he would like to meet a lawyer who had actually defended a young black man in a death penalty case forty years earlier. Interested, Gaines invited her to bring the lawyer to his house. She arrived, in Gaines's words, accompanied by a "Cajun fellow, probably in his seventies, bent, frail."

They sat together on the porch, and the lawyer told the author about Gruesome Gertie, about how the generator could be heard from blocks away, and about how the boy survived a botched execution. He recounted how he had taken the case from the supreme court of Louisiana all the way up to the U.S. Supreme Court in Washington, DC, and how he had failed again and again. One year later, he said, the boy was sent back to the electric chair. And killed.

Suddenly, Gaines observed, the old Cajun lawyer went silent, then brought his hands up to his face. The student moved closer, held him in her arms, and the lawyer laid his head on her shoulder. After a moment, he began to weep.

For the boy. For himself.

"Forty years later," Gaines noted, "he could still remember that generator, that chair."

Acknowledgments

I would most graciously like to thank the DeBlanc family for their cooperation over the years that it took to write this book. Lillian DeBlanc kindly shared many memories and stories about life with her husband Bertrand and opened a window into St. Martinville in 1946 that only she could. I would also like to thank the sons and daughters of Bertrand and Lillian that I spoke with—Veronica, Daniel, Catherine, Melanie, and Bertrand Jr. They were all generous with their time, and I would have only scraped the surface of this story without their help.

Helen Patton Wright, wife of the late J. Skelly Wright, was also kind enough to invite me to her home and share scrapbooks and memories of her husband's involvement in the Willie Francis case. Her son James Wright and nephew Jim Wright were also very helpful to me along the way.

I'm grateful that A. P. Tureaud Jr. spoke to me with so much insight and detail about his life in New Orleans, his father, and growing up in the incredible Tureaud family. I would also like to thank various members of the Francis, Resweber, Rousseve, Pecot, Simon, Dupois, Fuselier, Nassans, Duplantis, and Vincent families, as well as Diane Baker Godwin for speaking candidly about their relatives. I am especially appreciative of members of the Thomas family, who were gracious enough to speak with me about a painful time in their family's past.

Allan Durand, director of the documentary film *Willie Francis Must Die Again*, had safeguarded Bertrand DeBlanc's legal files and kindly allowed me to spend days in his office combing through and copying so many documents. Allan also provided rich insight into St. Martinville's past and Cajun life in general. Jeffrey Bowman, co-author (with Arthur S. Miller) of *Death by Installments: The Ordeal of Willie Francis*, invited both Allan and me into his Washington, DC, home to share pizza and unforgettable conversation about the Willie Francis case. No one knows more about the case than Jeff, and the gifted attorney was kind enough to help me navigate the sometimes-challenging questions that arose along the way. His assistance was most appreciated. "Louisiana Legend" Gus Weill might be the greatest conversationalist I've ever come across, and the time he spent talking to me was as rich as any visit to a library.

This book would not have been possible were it not for the many people of St. Martinville who tolerated, with great patience, my mispronouncing every Cajun name I came across. They are truly, as it has been said, the "most peaceable, happy people" on earth. James Akers is a wonderful storyteller and goldmine of St. Martinville history, and Velma Johnson proved to be an invaluable source with a mind for details of St. Martinville in the 1940s. I spent many hours with them at the St. Martinville Cultural Heritage Center, and I'm grateful they shared their memories with me.

Ella Vincent Lawrence always had the answers to my questions about everything from Cajun coffee, to street names, to bloodlines. My visits with Sue Martin, another lifelong resident of St. Martinville, were especially memorable. Sue invited me several times into her beautiful old house on the Bayou Teche, just a block from the courthouse where she worked in 1946. Her words painted pictures for me. James Theriot took me around town in his truck for an inspirational tour of St. Martinville. And the late Nolan "Cabbie" Charles did the same, opening my eyes to the parts of town in which he'd lived and worked his whole life before his death in 2006. Cabbie, I know, was very happy to learn that someone was going to tell the story of his old friend, Willie Francis. Hilton Butler, the former warden at Angola, patiently answered many questions and shared stories and details about the eleven death runs he made with Gruesome Gertie, several in the company of Captain Ephie Foster.

When a stranger from New York with a notepad in hand showed up at her door (the same door Andrew Thomas was walking toward before he was shot dead), Ione Guirard was kind enough to open it. I wasn't sure if I wanted to be the one to inform the current residents, if they didn't already know, that a murder had taken place on their property. Turned out, Ione knew a lot, and her generosity is most appreciated.

Others in and around St. Martinville who were helpful to me along the way were Andrew Stevens, Robert Adams, E. L. Guidry, Louie M. Cyr, and George Etie Jr. Thanks also to Burk Foster, Jenny Borders at Angola, Jessica Cormier at CODOFIL, and Dominique Durand.

Dr. Florent Hardy of the Louisiana State Archives is a true man of action—always an email away whenever I got stuck—and on countless occasions, he pointed me in the direction of people who could help.

I benefited from the help of three researchers, Elizabeth Kucich, Jennifer Bayhi, and Joanna Gohmann, who helped me track down people and documents in Louisiana while I was in New York. And thanks to my mother, Dorothy King, who proved to be an amateur genealogist extraordinaire.

In New Iberia, I had the privilege to meet Paul Schwing and the "World's Problem Solvers" at the famous Victor's Café. Paul treated me to a fine breakfast and, along with Clayton J. David and the other regulars, helped me understand and navigate 1940s New Iberia. James Lee Burke led me to another New Iberian trove of history and information in Morris Raphael, and Earl Robicheaux Sr. helped arrange a tour of the old New Iberia Parish jail, as well as providing details about the New Iberia Sheriff's Office. Monsignor Ronald Broussard and John Reedom at the St. Edward Catholic Church gave me background information on the Holy Ghost Fathers in New Iberia, but not before making me attend Sunday mass first. Father Hannigan would be delighted to learn that his old parish is still warm and lively and with hardly an open seat in the pews.

I would also like to thank the many librarians and staff at the following libraries and research centers, as they always seemed to go the extra mile: Amistad Research Center in New Orleans; Jane Vidrine at the University of Louisiana Lafayette Library, Mary Alice Fontenot Riehl Collection; Louisiana State University Paul M. Hebert Law Center in Baton Rouge; Schomburg Center for Research in Black Culture in New York; Moorland-Springarn Research Center at Howard University in Washington, DC; National Archives, Washington, DC; Library of Congress, Washington, DC; the New York Public Library–Humanities and Social Sciences Library; the Iberia Parish Library; and the St. Martinville Public Library.

As a nonlawyer writing a book that is heavily dosed in law, I needed help. I owe a great deal to the brilliant appellate lawyer Tom Burka, who showed me the way. David Darden and Matthew Boylan trained their legal eyes on this manuscript at various stages and provided invaluable suggestions and advice. This book also benefited from the encouragement and critiques of some trusted friends, including Karen Abbott, who knows a thing or two about telling stories and pushed me to tell this one better. Jim Wohl loves a good story as much as I do and didn't mind spending hours reading and discussing a work in progress. Thanks also to Dr. Nathaniel Ehrlich, Meg Leder, and Maureen Ogle for their insight and advice; to Tom Schmidt, who offered his Washington home to me whenever I was in town and who designed a fantastic map of St. Martinville for this book; and to Nick Barose, for support and friendship along the way. And a special thanks goes to as pure a gentleman as there is, Peter Skutches, who attacked my manuscript at various stages with a green pencil that usually sent me digging again. Every writer should be fortunate enough to have an erudite friend like Peter watching his or her back.

Early on, I wrote to an author I'd long admired—David J. Garrow, Pulitzer Prize–winning author of *Bearing the Cross: Martin Luther King Jr., and the Southern Christian Leadership Conference*— with the hope that he might offer a few words of advice or encouragement about my manuscript. Professor Garrow was extremely supportive and helpful, and I'll be forever grateful to him.

My longtime friend Carlo DeVito deserves all the credit for this book ever being put to pen and paper. He came across the story and thought I should look into it. I was reluctant, but he was persistent. He was right, as always. Thank you, Carlo.

I'd also like to thank Lara Heimert, Brandon Proia, Nicole Caputo, and Jodi Marchowsky at Basic *Civitas* for all their help and support. My editor, Chris Greenberg, was an enthusiastic advocate from the start. This book benefited tremendously from his critical eye. And I am extremely fortunate that this book attracted the attention of my agent, Farley Chase. It could not have been in better hands. Farley's passion for the story, his instinctive narrative vision and his persistence were encouraging at every stage.

In many ways, this book was a family project, and I thank my parents for the many times they were around for support and to babysit. Mary Jane Miles is our Evangeline Oak, and the upstate Kings—Ed, Janette, Emily, Eileen, and Jimmy—are a joy to be near.

Finally, my two daughters, Maddie and Liv, patiently put up with the fact that daddy wasn't spending all that time in his office writing a fabulous childrens' book, inspired by them. They are inspiring to me just the same, and beyond words. And my wife Lorna is the one I can always count on to help me see the light. My love and my best friend, she is one of a kind and I'm lucky to have her.

Notes and Sources

Among the dozens of books I read throughout my research, three were extraordinarily useful to me. *Death by Installments: The Ordeal of Willie Francis* by Arthur S. Miller and Jeffrey H. Bowman (in the series Contributions in Legal Studies published by Greenwood Press 1988) was an invaluable companion, and anyone who desires a more thorough understanding of the decisions and dynamics of the U.S. Supreme Court case, *State of Louisiana ex rel. Francis v. Resweber*, 329 U.S. 459 (1947), would be wise to seek out Miller and Bowman's book for further reading.

Adam Fairclough's *Race & Democracy: The Civil Rights Struggle in Louisiana, 1915–1972* (University of Georgia Press, 1995) is the quintessential text on Louisiana race and politics. And Liva Baker's *The Second Battle of New Orleans: The Hundred-Year Struggle to Integrate the Schools* (HarperCollins, 1996) sheds incomparable light on the work and lives of A. P. Tureaud and J. Skelly Wright, as well as the great city of New Orleans.

Bibliography

Ambrose, Stephen E. *To America: Personal Reflections to an Historian*. Simon & Schuster, 2003.

Arsenault, Bona. *History of the Acadians*. Lemeac, 1978.

Baker, Liva. *The Second Battle of New Orleans: The Hundred-Year Struggle to Integrate the Schools*. HarperCollins, 1996.

Bernard, Shane. *The Cajuns—Americanization of a People*. University of Mississippi Press, 2003.

Black, Elizabeth, and Hugo L. Black. *Mr. Justice and Mrs. Black: The Memoirs of Hugo L. Black*. Random House, 1986.

Brandon, Craig. *The Electric Chair: An Unnatural American History*. McFarland and Company, 1990.

Brasseaux, Carl A. *The Founding of New Acadia: The Beginnings of Acadian Life in Louisiana, 1765–1803*. Louisiana State University Press, 1987.

Capuder, Lawrence. *1896 in Le Petit Paris*. Little Paris Publishing Company, 1999.

Carleton, Mark T. *Politics and Punishment: The History of the Louisiana State Penal System*. Louisiana State University Press, 1971.

Chaze, Elliott. *The Golden Tag*. Simon & Schuster, 1950.

Coles, Robert. *Conversations with Robert Coles*, edited by Jay Woodruff and Sarah Carew Woodruff. University Press of Mississippi, 1992.

Conrod, Glenn R. *A Dictionary of Louisiana Biography*. Vol. 2. Louisiana Historical Association, 1988.

Essig, Mark. *Edison & The Electric Chair: A Story of Light and Death*. Walker and Company, 2003.

Fairclough, Adam. *Race and Democracy: The Civil Rights Struggle in Louisiana 1915–1972*. University of Georgia Press, 1999.

Francis, Willie, and Samuel Montgomery. *My Trip to the Chair*. 1947. Afro-American Pamphlets, Part 3, #148, Rare Book & Special Collections Division, Library of Congress, Washington, DC.

Freedman, Max, William Merritt Beaney, and Eugene Victor Rostow. *Perspectives on the Court*. Northwestern University Press, 1967.

Friendly, Fred W., and Martha J. H. Elliott. *The Constitution: That Delicate Balance*. Random House, 1984.

Gaines, Ernest J. *A Lesson before Dying*. Vintage Contemporaries, 1993.

Gaines, Ernest J. *Mozart and Leadbelly, Stories and Essays*, compiled and edited by Marcia Gaudet and Reggie Young. Knopf, 2005.

Gill, James. *Lords of Misrule: Mardi Gras and the Politics of Race in New Orleans*. University Press of Mississippi, 1997.

Gross, Samuel R., Kristen Jacoby, Daniel J. Matheson, Nicholas Montgomery, and Sujata Patil. "Exonerations in the United States 1989 through 2003." *Journal of Criminal Law and Criminology* 95, no. 2 (2005): 523–560.

Gunning, Sandra. *Race, Rape, and Lynching: The Red Record of American Literature, 1890–1912*. Oxford University Press, 1996.

Hollandsworth, James G. *The Louisiana Native Guards: The Black Military Experience during the Civil War*. Louisiana State University Press, 1998.

Irons, Peter. *A People's History of the Supreme Court: The Men and Women Whose Cases and Decisions Have Shaped Our Constitution*. Viking, 1999.

Jackson, Robert Houghwout. *Dispassionate Justice: A Snythesis of the Judicial Opinions of Robert H. Jackson*, edited by Glendon Schubert. Bobbs-Merrill Company, 1969.

Kane, Harnett T. *The Bayous of Louisiana*. Morrow and Company, 1943.

King, Edward. *The Great South: A Record of Journeys in Louisiana, Texas, the Indian Territory, et al.* The American Publishing Company, 1874.

Larroque, Charles. *Memories of St. Martinville.* Pelican, 1999.

Lawson, Steven F. *To Secure These Rights: The Report of President Harry S. Truman's Committee on Civil Rights.* Bedford/St. Martins, 2004.

Lemann, Nicholas. *Out of the Forties.* Texas Monthly Press, 1981.

Lewis, Anthony. *Gideon's Trumpet.* Random House, 1964.

Mann, Robert T. *Legacy to Power: Senator Russell Long of Louisiana.* iUniverse, 2003.

McConville, Sean. *English Local Prisons, 1860–1900: Next Only to Death.* Routledge, 1995.

Miller, Arthur Selwyn. *A Capacity for Outrage: The Judicial Odyssey of J. Skelly Wright.* Greenwood Press, 1984.

Miller, Arthur S., and Jeffrey H. Bowman. *Death by Installments: The Ordeal of Willie Francis.* Greenwood Press, 1988.

Miller, Henry. *The Air-Conditioned Nightmare.* New Directions Publishing Company, 1945.

Miller, Merle. *Plain Speaking: An Oral Biography of Harry S. Truman.* Black Dog & Leventhal Publishers, 2005.

Moran, Robert Earl. *One Hundred Years of Child Welfare in Louisiana, 1860–1960.* Center for Louisiana Studies, University of Southwestern Louisiana, 1980.

Morrill, William W. *American Electrical Cases*, vol. 2. M. Bender, 1889–1892.

Pederson, William D., and Norman W. Provizer, eds. *Leaders of the Pack: Polls & Case Studies of Great Supreme Court Justices.* Peter Lang Publishing, 2003.

Peltason, Jack Walter. *Fifty-Eight Lonely Men: Southern Federal Judges and School Desegregation.* University of Illinois Press, 1971.

Prejean, Sister Helen. *Dead Man Walking.* Vintage Books, 1993.

Prettyman, Barrett, Jr. *Death and the Supreme Court.* Harcourt, Brace and World, Inc., 1961.

Rushton, William Faulkner. *The Cajuns: From Acadia to Louisiana.* Farrar Straus Giroux, 1979.

Sifakis, Stewart. *Compendium of the Confederate Armies: Louisiana*. Facts on File, 1995.

Simon, James F. *The Antagonists: Hugo Black, Felix Frankfurter and Civil Liberties in Modern America*. Simon and Schuster, 1989.

Sindler, Allan P. *Huey Long's Louisiana*. Johns Hopkins Press, 1956.

Stevens, Alden. "Small Town America." *The Nation*, June 15, 1946.

Tolnay, Stewart E., and E. M. Beck. *A Festival of Violence: An Analysis of Southern Lynchings, 1882–1930*. University of Illinois Press, 1995.

Vidrine, Clyde C. *"Just Takin' Orders": A Southern Governor's Watergate*. Clyde C. Vidrine, Publisher, 1977.

Wallechinsky, David, and Irving Wallace. *The People's Almanac*. Doubleday, 1975.

Warren, Robert Penn. *All the Kings Men*. A Harvest Book, 1946.

Weill, Gus. *You Are My Sunshine: The Jimmie Davis Story*. Word Books, 1977.

Wexler, Laura. *Fire in a Canebrake: The Last Mass Lynching in America*. Scribner, 2003.

Wiecek, William M. "Felix Frankfurter, Incorporation, and the Willie Francis Case." *Journal of Supreme Court History* 26, no. 1: 53–66.

Woodruff, Jay, and Sarah Carew Woodruff. *Conversations with Robert Coles*. University Press of Mississippi, 1992.

Notes

prologue: the curse of st. martinville

ix *I'd been poring:* Prejean, 4.

ix *As Sister Helen:* Ibid.

x *The pictures:* Lee Russell, Photographic Collection, Library of Congress.

x *In the center:* Capuder, ix.

face of a killer

1 *If the truck: Oakland Tribune,* May 5, 1946.

2 *But there was no radio:* Interview, Hilton Butler.

2 *The truck was a:* Interview, Paul Cook, www.texaspowerwagon.com.

2 *Earlier that Thursday afternoon:* Interview, Hilton Butler.

2 *On most of these:* Ibid.

3 *Ephie Foster, forty-three years:* 1930 U.S. Census.

3 *Camp captains:* Carleton, 138.

3 *One captain was:* Ibid.

3 *Discipline, one report:* Ibid., 141, 139.

3 *Poor white:* Ibid., 144.

3 *Foster would:* Ibid.

3 *Venezia, thirty-eight:* 1920 U.S. Census.

3 *With "sallow:* Louisiana State Penitentiary Prison Records Book 38, Angola, Louisiana.

3 *By the time:* 1930 U.S. Census.

3 *In and out:* Louisiana State Penitentiary Prison Records Book 38; Louisiana Pardons Board Hearing transcripts, Supreme

Court Record, *Louisiana ex rel. Francis v. Resweber,* 329 U.S.
459 (1947), Appendix to Brief for Respondent, National
Archives, Washington, DC (hereinafter cited as Supreme
Court Record).

3 *Foster and Venezia were:* Interview, Hilton Butler.

4 *On Thursday nights:* Interview, Paul Schwing, Clayton J. David.

4 *In one case: Social and Economic Impacts of Outer Continental Shelf
Activities on Individuals and Families,* vol. 2: *Case Studies of
Morgan City and New Iberia, Louisiana,* U.S. Department of the
Interior, Minerals Management Service Gulf of Mexico OCS
Region.

4 *Past the antebellum homes:* Interview, Morris Raphael.

4 *places like:* Interview, Paul Schwing, Clayton J. David.

4 *The U.S. Department:* Miller and Bowman, 6.

4 *Sanitary conditions:* Carleton, 141.

4 *Mary M. Daugherty:* Ibid., 153.

5 *Housed in sweatboxes: The Advocate,* April 24, 2005.

5 *Prison understaffing:* Louisiana State Penitentiary Prison
Records Book 38.

5 *Expecting a storm:* Miller and Bowman, 7.

5 *Together they would:* Ibid., 7.

5 *Whippings and beatings:* Carleton, 136.

5 *Not long after:* Ibid.

6 *There was a bar:* Interview, Paul Schwing, Clayton J. David.

6 *Before midnight:* Interview, George Etie Jr.

6 *Locals knew:* Interview, Morris Raphael.

6 *Foster and Venezia:* Interview, George Etie Jr.

6 *It was getting late: Louisiana ex rel. Francis v. Resweber,* 329 U.S.
459 (1947), Petition for a writ of habeas corpus, Affidavit,
Louie M. Cyr., Interview, Louis M. Cyr, National Archives,
Washington, DC.

6 *In St. Martinville:* Interview, Louie M. Cyr.

6 *Then Foster invited: Louisiana ex rel. Francis v. Resweber,* 329
U.S. 459 (1947), Petition for a writ of habeas corpus, Affidavit,
Louie M. Cyr, National Archives, Washington, DC.

7 *Gruesome Gertie:* Interview, Butler.

7 *He knew that the boy:* Louisiana Pardons Board Hearing
transcripts, Appendix to Brief for Respondent (hereinafter
cited as Louisiana Pardons Board).

7 *Tomorrow, Foster:* Affidavit of Louie M. Cyr, Interview, Louie
M. Cyr.

like shines in a rooster's tail

Although it may not be difficult to imagine what Willie might have been thinking and feeling on the morning of his scheduled execution and throughout the day, given the dramatic circumstances, what he thought—or feared or recognized or wondered at or prayed for—need not be surmised at all. Not only did Willie respond openly to questions from the press, but with Samuel Montgomery, he also wrote a pamphlet about his incarceration and near execution that was published under the title *My Trip to the Chair*. Much of this chapter is derived from this pamphlet.

8 *His heart was:* Francis and Montgomery, 8.

8 *In contrast to:* Prettyman, 90.

9 *But there was a second:* Francis and Montgomery, 8.

9 *When they reached:* Ibid.

9 *Willie's mother:* Ibid., 6.

9 *"Mornin', Willie:* Ibid., 8.

9 *The inmate stepped:* Ibid.

9 *His new barber:* Ibid.

9 *Willie had often:* Interview, Mrs. Sidney DuPois Jr.

10 *"It's just a little:* Francis and Montgomery, 3.

10 *"They said I would:* Ibid., 5.

10 *He worried about:* Francis and Montgomery, 8.

11 *District Attorney L. O. Pecot:* E. L. Resweber/District Attorney files, *State of Louisiana v. Willie Francis*, in St. Martinville Courthouse.

11 *The language in:* Francis and Montgomery, 6.

11 *it struck Willie:* Ibid.

11 *"I guess he thought:* Ibid.

12 *On May 2:* Ibid.

12 *A frequent visitor:* 1930 U.S. Census.

12 *Father Hannigan was:* Francis and Montgomery, 6.

12 *You're a lucky fella, Willie: Wisconsin Rapids Daily Tribune*, July 1, 1946.

12 *Father Hannigan let:* Ibid.

12 *Unlike most people:* Francis and Montgomery, 6.

12 *Hannigan told Willie:* Ibid.

12 *This is your: Wisconsin Rapids Daily Tribune*, July 1, 1946.

12 *Besides, Father:* Ibid.

12 *The electric chair:* Ibid.

12   *It will only:* Ibid.
13   *You're not being:* Ibid.
13   *By the end:* Ibid.
13   *Nobody wants to:* Ibid.
13   *Just as the sun:* Ibid.
13   *He could have:* Ibid.
13   *But the youth was:* Ibid.
13   *Ozenne prompted:* Francis and Montgomery, 7.
13   *An hour later:* Ibid.
13   *"more ice cream:* Ibid.
13   *Now that the end:* Ibid.
13   *They never spoke: Statesville Daily Record* (North Carolina),
     January 14, 1947.
13   *After his dinner:* Francis and Montgomery, 7.
13   *Why was it:* Ibid.
13   *Father Hannigan had:* Ibid.
13   *And burning:* Ibid.
13   *Finally, Willie:* Ibid.
13   *He had promised:* Ibid.
13   *"Boy, you sure:* Ibid.
13   *Born into a Roman:* Ibid., 2.
14   *Willie knew that:* Ibid., 8.
14   *"God, tonight is the:* Ibid.
14   *That night, Willie:* Ibid.
14   *"Well, Willie:* Ibid, 9.
14   *Willie smiled:* Ibid.
15   *His stomach:* Ibid.
15   *Willie walked:* Interview, Earl Robicheaux.
15   *Sheriff Ozenne looked:* Francis and Montgomery, 9.
15   *The inmate who:* Ibid.
15   *The New Iberia:* Ibid.
15   *As the elevator:* Ibid.
16   *Transfer protocol:* Miller and Bowman, 4.
16   *Ozenne liked:* Ibid.
16   *His tongue:* Francis and Montgomery, 10.
16   *A large sign:* Photograph, John Vachon, 1943, Library of
     Congress.
16   *Willie looked down:* Francis and Montgomery, 10.
16   *"Don't worry, Willie:* Ibid.
16   *He was "more:* Ibid.
16   *The fields terrified:* Interview, Nolan Charles.

16   *After the sedan:* Francis and Montgomery, 10.
16   *"More than anything:* Ibid.
17   *For the drive:* Ibid.
17   *She was there:* Ibid.
17   *This morning: Weekly Messenger,* May 3, 1946.
17   *Many blacks:* Francis and Montgomery, 10.
18   *Over the years:* Burk Foster, "Louisiana's Last Hanging," *The Angolite,* Nov/Dec, 2001. Also, *Lafayette Advertiser,* March 25, 1983.
18   *A truck was:* Photographs taken by Bertrand DeBlanc, May 3, 1946.
18   *Captain Foster and:* Louisiana Pardons Board.
18   *Residents of:* DeBlanc photographs.
18   *Formidable-looking:* Interview, Hilton Butler.
18   *Foster decided:* Louisiana Pardons Board.
19   *An onlooker that day: Louisiana ex rel. Francis v. Resweber,* 329 U.S. 459 (1947), Petition for a writ of habeas corpus, Affidavit of Ignace Doucet, National Archives, Washington, DC.
19   *Foster then:* Chaze, 80. Chaze was a reporter who covered the execution of Willie Francis for the Associated Press in 1946–1947. His novel, *The Golden Tag,* contains several descriptions of the portable electric chair and the truck, which, photographs show, were accurate. I quote his description of the switchboard and the colors, since the photos are black and white and Chaze does not appear to stray from the details of the executioner's equipment in his novel.
19   *Venezia stayed:* Louisiana Pardons Board.
19   *Foster told:* Ibid.
19   *Certain that the chair:* Affidavit of Ignace Doucet.
19   *The three of them: Charleston Gazette,* May 10, 1947.
19   *"I wished I had:* Francis and Montgomery, 11.
19   *Thick black cables:* Chaze, 80.
19   *At its top:* Louisiana Pardons Board.
20   *Already this chair:* The Louisiana State Penitentiary Museum, Angola, Louisiana.
20   *And one woman: Lowell Sun,* August 4, 1942.
20   *"Look," she said: Times-Picayune,* February 4, 1998.
20   *The half-dozen:* Louisiana Pardons Board.
20   *Willie could feel:* Francis and Montgomery, 12.
20   *He met the gaze:* Friendly and Elliot, 164. Interview, Mrs. Sidney Dupois.

20   *"What are you:* Friendly and Elliot, 164.
20   *"I came to be:* Ibid.
20   *Cuffed and shackled:* Francis and Montgomery, 11.
20   *He had instructed:* Interview, Velma Johnson.
20   *Willie had attended:* Alden Stevens, "Small-Town America: II.
      St. Martinville, Louisiana," *The Nation,* June 15, 1946.
20   *Sitting beside him:* Francis and Montgomery, 11.
20   *In "rich, round:* Lemann, 90.
21   *Outside the jail:* Miller and Bowman, 7.
21   *Already exhausted:* Ibid.
21   *Francis had spent:* Ibid.
22   *This time:* Francis and Montgomery, 11.
22   *Willie broke into:* Ibid., 12.
22   *Carrying a view:* Interview, Velma Johnson.
23   *"A beaten animal:* Louisiana Pardons Board.
23   *"Is there anything:* Ibid.
23   *Father Rousseve again:* Affidavit, Sidney Dupois.
23   *A sudden movement:* Francis and Montgomery, 12.
23   *Black and thick:* The Louisiana State Penitentiary Museum at
      Angola.
23   *The man then:* Louisiana Pardons Board.
23   *"It hurts me:* Friendly and Elliot, 164.
23   *"It'll hurt more:* Ibid.
24   *When the needle:* Affidavit, Maurice Rousseve.
24   *Good-bye, Willie:* Ibid.
24   *Willie, surprised:* Francis and Montgomery, 12.
24   *In a grandiose:* Miller and Bowman, 9.
24   *Willie's hands:* Louisiana Pardons Board.
24   *It felt like:* Francis and Montgomery, 12.
25   *"It's no use:* Louisiana Pardons Board.
25   *"Well, we'll give:* Miller and Bowman, 9.
25   *"Give me some more:* Louisiana Pardons Board.
25   *"I'm giving you all:* Ibid.
25   *"Take it off!: Charleston Daily Mail,* May 4, 1946.
25   *"You're not supposed:* Ibid.
25   *"I AM N-N-NOT:* Louisiana Pardons Board.
25   *Willie believed:* Francis and Montgomery, 13.
26   *"It seemed like:* Ibid.
26   *His head was:* Ibid.
26   *I'm not dead:* Ibid.
26   *"Quivering with fright: The Port Arthur News,* May 5, 1946.

26 *"I just want:* Louisiana Pardons Board.
26 *Word traveled:* Interview, Velma Johnson.
27 *Instead, he climbed:* Interview, Nolan Charles.
27 *Back in Sheriff:* Louisiana Pardons Board.
27 *LeBlanc considered: Times-Picayune,* May 4, 1946.
27 *"On one side: Miami Herald,* May 5, 1946.
27 *The decision:* Miller and Bowman, 10.
27 *The officials:* Ibid.
27 *Davis suggested:* Louisiana Pardons Board.
28 *After receiving:* Miller and Bowman, 11.
28 *"It's sort of like:* Francis and Montgomery, 13.
28 *How can they:* Miller and Bowman, 11.
28 *On unsteady legs:* Louisiana Pardons Board.
28 *"I missed you:* Affidavit, Ignace Doucet.
28 *Willie smiled:* Francis and Montgomery, 13.
28 *"The Lord was:* Louisiana Pardons Board.
29 *"They couldn't kill:* Affidavit, Louie M. Cyr.
30 *"Yes," Father:* Francis and Montgomery, 14.
30 *"Father," Willie: Wisconsin Rapids Daily Tribune,* July 1, 1946.
30 *Sheriff Resweber, when: Post-Standard,* May 4, 1946.
30 *Willie was lying:* Chaze, 70. I use Chaze's description again
from his novel, since Chaze would be one of those reporters,
and photographs show him trailing Willie in a brown hat.
30 *"Willie! What was:* Miller and Bowman, 12.
31 *"They walked me: Time* (magazine), July 14, 1946.
31 *"The electric: Wisconsin Rapids Daily Tribune,* July 1, 1946.
31 *"How'd it feel: Berkshire Evening Eagle,* July 1, 1946.
31 *"Plumb mizzuble:* Ibid.
31 *"God fool'd with: Time* (magazine), July 14, 1946.
31 *"The Lord was: Miami Herald,* May 5, 1946.
31 *"What was it like:* Miller and Bowman, 12.
31 *Willie responded:* Ibid.
31 *"Like you got: Wisconsin Rapids Daily Tribune,* July 1, 1946.
32 *"I reckon:* Ibid.
32 *"What a miracle: Chicago Defender,* August 31, 1946.
32 *"I'd be happy: Berkshire Evening Eagle,* July 1, 1946.
32 *Willie's picture:* See *Chicago Defender,* June 8, 1946; *Pittsburgh Courier,* May 24, 1946; *Zanesville Signal,* May 4, 1946; *Reno Evening Gazette,* May 9, 1946.
32 *One reporter: Louisiana Weekly,* May 15, 1946.
33 *"He made sure:* Interview, Velma Johnson.

33   *Of Course I Am:* A photograph taken on the evening of May 3, 1946, shows Willie standing in front of his cell wall where these words can be seen clearly.

to dry the tears of those who still weep here

34   *Inside the Francises':* United Press International, May 9, 1946.
34   *"Merci Dieu!":* Ibid.
34   *"Le bon Dieu":* Ibid.
35   *So Frederick Francis:* Miller and Bowman, 13.
35   *He looked down:* United Press International, May 9, 1946.
35   *Then, with all:* Miller and Bowman, 13.
35   *On Saturday:* Friendly and Elliot, 165. Also interview, Veronica DeBlanc.
35   *The man at:* 1910 U.S. Census.
36   *Frederick Francis's:* Based on U.S. Census information. Name changes were common following Reconstruction, as freedmen took the surnames of former owners, sometimes with modifications.
36   *Though slavery:* Lemann, 85.
36   *Most whites:* Ibid., 86.
37   *The son of a:* Bertrand's biographical material is based on interviews with various DeBlanc family members, as well as U.S. Census information.
38   *"He was there:* Interview, Lillian DeBlanc.
38   *"His hero was:* Ibid.
38   *the French Cajuns:* National Socialist White People's Party (NSWPP) Manual, 2nd ed., April 1998.
38   *But Long took a:* Moran; also, Mann.
39   *Like DeBlanc:* Bernard, 6.
39   *Captain Robert L.:* Ibid.
40   *"I have to go, too!":* Interview, Lillian DeBlanc.
40   *General Dwight: Weekly Messenger,* October 26, 1945.
40   *In October:* Ibid.
40   *Still, money:* Interview, Lillian DeBlanc.
40   *On the morning:* Friendly and Elliot, 165.
41   *"No," DeBlanc:* Ibid.
41   *He was described:* Sifakis.
41   *In May of 1867:* Gill.
42   *DeBlanc founded: The Handbook of Texas,* Texas State Historical Association, The General Libraries at the University of Texas at Austin, 1999.

42   *These, mounted: Republican Campaign Text Book*, 1882, published by the Republican Congressional Committee.
43   *McEnery responded:* Office of the Louisiana Secretary of State, Louisiana Governors biography, www.sos.louisiana.gov.
43   *"What is behind: Lafayette Advertiser*, March 8, 1873.
43   *After the election:* Ibid.
44   *"If white people: Galveston Daily News*, January 29, 1875.
44   *A story in* Scribner's: King.
44   *Indeed, it was estimated:* Gunning.
44   *There a crowd: New York Times*, November 10, 1883.
44   *"Legend has it:* Interview, James Akers.
45   *Perhaps weighing:* Interview, Lillian DeBlanc.
45   *Moments after:* Friendly and Elliot, 165.
45   *"Yes, I was there:* Ibid.
46   *"I know you:* Ibid.
46   *"The question of:* Ibid.
46   *Broussard's final:* Ibid.
46   *"I don't need it:* Ibid.
47   *He and Andrew:* Lemann, 90.
47   *He was overseas:* Interview, Lillian DeBlanc.
48   *"This is the most:* Friendly and Elliot, 166.

so many heart-breaking scenes

In this chapter I rely on several works, including Bona Arsenault's *History of the Acadians*, Carl A Brasseaux's *The Founding of New Acadia*, and William Faulkner Rushton's *The Cajuns: From Acadia to Louisiana*.

50   *Daniel Subercase:* Arsenault.
50   *An English surveyor:* Alice Ferguson, "French Acadians Settle in to the New World, Part I," *Louisiana Daily Advertiser*, June 6, 1994.
50   *Major Charles Lawrence:* Brasseaux.
51   *Presenting "His:* Arsenault.
51   *He concluded: Louisiana Daily Advertiser*, June 6, 1994.
51   *Winslow himself:* Arsenault.
52   *Winslow wrote: Louisiana Daily Advertiser*, June 6, 1994.
53   *Lured by the rich:* Ibid.
53   *In marshes:* Rushton.
53   *The French and Creoles:* Brasseaux.
54   *Unlike the English:* Fairclough, 2.
54   *By 1820:* Hollandsworth.

54 *Acadians, or Cajuns:* Rushton.
54 *Despite the:* Brasseaux.
55 *Negroes were viewed:* Ibid.
55 *Cajuns voluntarily:* Ibid.
55 *"Prior to the late:* Ibid.
56 *Supporting it all:* Henry Miller, 97.
57 *Miller passed:* Ibid., 105.

a short story

59 *With World War: Time* (magazine), July 31, 1944.
59 *Elsewhere were: Weekly Messenger,* August 31, 1944.
59 *Another piece: Weekly Messenger,* October 27, 1944.
60 *And the obituary:* Ibid.
60 *By 8:45 a.m.:* Coroner's Inquest Held before Dr. S. D. Yongue, Coroner of St. Martin Parish, Louisiana, on the 8th Day of November, 1944, St. Martin Parish Court Records (hereinafter cited as Coroner's Inquest).
60 *"You better go:* Ibid.
60 *"If the car:* Ibid.
61 *"Yes, sure he:* Ibid.
61 *"It sounded:* Ibid.
61 *"They came fast:* Ibid.
62 *"There was a car:* Ibid.
62 *His father, Albert:* 1910 U.S. Census.
62 *In 1920:* 1920 U.S. Census. Also, interview, Shirley Romero.
62 *Also living in:* 1930 U.S. Census.
63 *Eastin had also:* Bob Hamm, "The Man Who Cheated the Chair . . . for a While," *Lafayette Daily Advertiser,* April 25, 26, 1993.
63 *The dinner was:* Ibid.
63 *"Cordial" and:* Interviews, Shirley Romero, James Akers, Lillian DeBlanc.
63 *"No one,":* Weekly Messenger, November 10, 1944.
63 *Playing at the: Lafayette Daily Advertiser,* April 25, 26, 1993.
63 *After turning off: State of Louisiana, ex rel. Willie Francis Petitioner v. E. L. Resweber, Sheriff of the Parish of St. Martin, Louisiana, et al.,* In Opposition to the Writ Granted, Supreme Court of the United States, October Term, 1946, No. 142, 8.
63 *Thomas was jumped: Weekly Messenger,* November 10, 1944.
63 *One bullet:* Coroner's Inquest.

63   *Two more:* Ibid.
63   *There was no:* Ibid.
64   *On Thursday: Weekly Messenger,* November 10, 1944.
64   *Andrew Thomas was laid:* Ibid.
64   *Mr. Thomas' death:* Ibid.
65   *In the same:* Ibid.
65   *State Representative: Lafayette Daily Advertiser,* April 25, 26, 1993.
65   *A white couple:* Ibid.
65   *The woman was:* Ibid.
65   *A lifelong bachelor:* Interview, Nolan Charles, James Theriot.
65   *The gossip was:* Coroner's Inquest.
65   *"We would like:* Ibid.
66   *"I saw his:* Ibid. The remainder of this exchange between Dr. Yongue and Alvin Van Brocklin is transcribed in the Coroner's Inquest.
66   *Both husbands:* Interview, Genevieve Duplantis Lasseigne.
66   *"Did you ever:* Coroner's Inquest.
66   *Even though:* 1930 U.S. Census.
67   *Chief Thomas:* Interview, Charles Fuselier.
67   *This was the first:* Interview, Allan Durand.
67   *Louis Nassans:* Interview, Genevieve Duplantis Lasseigne.
67   *In each issue: Weekly Messenger,* September 24, 1944.
67   *A November 24: Weekly Messenger,* November 24, 1944.
68   *During a meeting:* Louisiana Pardons Board.
68   *According to Resweber:* Ibid.
68   *On the evening: The Port Arthur News,* August 6, 1945.
68   *Just a few blocks:* Appendix to Brief for Respondent, Pecot.
69   *Instinctively, he ducked:* Miller and Bowman, 19.
69   *Detective Edmund Oster: The Port Arthur News,* August 6, 1945.
69   *Once in custody:* Miller and Bowman, 19.
69   *Nonetheless, Goldsmith: The Port Arthur News,* August 6, 1945.
69   *According to Goldsmith:* Ibid.
69   *Willie replied that he:* Miller and Bowman, 19.
70   *(Eight days after:* St. Martin Parish District Attorney files, St. Martinville Courthouse.
70   *Clearly not written:* Ibid.
70   *Written in childlike:* Ibid.
71   *They told Goldsmith: The Port Arthur News,* August 6, 1945.
71   *On the trip:* Appendix to Brief for Respondent, Pecot.

71   *He scrawled:* St. Martin Parish District Attorney files, St. Martinville Courthouse.

72   *News of Willie: Weekly Messenger,* August 6, 1945.

72   *Instead, Francis:* Ibid.

72   *The* Louisiana Weekly: *Louisiana Weekly,* January 17, 1947.

72   *According to the:* Appendix to Brief for Respondent, Pecot.

72   *The pistol:* Ibid.

72   *Police also:* Ibid.

73   *So St. Martin:* Ibid.

73   *Indeed, Sheriff:* St. Martin Parish District Attorney files, St. Martinville Courthouse.

73   *To ensure:* Appendix to Brief for Respondent, Pecot.

73   *Detentions such:* Fairclough, 118.

those slips will happen

74   *Inmates sometimes:* Interview, James Akers.

74   *On May 18: New York Times,* May 18, 1882.

75   *From the Reconstruction:* Tolnay and Beck.

75   *A story in: The Nation,* October 30, 1935.

75   *A little more:* Ibid.

76   *And in January:* Ibid.

76   *The eight:* Ibid.

76   *Sheriff J. L. Brock:* Ibid.

76   *Wilkins documented:* Roy Wilkins, "Louisiana's Black Utopia," *The Crisis Magazine,* February 1935.

78   *And the sheriff's:* Unknown Subjects, Eviction of Negro Civil Rights Leaders, New Iberia, Louisiana, May 17, 1944, FBI File 44–999, Records Group 60, National Archives II, College Park, MD (hereinafter cited as FBI File 44–999).

the abysmal darkness

79   *It was the first:* Miller and Bowman, 8.

79   *Judge James Dudley:* Conrod, 744.

80   *While studying:* Capuder, 153.

80   *In 1953, eight: Indiana Evening Gazette,* November 14, 1959.

80   *When Willie:* State of Louisiana, Parish of St. Martin, *State of Louisiana v. #2161 Willie Francis,* Minutes of Court, Mina G. Willis, Deputy Clerk of Court (hereinafter cited as Minutes of Court).

ff NOTES

80 *The prosecution:* Louisiana Pardons Board.
80 *He was, according:* Ibid.
81 *Yet the defense:* Miller and Bowman, 23.
81 *He described:* Supreme Court Record, 9.
81 *Mestayer and Parkerson "requested:* Minutes of Court; and Miller and Bowman, 23.
81 *As it turned:* Miller and Bowman, 23.
81 *District Attorney:* Louisiana Pardons Board.
82 *Nor did the:* Supreme Court Record, 9.
82 *The first entry:* Minutes of Court.
82 *He ordered:* Ibid.
82 *At that time:* Ibid.
83 *Twelve white men:* Ibid.
83 *District Attorney:* Louisiana Pardons Board.
83 *He would add:* Ibid.
83 *In fact, at:* 1930 U.S. Census.
83 *(Just two years:* Interview, James Theriot.
83 *Another juror:* Interview, James Theriot, Sue Martin.
83 *Several of the:* Interview Sue Martin.
84 *Pecot's notion:* Louisiana Pardons Board.
84 *Aside from Dr.:* Minutes of Court.
84 *Pecot would:* Louisiana Pardons Board; and Coroner's Inquest.
85 *In response:* Minutes of Court.
86 *Once the State:* Ibid.
86 *Either way:* Ibid.
86 *They did not:* Coroner's Inquest.
87 *According to:* Louisiana Pardons Board.
87 *Its eight:* Supreme Court Record, 7 and 9.
88 *District Attorney:* Louisiana Pardons Board.
88 *Resweber responded:* Ibid.
89 *The New Orleans: Louisiana Weekly,* November 14, 1946.
89 *This was borne:* Ibid.
90 *Bertrand DeBlanc's:* Bertrand DeBlanc's case files.
90 *Other white:* Interview, Margaret Bonin.
90 *"Willie didn't:* Allan Durand's documentary, *Willie Francis Must Die Again,* France-America Film Group, 2006. Also, interview, Nolan Charles.
90 *When Charles told:* Interview, Nolan Charles.
91 *The President's:* Lawson, 66.
91 *In the early:* Interview, Jason, Schubert, Curator J. M. Davis Arms and Historical Museum, Claremont, Oklahoma.

91   *Smith & Wesson:* Interview, Roy Jinks, Smith & Wesson company historian. August Fuselier's pistol was probably a prewar Smith & Wesson .38 regulation police model. Since his holster had threads cut to accommodate the pistol, it was probably the four-inch barrel model, which had the capacity for five rounds.

91   *Furthermore the St. Martinville: Weekly Messenger,* November 10, 1944.

92   *It was purchased:* Interview, Ione Guirard.

92   *According to:* Coroner's Inquest.

92   *On June 25:* St. Martin Parish Court Records, St. Martinville Courthouse. *Weekly Messenger,* June 26, 1937. Also, interview, E. L. Guidry.

93   *The architect:* Interview, E. L. Guidry.

93   *With the barrel:* Ibid.

93   *The two argued: Weekly Messenger,* June 26, 1937.

93   *His uncle:* Interview, James Akers.

93   *"Mr. Peeters,": Weekly Messenger,* July 2, 1937.

94   *The minutes:* Minutes of Court.

94   *The jury of twelve: The Port Arthur News,* September 16, 1945.

94   *The sheriff:* Minutes of Court.

95   *When Judge Simon:* Ibid.

95   *Mestayer and:* Ibid.

95   *Judge Simon then:* Ibid.

95   *Standing before:* Ibid.

95   *Simon then:* Ibid.

95   *According to:* Ibid.

96   *The very last:* Ibid.

96   *Governor Jimmie Davis:* Weill; and Minutes of Court.

we do not have any bad
negroes here any more

97   *"A few of them:* Stevens. Much of Alden Stevens's interview with Father Maurice Rousseve is recounted here with permission of *The Nation.*

97   *Rousseve explained:* Ibid.

98   *Stevens told:* Ibid.

98   *"We have no:* Ibid.

98   *Maurice Louis:* Interview, Sister Mary Theresa Vincent Rousseve. Also, Brother Dennis Newton, S.V.D., *The Historical*

Significance of St. Augustine's Seminary. Also, Marcia Stein, Rev. Maurice Rousseve, S.V.D., *The Early Days*, 2003. Also, Sister Mary Anthony Scally, R.S.M., *Negro Catholic Writers (1900–1943) A Bio-Bibliography*, 1945. Pamphlets courtesy of St. Augustine's Seminary, Bay St. Louis, Mississippi.

99   *Stevens asked:* Stevens.
100 *"The people here:* Ibid.
100 *Rousseve had:* Ibid.
100 *"A doctor:* Ibid.
100 *Father Rousseve clearly:* FBI File 44–999.
100 *Later he wrote:* Stevens.
101 *In the spring:* Fairclough, 89.
101 *Hardy's reputation:* Ibid.
101 *In early 1944:* Ibid., 85.
101 *The NAACP:* Ibid., 88.
101 *Blacks, it was:* Ibid., 86.
102 *On May 7, 1944:* Ibid., 89.
102 *Convinced the school's:* Ibid.
102 *On May 15:* FBI File 44–999.
102 *According to Hardy's:* Ibid.
102 *"You yellow:* Ibid.
102 *Porter then:* Ibid.
102 *When Hardy:* Ibid.
102 *Ozenne, a rugged:* Interview, Paul Schwing, Clayton J. David.
102 *They then:* FBI File 44–999.
103 *It was located:* Fairclough, 88.
103 *At the Negro:* FBI File 44–999.
103 *Hardy told:* Ibid.
103 *Hardy received:* Ibid.
103 *The NAACP:* Ibid.
104 *Lourd later said:* Ibid.
104 *The June 3, 1944: Louisiana Weekly,* June 3, 1944.
104 *Ozenne, meanwhile:* FBI File 44–999.
104 *The FBI reports:* Ibid.
104 *"Get in that:* Ibid.
104 *"Knowing Gus Walker:* Ibid.
104 *Echoing the:* Ibid.
105 *His expulsion:* Ibid.
105 *Faulk told Dr. Dorsey:* Ibid.
105 *"It will be:* Ibid.
105 *One of the:* Ibid.

106   *According to:* Ibid.
106   *Mrs. Cyrus Broussard:* Ibid.
106   *The five jury:* Ibid.
106   *In June of:* PM, June 18, 1944.
106   *Ozenne, a:* Ibid.
107   *J. Edgar Hoover:* FBI File 44–999.
107   *"It seems about:* Ibid.
107   *FBI Special Agent:* Ibid.
107   *The following exchange:* PM, June 18, 1944.
108   *Among the many:* FBI File 44–999.
109   *A raid, they:* Ibid.
109   *Father Joseph P. Lonergan:* Ibid.
109   *Lonergan stated:* Ibid.
110   *The fact:* Ibid.
110   *Their fear:* Ibid.
110   *In a report:* Ibid.
110   *(Ironically, Truman:* Merle Miller.
111   *With the departures:* Fairclough, 97. Also, FBI File 44–999.
111   *Certainly, Ozenne:* Fairclough, 96.
111   *Judge S. O. Landry:* FBI File 44–999.
111   *Tom C. Clark's:* Ibid.
112   *Odds are:* Interview, Paul Schwing, Clayton J. David. Also, U.S. Social Security Death Index.
112   *Sheriff Resweber even:* Louisiana Pardons Board.
112   *Fuselier had stated:* Ibid.
113   *On yet another:* Ibid.
113   *He gave Resweber:* Ibid.
113   *Concluding that:* Ibid.
114   *"I took a:* Willie Francis Port Arthur, Texas Confession, St. Martin Parish Court Records.
114   *"It was a:* Louisiana Pardons Board.
114   *"Andrew Thomas:* Associated Press photograph. Also, *The Daily Times-News*, May 4, 1946. Also, Willie Francis Resweber Confession, St. Martin Parish Court Records.
114   *"I wasn't after:* The Daily Times-News, May 4, 1946.

for heaven's sake he's just a kid

115   *The petition:* Writ of Habeas Corpus, May 7, 1946, Supreme Court Record.
116   *Anticipating Simon's:* Miller and Bowman, 30.

116 *By noon the:* Ibid.
116 *Sheriff Resweber told: Times-Picayune*, May 8, 1946.
116 *DeBlanc told:* Ibid.
116 *For one: Wisconsin Daily Tribune*, May 9, 1946.
117 *A nineteen-year-old:* St. Martin Parish Court Records.
117 *An anonymous:* Ibid.
117 *A writer:* Ibid.
117 *A man in:* Ibid.
117 *After all:* Ibid. Also, Miller and Bowman, 32.
117 *But most:* St. Martin Parish Court Records.
117 *According to: Times-Picayune*, May 9, 1946.
117 *One writer:* Miller and Bowman, 33.
117 *Bertrand DeBlanc made: Times-Picayune*, May 5, 1946.
117 *NAACP attorney: Times-Picayune*, May 8, 1946.
118 *On May 6:* NAACP Records, Collections of the Manuscript
      Division, Library of Congress (hereinafter cited as NAACP
      Records).
118 *Alexander Pierre Tureaud:* Fairclough, 65.
118 *DeBlanc met:* NAACP Records.
118 *The NAACP:* Ibid.
118 Louisiana Weekly: Interview, A. P. Tureaud Jr.
118 *The tension: Louisiana Weekly*, May 16, 1946.
119 *Tureaud also:* NAACP Records.
119 *The* State Times: *State Times*, May 8, 1946.
119 *Bertrand DeBlanc quickly:* Bertrand DeBlanc's case files.
120 *"The city wasn't:* Interview, Robert Adams.
120 *Indeed, Father:* Lemann, 95.
120 *On the morning:* United Press International, May 8, 1946.
120 *Later that day:* Miller and Bowman, 31. Also, NAACP Records.
121 *O'Neill saw:* Miller and Bowman, 31.
121 *After a long:* Ibid.
121 *Willie's family:* United Press International, May 9, 1946.
121 *Meanwhile, Willie:* Ibid.
121 *As the criticism: Weekly Messenger*, May 10, 1946.
123 *He also believed:* Bertrand DeBlanc's Case Files.
123 *When Tureaud:* NAACP Records.
124 *Highly motivated:* Ibid.
124 *White would later:* Ibid.
124 *On May 15, 1946:* Miller and Bowman, 34.
124 *The court reasoned:* Ibid.

124   *"Things look: Philadelphia Tribune*, May 18, 1946. Also, *Statesville Daily Record* (North Carolina), May 18, 1946.
125   *"My client: Post-Standard*, May 16, 1946.

nothing against the boy

126   *He didn't much:* Interview, Veronica DeBlanc.
126   *"No, thank you,":* Ibid.
128   *Pecot, who would:* Louisiana Pardons Board.
128   *Alexander Pierre Tureaud:* Fairclough, 67.
128   *Homer A. Plessy:* Baker, 36.
128   *As a result:* Ibid., 38.
129   *Two years:* Fairclough, 6.
129   *By 1904:* Ibid.
129   *One of eleven:* Baker, 46.
129   *They attended:* Ibid., 47.
129   *And with:* Ibid., 48.
129   *By 1919:* Ibid., 49.
129   *Directionless yet ever:* Ibid., 50.
130   *Aspiring to:* Ibid., 51.
130   *It took years:* NAACP Records.
130   *One state judge:* Baker, 52.
130   *Five feet six inches:* Ibid., 54.
130   *When he was:* Fairclough, 10.
130   *Eventually, the:* Baker, 138.
131   *On those occasions:* Ibid., 140.
131   *Discriminatory practices:* NAACP Records.
131   *Working alongside:* Ibid.
131   *As a light-skinned:* Fairclough, 16.
132   *Certainly if:* Ibid., 17.
132   *As Huey Long:* Ibid.
132   *He had taken:* Baker, 59.
132   *He had once:* Fairclough, 17.
133   *The State's first:* Louisiana Pardons Board.
133   *Bazer then introduced:* Ibid.
134   *Bazer told the board:* Ibid.
134   *Yongue informed the board:* Ibid. Yongue's exact testimony before the Pardons Board is presented as dialogue in quotations, as is that of the board.
135   *The State next:* Louisiana Pardons Board.
135   *"We set the chair:* Ibid.

135 *"We started:* Ibid. Venezia's exact testimony before the board is presented as dialogue in quotations, as is that of the board.

137 *As he was being: Washington Post,* May 12, 1946.

137 *After he recalled:* Louisiana Pardons Board. Resweber's exact testimony before the board is presented as dialogue in quotations, as is that of the board.

141 *"You did not:* Louisiana Pardons Board.

141 *J. Edgar Hoover:* Lawson, 67.

142 *Durand told:* Rebecca Agule, "The Two Deaths of Willie Francis," *The Record* (independent newspaper at Harvard Law School), November 16, 2006.

142 *Father Maurice Rousseve, too:* Lemann, 95.

142 *"Does he act:* Louisiana Pardons Board.

142 *"Sheriff, does he:* Ibid. Resweber's exact testimony before the board is presented as dialogue in quotations, as is that of the board.

144 *"What do you:* Ibid. Ozenne's exact testimony before the board is presented as dialogue in quotations, as is that of the board.

144 *The* Philadelphia Tribune: *Philadelphia Tribune,* June 4, 1946.

145 *The article:* Ibid.

145 *Both Mr. and Mrs.: Louisiana Weekly,* May 16, 1946.

145 *Likewise, stories: Chicago Defender,* June 8, 1946.

145 *A. P. Tureaud himself:* NAACP Records.

145 *A study published:* Gross et al.

145 *Twenty-one percent:* Ibid.

145 *The study:* Ibid.

145 *According to:* Ibid.

145 *The report concludes:* Ibid.

murder at midnight

147 *"The consensus: Philadelphia Tribune,* June 4, 1946.

147 *She wrote:* Jessyl Taylor, "Was This an Act of God?" *World's Messenger,* undated photocopy of article in the files of Bertrand DeBlanc.

148 *Taylor added:* Ibid.

148 *"Did he [Willie]:* Louisiana Pardons Board. Ozenne's exact testimony before the board is presented as dialogue in quotations, as is that of the board.

149 *In 1984:* A. Miller, 27.

149 *There is writing:* Associated Press photograph taken May 3, 1946.

150 *("Morris" could be: Traverse City Record-Eagle,* January 14, 1947.

151 *"In your opinion:* Louisiana Pardons Board.

151 *When Tureaud had:* Ibid.

152 *August Fuselier was born:* 1900 U.S. Census. Also, material and quotes were taken from three St. Martinville residents who wished to remain anonymous.

152 *Father Maurice Rousseve believed:* Lemann, 93.

153 *Aside from:* Ibid.

153 *Reportedly, he walked:* Ibid.

153 *Among them:* Several St. Martinville residents, on separate occasions, indicated that Lena Foti was Fuselier's mistress. Again, their names are withheld here.

153 *Fuselier's car:* Ibid. Also, Louisiana Pardons Board.

153 *After the board:* Louisiana Pardons Board.

154 *Otherwise, he reasoned:* Ibid.

154 *In Louisiana:* Ibid.

154 *"Society looks:* Ibid.

154 *"Is it not a fact:* Ibid. Pecot's exact testimony, as well as that of Tureaud's, is presented as dialogue in quotations.

a boy on the threshold of eternity

158 *Among them was that:* Louisiana Pardons Board.

158 *In a similar:* Ibid.

158 *Doucet added:* Ibid.

158 *Like Father Rousseve:* Ibid.

158 *Indeed, "a parade: Nevada State Journal,* June 1, 1946. Also, *Chicago Defender,* June 8, 1946.

159 *DeBlanc then argued:* Louisiana Pardons Board. Also, Miller and Bowman, 39.

159 *Then, invoking:* Louisiana Pardons Board.

159 *"There is the:* Ibid.

159 *DeBlanc proceeded by: New York Times,* February 24, 1885. Also, McConville, 417.

160 *Then there was:* Wallechinsky and Wallace.

161 *Bertrand DeBlanc next:* Louisiana Pardons Board. Also, *New York Times,* February 10, 1921.

161 *DeBlanc pleaded:* Louisiana Pardons Board. DeBlanc's address to the board is presented as dialogue in quotations.

162   *I show you:* Louisiana Pardons Board.
163   *Here is a boy:* Ibid.
163   *"When they saw:* Friendly and Elliot, 167.
163   *What assurance:* Louisiana Pardons Board.
165   *You, gentlemen:* Ibid.
166   *The young lawyer: Chicago Defender*, June 8, 1946.
166   *The fate of the:* Ibid.
166   *A story in:* Ibid.

praying harder than ever

167   *"I guess the:* Friendly and Elliot, 167.
167   *Dr. A. O. Wilson: Chicago Defender*, June 8, 1946.
167   *He'd contacted:* Miller and Bowman, 42.
168   *J. Skelly Wright, the second:* A. Miller, 14.
168   *The son of:* Interview, Helen Patton Wright. Also, Baker, 89.
168   *It was, in:* Baker, 89.
168   *Except for an uncle:* Ibid. Also, interview, Helen Patton Wright.
168   *His older:* Interview, Jim Wright.
169   *Uncle Joe, in turn:* Baker, 95.
169   *After the assassination:* Ibid., 96.
169   *Wright, in his:* Interview, Helen Patton Wright.
169   *When the Japanese:* Baker, 101.
169   *The daughter of:* Ibid., 102. Also, interview, Helen Patton Wright.
170   *With bright blue eyes:* Interview, Helen Patton Wright.
170   *He hoped a:* Baker, 89.
170   *On one such occasion:* Interview, Helen Patton Wright.
170   *"Foolish," she later:* Ibid.
170   *It was upon:* Baker, 88.
171   *Until then:* Baker, 92. Also, Rosa Freeman Keller Papers, Amistad Research Center, New Orleans, Louisiana.
171   *He'd never sat:* Baker, 93.
171   *Wright himself would:* Ibid., 94.
171   *"The Negro:* Ibid., 106.
171   *Across the street:* Interview, Jim Wright, Helen Wright.
171   *"They couldn't see to:* Interview, Helen Wright.
172   *"When you go to:* Baker, 107.
172   *By early June:* Interview, Jim Wright.
172   *Retainers from:* Baker, 107. Also, interview, Jim Wright.
172   *President Eisenhower would:* Ambrose, 201.

172 *If the news:* Miller and Bowman, 42.
173 *In a letter:* Ibid.
174 *Once Willie had regained: Joplin Globe,* June 12, 1946.
174 *The Court would indeed:* Supreme Court Record.
174 *It was a mistake:* Prettyman, 111.
175 *"Every time he:* Francis and Montgomery, 15.
175 *"I guess I like:* Ibid.
175 *Asked for his: Joplin Globe,* June 12, 1946.
175 *"I'm tickled:* Prettyman, 112.
175 *"I had to agree:* Francis and Montgomery, 14.

get to the law

176 *Chief Justice Harlan Fiske Stone:* Pederson and Provizer, chapter by Theodore M. Vestal, "Harlan Fiske Stone: New Deal Prudence."
177 *When Justice Black:* Simon, 160.
177 *Justice Stone had suggested:* Ibid.
177 *"If this:* Ibid., 161.
177 *Shortly thereafter:* Jackson, 168.
178 *Indeed, Justice William O. Douglas:* Simon, 165.
178 *Some columnists:* David Lawrence, editorial, *Charleston Daily Mail,* June 19, 1946.
178 *Senator Scott Lucas: Reno Evening Gazette,* June 12, 1946.
179 *In 1937: Palko v. Connecticut,* U.S. Supreme Court, 302 U.S. 319 (1937).
179 *Furthermore, in 1908: Twining v. New Jersey,* 211 U.S. 78 (1908).
180 *As a result: Encyclopedia Britannica,* Encyclopedia Brittanica Online, retrieved October 11, 2007, http://www.britannica.com/eb/article–9015461.
181 *Writing for the majority:* Black and Black.
182 *Walter Gobitis and his family:* Simon, 107. (The Gobitas' name was misspelled in Court records. For the sake of clarity, I use the Court spelling,)
183 *Walter Gobitis sued:* Ibid., 106.
183 *Immensely proud:* Ibid., 109.
183 *Although he might personally:* Ibid., 108.
183 *The* Gobitis *decision:* Ibid., 113.
184 *Three years later:* Ibid., 117.
184 *An appeal to the: In re Kemmler,* U.S. Supreme Court, 136 U.S. 436 (1890).
185 *With his legal options: New York Herald,* August 7, 1890.

185   *One newspaper:* New York Times, August 7, 1890. Also *New York World*, August 7, 1890.
186   *Luckily for Wright:* Miller and Bowman, 72.
186   *Emily Branch had recently:* NAACP Records.
186   *Responding to a letter:* Ibid.
186   *A few weeks earlier:* Ibid.
186   *Thurgood Marshall believed:* Ibid.
186   *Two days:* Ibid.
187   *The next day:* Ibid.
187   *Skelly Wright, who had:* Interview, Helen Wright.
187   *"Oyez! Oyez!:* Miller and Bowman, 69.
188   *The first interruption:* Ibid., 70.
188   *Doesn't the sheriff:* Ibid.
188   *Frankfurter nodded:* Ibid.
188   *Wright proceeded:* Ibid.
188   *Wright argued:* Ibid., 70–71.
188   *"A second execution:* Ibid., 71.
189   *Justice Reed jumped in:* Miller and Bowman, 71. No transcripts of *Louisiana ex rel. Francis v Resweber* exist. Exchanges between the Supreme Court justices and Wright, Pecot, and Culligan are derived, in part, from Miller and Bowman's reconstruction of oral arguments in their book, *Death by Installments: The Ordeal of Willie Francis.*
189   *"Why don't you:* Susan L. Carney, and Helen Patton Wright, "Oral History Project," The Historical Society of the District of Columbia Circuit, October 1995–April 1996.
189   *"If the State of Louisiana:* Miller and Bowman, 71.
190   *"Why are these:* Ibid., 72.
190   *The State advanced:* Ibid.
191   *"We know:* Ibid.
191   *"Get to the law:* Ibid.
191   *Culligan, chastened and stunned:* Ibid.
191   *"Just how many:* Ibid., 73.
191   *He said that Black's:* Ibid.
192   *"The Justices seemed:* Prettyman, 115.
192   *If Black's question:* Miller and Bowman, 73.

weeping no tears

194   *The next to vote:* Simon, 178.
194   *He would indeed:* Ibid.
194   *Skelly Wright would later:* Friendly and Elliot, 170.

194   *"Why Black:* Miller and Bowman, 108.
195   *"This is not:* Ibid., 77.
195   *Strangely, that consideration:* Ibid.
196   *Burton, in fact:* Baker, 113–114.
197   *"Accidents happen:* Judgment of the Court, 329 U.S. 459.
197   *Indeed, Reed's opinion:* Miller and Bowman, 80.
198   *In fact, Reed:* Wiecek, 3.
198   *As to the issue:* Judgment of the Court, 329 U.S. 459.
198   *Nor could any:* Miller and Bowman, 83.
198   *The Supreme Court in* Kemmler: Ibid.
199   *Burton felt strongly:* Judgment of the Court, 329 U.S. 459.
199   *As Miller and Bowman:* Miller and Bowman, 83.
200   *Justice Douglas was the first:* Ibid., 84.
200   *As Burton had written:* Dissenting Opinion, 329 U.S. 459.
201   *"I have to hold:* Miller and Bowman, 91.
201   *He also reiterated:* Ibid.
201   *Desperately trying to hold:* Ibid., 93.
202   *As something:* Ibid., 96.
202   *Frankfurter opposed constitutional:* The "shock the conscience
      test" would later play out in *Rochin v California* (1952), with
      Black taking issue with the vagaries that permitted judges to
      apply subjective judgment to decisions.
203   *That Reed chose:* Miller and Bowman, 99.
203   *Meanwhile, Frankfurter:* Ibid., 93.
204   *Burton himself was:* Ibid.
204   *On December 31:* Ibid., 94
205   *"And, in a case:* Ibid.
205   *"All this is purely:* A. Miller, 33.
205   *In his memorandum:* Ibid., 34.
205   *"I am sorry:* Ibid.

just like a movie star

206   *DeBlanc would visit:* Interview, Gus Weill.
206   *Sheriff Ozenne believed:* Louisiana Pardons Board.
207   *Willie wrote:* St. Martin Parish Court Records.
209   *Around that time: Dunkirk Evening Observer,* January 14, 1947.
210   *"When I got:* Friendly and Elliot, 168.
210   *"Skelly was crushed:* Interview, Helen Wright.
211   *A letter from:* Bertrand DeBlanc Case Files. Also, *Edwardsville
      Intelligencer,* January 16, 1947.

211   *"If anybody's gonna:* Edwardsville Intelligencer, January 16, 1947.
211   *Another letter:* Jessyl Taylor, "Was This an Act of God?" *World's Messenger*, undated photocopy of article in the files of Bertrand DeBlanc.
211   *"We cannot judge:* Ibid.
212   *This is my last:* Ibid.
212   *Willie then wrote:* Ibid.
212   *Dear Mrs. Taylor:* Ibid.
213   *He later told:* Ibid.
213   *It was evident:* Miller and Bowman, 114, 116.
213   *With all the attention:* Francis and Montgomery, 14.
213   *A song about:* Bertrand DeBlanc Case Files.

better with an ax

215   *By the early:* Brandon, 28.
215   *Much of the debate:* Ibid.
215   *While most northern states:* Encyclopedia Brittanica, 11th ed., vol. 16, Cambridge University Press, 1911, p. 812.
216   *Until William Kemmler:* Brandon, 27.
216   *In most cases:* Ibid., 26.
216   *Dangling from:* Ibid.
216   *Increasingly, public hangings:* Essig, 78.
216   *Toward the end:* Morrill, 840.
216   *Southwick had secured:* Essig, 94.
217   *Southwick would soon:* Brandon, 166.
217   *Undaunted, Southwick pleaded:* Essig, 116.
217   *He and George Westinghouse:* Brandon, 7.
217   *He recommended:* Essig, 117.
217   *Killing criminals:* Essig, 3.
217   *"It will be:* Ibid.
218   *A crowd of 1,500:* Essig, 279.
218   *Westinghouse was understandably:* Brandon, 9.
218   *But Edison had:* Ibid., 10.
218   *After the death:* Essig, 123, 250.
218   *Once Kemmler was secured:* Essig, 251.
219   *When the current:* Ibid.
219   *His mouth "twisted:* Ibid.
219   *The "father of:* Ibid., 252.
219   *"Great God!":* Ibid.
219   *A "purplish:* Ibid.

219 *Southwick wheeled:* Brandon, 177.
219 *The current was:* Essig, 257.
219 *Thomas Edison was less:* Brandon, 185.
219 *George Westinghouse, however:* Ibid.
220 *By then, too:* Ibid., 226.
220 *On February 9, 1934: Los Angeles Times,* July 1, 1934. Also, *Syracuse Herald,* February 9, 1934.
220 *Following the lead:* Interview, Burk Foster, regarding a 1988 memo from Roger Thomas, former assistant warden at Angola.
220 *The following month:* Ibid.
220 *Four escaped convicts:* Burk Foster, "Louisiana's Last Hanging," *The Angolite,* November/December, 2001.
221 *After that point: Los Angeles Times,* July 1, 1934.
221 *A cruel irony:* Miller and Bowman, 116.
221 *Davis's executive counsel: Times-Picayune,* January 14, 1947.
221 *The news was:* Ibid.
221 *"It's the same:* Ibid.
222 *"This time it'll be: Traverse City Record-Eagle,* January 14, 1947.
222 *"No, thanks: Times-Picayune,* January 14, 1947.
222 *"Here speak the: Pittsburgh Courier,* undated photocopy, Bertrand DeBlanc Case Files.
222 *Once he'd composed: Times-Picayune,* January 14, 1947.
222 *Reporters visited: Times-Picayune,* January 14, 1947.
222 *"Death and me:* Ibid.
222 *Did he have nightmares:* Francis and Montgomery, 14.
222 *Willie told another: Times-Picayune,* January 14, 1947.
223 *Echoing the thoughts:* Ibid.
223 *"Five of the:* Francis and Montgomery, 16.
223 *One reporter wondered:* Ernest J. Wright, undated *Louisiana Weekly* editorial, Bertrand DeBlanc Case Files.

strong and easy boy

224 *One writer in Louisiana:* NAACP Records.
224 *"Where five men:* Miller and Bowman, 118. For details of Felix Frankfurter's extrajudicial machinations, I relied heavily on this book, as the authors compiled a most detailed and accurate examination of the Supreme Court Justices' correspondence.
224 *Especially critical: Pittsburgh Press,* January 14, 1947.

225 *James Marlow: Times-Picayune,* January 14, 1947.
227 *The* Norfolk State News*: Miller and Bowman, 119.
227 *"It would be:* Ibid.
227 *Noted radio:* Unidentified photocopy of news story regarding Winchell's plea on behalf of Willie Francis, Bertrand DeBlanc Case Files.
227 *Conceding that: Washington Post,* February 24, 1947.
227 *The* Times-Picayune*: Times-Picayune,* January 14, 1947.
227 *And in Birmingham: The Age-Herald,* January 15, 1947.
228 *White wrote: Mansfield New-Journal,* January 19, 1947.
229 *White said the column:* NAACP Records.
229 *An indignant Thurgood Marshall:* Ibid.
229 *Knowing well:* Ibid.
229 *Among others:* Ibid.
230 *Marshall wrote Daniel Byrd:* Ibid.
230 *"If the Pope:* Ibid.
230 *Byrd felt that:* Ibid.
230 *Bishop Jules B. Jeanmard:* Ibid.
230 *Bishop Jeanmard closed:* Ibid.
230 *Coming off the term:* Miller and Bowman, 43.
231 *Reflecting the emotional tone:* Ibid., 123.
231 *Adrian Conan Doyle:* Felix Frankfurter Papers, Manuscript Division, Library of Congress.
231 *In his concurrence:* Supreme Court Record.
231 *In fact, thousands:* Wiecek, 6.
231 *More puzzling:* Felix Frankfurter Papers, Manuscript Division, Library of Congress.
232 *In a later case:* Miller and Bowman, 109.
232 *Frankfurter ruled:* Ibid., 110.
232 *Despite Frankfurter's often:* Wiecek, 6.
232 *Of course, so:* Miller and Bowman, 111.
232 *She wrote:* Felix Frankfurter Papers, Manuscript Division, Library of Congress.
233 *"You will permit:* Ibid.
233 *However much Frankfurter:* Wiecek, 6. Also Miller and Bowman, 124.
233 *Perhaps guided:* Freedman, Beaney, and Rostow, 15.
233 *In his concurring:* Felix Frankfurter Papers, Manuscript Division, Library of Congress.
233 *A highly respected:* Ibid.
234 *In 1938:* Miller and Bowman, 125.

234 *Noting further:* Ibid.
234 *Then, more particularly:* Felix Frankfurter Papers, Manuscript Division, Library of Congress.
234 *Frankfurter acknowledged:* Ibid.
234 *"This cause has been:* Miller and Bowman 126.
235 *"It is difficult:* Felix Frankfurter Papers, Manuscript Division, Library of Congress.
235 *When Frankfurter mailed:* Miller and Bowman, 125.
235 *Shortly after receiving:* Ibid., 126.
235 *Certainly, for:* Ibid., 127.
236 *These considerations:* Ibid.
236 *Lemann concluded:* Ibid.
236 *As Miller and Bowman:* Ibid.
236 *With it, he included:* Felix Frankfurter Papers, Manuscript Division, Library of Congress.
236 *"You could not have:* Miller and Bowman, 128.
237 *Throughout his career:* Ibid.
237 *As Miller and Bowman write:* Ibid., 130.

a disgraceful and inhuman exhibition

238 *Sitting at his desk:* Miller and Bowman, 132.
238 *The amendment:* Bertrand DeBlanc Case Files.
238 *The Supreme Court rules:* Miller and Bowman, 132.
239 *It seemed that he:* NAACP Records.
239 *Walter White thought the:* Ibid.
239 *But Thurgood Marshall pointed:* Ibid.
239 *Amused as Cyr:* Interview, Louie M. Cyr.
239 *It was a shame:* Miller and Bowman, 132.
239 *Cyr's remark left:* Ibid.
240 *While Etie had witnessed:* Affidavit, Louie M. Cyr.
240 *Etie had described:* Ibid.
240 *It was Etie's:* Ibid.
240 *Not many hours:* Ibid.
240 *It was bad enough:* Supreme Court Record.
241 *He managed to find:* Affidavit, Ignace Doucet.
241 *He also confirmed:* Ibid.
241 *DeBlanc attempted:* Miller and Bowman. 133.
241 *Secretary Lawrence Sauer: Louisiana Weekly,* undated photocopy.
242 *"I'm gonna die: Washington Times Herald,* April 23, 1947.
242 *He filed papers:* Miller and Bowman, 134.

243 *This change of heart: Louisiana Weekly*, undated photocopy.
243 *Any short-term affection:* St. Martin Parish Court Records.
244 *The next morning:* Ibid.
244 *"Well, I guess: Times-Picayune*, May 7, 1947.
245 *The sheriff asked Blackie:* Ibid., May 8, 1947.
245 *After studying the opinions:* Miller and Bowman, 136.
246 *Neither Wright:* Prettyman, 306.
246 *The Court managed:* Ibid.
246 *When it was determined:* Ibid.
246 *According to Wright's petition:* Supreme Court Record.
246 *It was "negligence:* Ibid.
246 *He added, "The scene:* Ibid.
247 *Wright concluded by accusing:* Miller and Bowman, 136.
247 *The justices gathered:* Prettyman, 305.
247 *The Court convened:* Miller and Bowman, 137.
247 *As he read:* Ibid.
247 *Vinson referred:* Ibid.
248 *Wright slumped forward:* Ibid.
248 *"Abstract principles:* Ibid.
248 *Vinson continued, "In:* Supreme Court Record.
248 *Both Wright and DeBlanc:* Miller and Bowman, 138.

my hell on earth

250 *"I used to walk: Times-Picayune*, May 9, 1947. The beginning of this chapter is derived from Associated Press reporter Elliott Chaze's May 8 interview with Louise Francis.
251 *The reporter was:* Chaze.
252 *Chaze reported: The Lowell Sun*, August 4, 1942.
252 *Willie was sitting calmly: Times-Picayune*, May 9, 1947.
252 *Neither he nor Chaze:* Ibid.
252 *"But tomorrow noon:* Ibid.
252 *HORRIBLE!: Weekly Messenger*, August 15, 1891.
253 *Mrs. Robertson's throat:* Ibid.
253 *"Miss Belle," the paper:* Ibid.
253 *Justice Ralph DeBlanc:* Ibid.
253 *The next day:* Ibid.
253 *The paper added that:* Ibid.
253 *Doubts lingered: Weekly Messenger*, August 22, 1891.
254 *"Most of our people: Weekly Messenger*, August 29, 1891.
254 *Still, the paper:* Ibid.

254 *"Someone lied:* Ibid.

254 *Indeed, the paper doubted:* Ibid.

254 *Brought before the bar: Weekly Messenger,* August 22, 1891.

254 *During the "Republican reign: Weekly Messenger,* March 25, 1893.

254 *They deliberated:* St. Martin Parish Court Records, 182.

254 *Michel took the verdict: Weekly Messenger,* October 1, 1892.

255 *In September of 1892: Weekly Messenger,* February 20, 1892.

255 *The testimony: Weekly Messenger,* March 25, 1893.

255 *They deliberated:* St. Martin Parish Court Records, 182.

255 *It was the first: Weekly Messenger,* March 4, 1893.

255 *"We were expecting:* Ibid.

255 *Michel was described:* Ibid.

256 *He was calm:* Ibid.

256 *He said further:* Ibid.

256 *Michel professed:* Ibid.

256 *Town lore:* Interview, James Akers.

256 *Many people in St. Martinville: Weekly Messenger,* June 3, 1893.

256 *Other townspeople:* Ibid.

256 *Officers kept the news:* Ibid.

256 *Perhaps, the* Messenger: Ibid.

257 *"The public seem to: Weekly Messenger,* January 28, 1893.

257 *On Friday: Lafayette Advertiser,* March 25, 1893.

257 *He had a hearty: Weekly Messenger,* March 25, 1893.

257 *Michel asked the sheriff:* Ibid.

257 *Louis Michel looked:* Ibid.

257 *Most papers:* Essig, 83. Also, Brandon, 27.

258 *This oral tradition: Lafayette Advertiser,* April 25, 26, 1993.

258 *After Michel had drunk: Weekly Messenger,* March 25, 1893.

258 *He avouched:* Ibid.

258 *A "black cap":* Ibid.

258 *At 12:20: Lafayette Advertiser,* April 25, 26, 1993.

258 *The astonished crowd:* Ibid.

258 *When the hole:* Ibid.

258 *"Louis was bold:* Ibid.

258 *The following week: Weekly Messenger,* April 1, 1893.

259 *On April 8, 1893: Lafayette Advertiser,* April 8, 1893.

259 *"It is hoped:* Ibid.

259 *Sheriff Gilbert Ozenne allowed: Times-Picayune,* May 9, 1947.

259 *Then Sheriff Ozenne brought:* Ibid.

260 *Willie told a reporter: Lafayette Advertiser,* April 25, 26, 1993.

260　*Only now the Lord: Lima News*, May 8, 1947.

260　*"Now I'm ready:* Ibid.

260　*"Who would think: Time*, May 19, 1947.

260　*"The whole thing: Charleston Daily Mail*, May 8, 1947.

260　*Willie didn't mind:* Francis and Montgomery, 5.

261　*He'd been asked:* Jessyl Taylor, "Was This an Act of God?" *World's Messenger*, undated photocopy of article in the files of Bertrand DeBlanc.

ruining my life

262　*Dr. Sidney Yongue pointedly:* Coroner's Inquest.

262　*An opponent:* Interview, Sue Martin.

263　*"Mrs. Zie was trying:* Ibid.

263　*In his testimony:* Coroner's Inquest.

263　*Akers says that the happily:* Interview, James Akers.

263　*In it, Akers said:* Ibid.

264　*"It was bad:* Interview, Genevieve Duplantis Lasseigne.

264　*"Andrew was a family:* Ibid.

264　*"We'd watch the games:* Ibid.

264　*"Besides," she told Akers:* Interview, James Akers.

265　*Nolan "Cabbie" Charles:* Interview, Nolan Charles.

265　*Though segregation:* Interview, Otis Thomas.

265　*"My father, as chief:* Ibid.

265　*The boy was fifteen-year-old:* Interview, Genevieve Duplantis Lasseigne.

266　*"I didn't work:* Francis and Montgomery, 5.

266　*"I would run:* Ibid.

266　*Stella had been:* Interviews with various DeBlanc family members, including Daniel DeBlanc, Lillian DeBlanc, Catherine DeBlanc, Ella Vincent Lawrence, and Diane Baker Godwin.

266　*In a back room:* Interview, DeBlanc family members.

267　*"Aunt Stella was very:* Interview, Daniel DeBlanc.

267　*Though she does not:* Jessyl Taylor, "Was This an Act of God?" *World's Messenger*, undated photocopy of article in the files of Bertrand DeBlanc.

267　*Taylor wrote:* Ibid.

268　*"That was it:* Interview, Daniel DeBlanc.

268　*That was the question:* Ibid.

268　*("DeBlanc's word:* Interview, Gus Weill.

268   *DeBlanc responded that he:* Bertrand DeBlanc Case Files.
268   *Weill then referred:* Ibid.
268   *"What did he mean:* Bertrand DeBlanc Case Files. Also, interview, Gus Weill.
268   *Nearly forty years later:* Interview, Gus Weill.
268   *Weill later added:* Ibid.

see you on the other side

269   *"I'm wearing: Time* (magazine), May 19, 1947.
270   *Chaze wrote that Willie: Dixon Evening Telegraph,* May 9, 1947.
270   *Willie turned his head:* Ibid.
270   *Chaze noted:* Ibid.
270   *The* Weekly Messenger: *Weekly Messenger,* May 9, 1947.
270   *An article just above:* Ibid.
271   *The two men:* Associated Press photograph depicting Guilbeaux, Resweber, Chaze, and Willie.
271   *"It's a long: Times-Picayune,* May 9, 1947.
271   *Farther than thirteen: Dixon Evening Telegraph,* May 9, 1947.
272   *"I'm goin' to: Daily Times-News* (Burlington, NC), May 9, 1947.
272   *Even though Francis: Washington Post,* May 10, 1947.
272   *None of them:* Ibid.
272   *"How are you:* Ibid.
272   *"I feel good:* Ibid.
272   *Then Willie "must:* Ibid.
272   *"I hope we have:* Ibid.
272   *"You folks got:* Ibid.
272   *"They ought to:* Ibid.
272   *Looking "haggard: Dixon Evening Telegraph,* May 9, 1947.
273   *He had had enough:* Friendly and Elliot, 171.
273   *"I can still stop: Washington Post,* May 10, 1947.
273   *"No, Mr. B-B-Bertrand:* Miller and Bowman, 139.
273   *DeBlanc heard in:* Ibid.
273   *Staring out the window:* Friendly and Elliot, 171.
273   *"I'm ready to die: Washington Post,* May 10, 1947.
274   *One front-page headline: The Lowell Sun,* May 9, 1947.
274   *A big, tall Texan:* Interview, Hilton Butler.
274   *Unlike Mississippi's: Time* (magazine), January 18, 1943.
274   *And unlike Jimmy Thompson:* Ibid.
274   *Hilton Butler: The Angoline,* January/February, 1991.
275   *"That's the way:* Ibid.

275   *Captain Ephie Foster would:* Interview, Hilton Butler.
275   *He remained employed:* Ibid.
275   *He would later tell: Lima News,* May 9, 1947.
275   *DeBlanc was present:* Miller and Bowman, 139.
275   *Hannigan continued:* Ibid.
276   *"I'm hungry: Lima News,* May 9, 1947.
276   *"I brought him: Washington Post,* May 10, 1947.
276   *Years later:* Interview, George Etie Jr.
276   *By now, a crowd: Washington Post,* May 10, 1947.
276   *Among the crowd:* Ibid.
276   *Though the mood:* Ibid.
276   *He could hear:* Ibid.
277   *When Willie entered:* Ibid.
277   *Chaze reported:* Ibid.
277   *Twice he wiped:* Ibid.
277   *He snapped:* Ibid.
277   *It was Sidney Dupois:* Miller and Bowman, 141.
278   *"Fine, Willie:* Ibid.
278   *"Well, you tell:* Ibid.
278   *"Are the straps: Chicago Defender,* May 17, 1947.
278   *"Everything is all right:* Ibid.
278   *"Nothing at all: Washington Post,* May 10, 1947.
278   *"Good-bye, Willie:* Ibid.
278   *When the 2,500:* Ibid.
278   *The jolt picked him:* Ibid.
278   *"Are you sure:* Bertrand DeBlanc Case Files, undated
        photocopy.
278   *"He's dead:* Ibid.
278   *Louisiana Taylor Francis: Pittsburgh Courier,* May 17, 1947.
279   *Just after noon:* Ibid.
279   *Alone on the:* Ibid.

the nerve to kill a man

280   *Andrew Thomas had left:* Interview, Shirley Romero.
281   *"Everyone came out:* Interview, Nolan Charles.
281   *And that's how:* Interview, James Akers.
281   *Standing before:* Friendly and Elliot, 166.
281   *Francis would outlive:* Social Security Death Index.
281   *Although a small story: Weekly Messenger,* May 9, 1947.
282   *The* Messenger *quoted:* Ibid.

282   *August Fuselier may have:* Lemann, 93.
282   *According to the prosecution, Andrew:* Supreme Court Record.
283   *According to the prosecution, "The:* Ibid.
283   *The sheriff claimed:* Louisiana Pardons Board.
283   *According to Willie:* Francis and Montgomery, 5.
283   *In his confession:* Willie Francis Port Arthur, Texas Confession.
284   *Nor did he ever:* Jessyl Taylor, "Was This an Act of God?"
        World's Messenger, undated photocopy of article in the files of
        Bertrand DeBlanc.
284   *On the night: Daily Times-News*, May 4, 1946.
285   *In his letter:* Jessyl Taylor, "Was This an Act of God?" *World's
        Messenger*, undated photocopy of article in the files of Bertrand
        DeBlanc.
285   *"Do you think: Traverse City Record-Eagle*, January 14, 1947.
285   *It would seem:* Ibid.
285   *"He would be:* Ibid.
285   *"I was convinced:* Lemann, 90.
286   *A "strict constitutionalist:* Interview, Gus Weill.

no matter how small

288   *Willie Francis was one:* Louisiana State Penitentiary Museum at
        Angola.
288   *Just as many:* Lemann, 90.
289   *Rousseve suggested, too:* Ibid., 91.
289   *"Anyway," Rousseve said:* Ibid., 93.
289   *Bertrand DeBlanc had demonstrated:* Ibid., 95.
289   *"The sad part:* Ibid.
289   *"My approach:* Ibid., 89.
290   *"He would get:* Interview, Veronica DeBlanc.
290   *He solemnly gazed:* Friendly and Elliot, 171.
290   *The decision was 5–4: Washington Post*, March 2, 2005.
291   *In his dissent:* Ibid.
291   *It was the "second:* A. Miller, 206.
291   *Late in his life:* Baker, 477.
292   *Tureaud was, as historian:* Fairclough, 67.
292   *In the early 1960s: Journey for Justice: The A. P. Tureaud Story*,
        documentary film, Rachel L. Emanuel and Denise Barkis-
        Richter, Louisiana Public Broadcasting, 2004.
292   *Whereas blacks had to:* Ibid.
293   *Wright was thrown:* Baker.

293 *Having run out of:* Ibid., 330.
293 *When the board:* Ibid., 331.
293 *Wright devised:* Ibid.
293 *The desegregation:* Ibid.
294 *He issued a statement:* Ibid., 335.
294 *On May 17:* Ibid., 333.
294 *Tureaud, meanwhile:* Ibid., 346.
294 *Governor Jimmie Davis, who:* Ibid., 350.
294 *Everywhere placards: Wall Street Journal,* November 16, 1960. Also, *Washington Post,* November 21, 1960.
295 *Wright estimated: Wall Street Journal,* November 16, 1960, Also, Baker.
295 *On the back:* Interview, Helen Patton Wright.
295 *Meanwhile, Tureaud and:* Baker, 394.
295 *A mass desegregation:* Ibid.
295 *Skelly Wright summoned:* Baker, 399.
296 *The writer John Steinbeck:* Fairclough, 248.
297 *School staff:* Coles, 55.
297 *He and Tureaud both:* A. Miller, 206.
297 *"Lots of people:* Peltason, 221.
297 *In 1962:* Baker.
297 *Kennedy ranked:* A. Miller, 206.
297 *Nearly forty years:* Ibid., 73. Also, Friendly and Elliot, 171.
298 *In words that stand:* Baker, 493.
298 *As Wright observed:* A. Miller, 208.
298 *To state his credo:* Ruth Bader Ginsberg transcript as speaker at Judge Robert A. Ainsworth Jr. Memorial Lecture, "Four Louisiana Giants in the Law," February 4, 2002.
299 *The caste system:* Lemann, 99.
299 *It would be achieved:* Baker, 169.
299 *In 1986:* Gaines, *Mozart and Leadbelly,* 52.
300 *She arrived:* Ibid., 58.
300 *"Forty years later:* Ibid., 59.

Index